SCIENCE AS INQUIRY

ACTIVE LEARNING, PROJECT-BASED, WEB-ASSISTED, AND ACTIVE ASSESSMENT STRATEGIES TO ENHANCE STUDENT LEARNING

Jack Hassard, Ph.D.

Georgia State University

Good Year Books

An Imprint of Pearson Learning

This book is dedicated to my wife, Mary-Alice.

Cover: PhotoDisc, Inc.; Interior: Unless otherwise acknowledged, all photos are property of Scott, Foresman and Company.
Photo credits: 1.1 Paul Conklin/Photo Edit; 4.6 Gale Zucker/Stock Boston; 5.1 Kathy Sloane/Photo Researchers; 5.7a NASA; 6.1 Barbara Rios/Photo Researchers; 6.3 A. Ramey/Photo Edit; 7.1 Spencer Grant/Stock Boston; 8.1 David Young-Wolff/Photo Edit; 9.8 Bohdan Hrynewych/Stock Boston; 9.9 Phyllis Picardi/Stock Boston.

Good Year Books
are available for most basic curriculum subjects plus many enrichment areas. For more Good Year Books, contact your local bookseller or educational dealer. For a complete catalog with information about other Good Year Books, please write:

Good Year Books
299 Jefferson Road
Parsipanny, NJ 07054

Executive Editor: Judy Adams
Editorial Manager: Suzanne Beason
Project Editor: Roberta Dempsey
Production/Manufacturing Director: Janet Yearian
Production/Manufacturing Coordinators: Fiona Santioanni/Karen Mancinelli
Design Director: Phyllis Aycock
Composition and line art: Chris O/Joan Olson

Book design by Foster Design.
Cover illustration assembled by Jack Foster.
Line art by Douglas Klauba. Electronic art by Karen Kohn and Associates.
Art copyright © 2000 Good Year Books, an imprint of Pearson Learning.
Copyright © 2000 Jack Hassard.

ACKNOWLEDGMENTS

Many educators have contributed to the development of this book. To begin, I would like to acknowledge the Bureau of Education and Research (BER) with whom I have had an association since 1990. BER is the largest provider of inservice education for teachers in North America. I wish to express my professional and personal thanks to Dr. Frank Koontz, Director of Programs at BER. In 1990 Frank asked me if I would be interested in conducting a seminar on cooperative learning and science teaching. As part of the BER strategy, I was to write a handbook that would be distributed to the science teachers attending the seminar. Frank helped throughout the process of developing the handbook, and has served as my teaching coach for the past eight years. His dedication and commitment to quality instruction contributed not only to the development of the seminars but also to the development of my abilities as a teacher. It is through the three separate seminars that I conducted for the BER that I came to formulate this book. Without Frank Koontz and the BER, *Science as Inquiry* would not have been written.

Two educators helped me draft parts of the manuscript. First, I wish to thank Mr. Daniel Whitehair, who, at the time of our collaboration, was a graduate student in science education at Georgia State University. Daniel's work on the book was invaluable. Daniel helped to develop the lesson plans based on the constructivist model of learning that constitute the last chapters of the book. He accomplished this task by taking large pieces of newsprint with brief outlines of teaching ideas written on them and turning them into polished, interesting, and provocative science lessons. Second, I wish to thank Dr. Nydia Hanna, a colleague at Georgia State University. Nydia prepared the introductory materials for Chapter 3, Fuzzy Situations. I hope you will find these fuzzy situations as intriguing an approach to critical and creative thinking as I did.

I was very fortunate that Roberta Dempsey was the project editor for *Science As Inquiry*. In fact, she was the person within Good Year that moved the book from my initial manuscript submission to the published book. She worked with me throughout the entire process, and without her the book would not have been published, nor would it have taken on the form presented here.

I wish to acknowledge the graduate students and graduates of the TEEMS (Teacher Education Environments in Mathematics and Science) program at Georgia State University, all of whom used earlier versions of this book (in the form of two of the handbooks written for the BER), thus providing valuable feedback that helped me improve the materials. Further, a number of these students contributed materials that I've included in this book; their names appear with the material they provided.

Dr. Marlene Hapai, Professor and head of the Natural Sciences Division at the University of Hawaii, invited me to teach in her Eisenhower science certification program for K–12 science teachers during the summers from 1993 through 1997. I thank her for providing this wonderful opportunity to teach in paradise; to collaborate with my dear friend, Dr. Joe Abruscato of the University of Vermont; and to use the materials over an extended period of time that would form the basis of this book.

I had the opportunity to work with teachers in the Savannah, Georgia, school district on cooperative and active learning strategies. I wish to thank Dr. Harris Lintini, Director of the Oatland Island Environmental Center, for making these opportunities available to me during the summers of 1991, 1992, and 1993. I also want to acknowledge Ken Royal, Sarah Crim, Charles Eich, and Salyon Johnson, who provided insights and allowed me to use their comments on the implementation of the Internet in their classes.

Finally, I wish to thank all of the science teachers who attended my seminars—those sponsored by the Bureau of Education and Research, as well as those sponsored by the more than fifty school districts in the United States with which I have had the privilege to work. The dedication and commitment to science teaching evident in these educators is truly inspiring. Thank you.

Dr. Jack Hassard

CONTENTS

For nearly ten years, I have been presenting to middle and high school educators seminars on science teaching. The seminars were originally created for teachers attending one-day presentations sponsored by the Bureau of Education and Research.[1] At these seminars, which were held in more than thirty states, teachers received a handbook designed by me as an active learning tool to complement and support the content of the program. The seminars were also presented directly to teachers in more than fifty school districts in various parts of the United States, including New York City, Chicago, Atlanta, St. Louis, Dayton, Columbia, Hartford, and Chattanooga. In all, the seminars have been seen by more than 15,000 science teachers in grades K–12. The seminars, along with the courses I taught at Georgia State University and the University of Hawaii, have been invaluable sources of knowledge on which I have relied heavily in developing *Science as Inquiry*.

Science as Inquiry, then, weaves together the best ideas exchanged at the seminars and in the classroom into a single, integrated book for school science.

THE FOCUS OF SCIENCE TEACHING

One of the things I asked teachers attending the seminars is what they look for as evidence that students in their classes are really learning. What I found is that there is a great deal of consistency in teachers' responses. Time and again, teachers cited the following signs/indicators of student learning:

- "When their eyes light up!"
- "By the kinds of questions they ask in class."
- "If they can relate what we are doing in here to what is going on out there."
- "By their body language."
- "If they can explain the concept to other students in class."

---

[1] *Bureau of Education and Research, 915 118th Ave., SE, Bellevue, WA 99009.*

- "If each can apply what they are learning here to his or her own life."

Very rarely did teachers mention the score that a student gets on a test. This is not to say that teachers didn't think tests were important, but rather that there were other "signs" indicative of student learning and that, in some cases, these signs were more important than test scores. To me, this signaled a group of teachers who looked at assessment in broad terms and recognized that assessment is a holistic process that involves more than exam and quiz scores.

In 1995 the National Academy of Science published the National Science Education Standards. This document helps all teachers focus on the nature of science teaching and compare current practice with future goals and aspirations.

How did what the teachers had to say about science teaching compare with statements in the National Science Education Standards? Science teaching, according to the authors of the Standards, should educate students who:

1. Use scientific principles and processes appropriately in making personal decisions.
2. Experience the richness and excitement of knowing about and understanding the natural world.
3. Increase their economic productivity.
4. Engage intelligently in public discourse and debate about matters of scientific and technological concern.

My experience talking with and listening to teachers across the country suggests that science teaching should focus on relating science to students' personal and social concerns, and that science teaching should give students opportunities to experience the process the richness and excitement of science.

In bringing together a variety of teaching strategies and activities, *Science as Inquiry* will contribute to the development of a science education program that helps us reach these goals.

Underlying all of science, no matter what discipline, is the spirit of inquiry—something the authors of the National Science Education Standards placed high on the list of expected outcomes of science. It is this spirit of inquiry that is the central theme of this book.

GOOD SCIENCE TEACHING

Is there a single approach to good science teaching? No! Are there general principles upon which we can agree? Yes! This is an important point, because these principles are actually beliefs that we hold about science teaching, and beliefs guide and influence the way we teach.

Early on in the teaching seminars, I often asked teachers to discuss their concept of "good science teaching." Working in small groups, teachers talked briefly among themselves about this question. Based on these discussions, teachers came up with the following characteristics of good science teaching:

- It must focus on hands-on and minds-on strategies.
- It is interesting and fun.
- The content is applicable to students' lives and communities.
- It is process-oriented.
- It uses active learning approaches.
- Students are active learners.

To contrast teachers' ideas with students' ideas on this question, I presented some findings reported by Charles Eich.[2] In his eighth-grade class, Eich asked students to identify what they thought made for a good science class. He went on to tell the students that the criteria they developed would be the principles that would guide his instruction. Here is what his students came up with:
- Relies less on lectures and notes and more on "hands-on" experiments

- Allows for outdoor settings in which to learn and experiment
- Has review games and review guides
- Assigns one fun long-term project during the year
- Does not work out of the book all of the time
- Allows students to work in groups
- Provides time to discuss and debate topics

Clearly, the similarity in beliefs between students and teachers is significant. Notice that students identified processes that we as science educators think are important, especially the opportunity to work in cooperative groups, and to discuss and debate scientific ideas.

As a final point of comparison, I presented the characteristics of good science teaching described in the National Science Education Standards. According to our colleagues at the national level, standards for good science teaching are as follows:

1. Science education for students should be inquiry-oriented.
2. As inquiry science teachers, we should guide and facilitate science learning by:

- Focusing and supporting student inquiries
- Orchestrating discourse between students about scientific ideas
- Challenging students to take responsibility for their own learning and to work collaboratively
- Encouraging and modeling the skills of inquiry as well as curiosity, openness to new ideas, and skepticism

3. An ongoing assessment of our teaching and the learning of our students should be in place.
4. We should know how to design and manage a learning environment conducive to inquiry learning.
5. As science teachers, we should develop a

---

[2] *According to students in Charles Eich's eighth-grade Earth science class, Hightower Trail Middle School, Marietta, Georgia.*

community of learners in our class that pro motes inquiry and the attitudes and values conducive to science learning.[3]

THEMES OF THIS BOOK

Science as Inquiry is designed around four themes that are based on contemporary goals of science teaching and the characteristics of "good" science teaching:

Active Learning

This concept is connected to the way we think students learn science. There is no doubt that students come to science classes from varied backgrounds and with different skills and abilities. Science teaching that engages students in activities that draw on multiple abilities and learning styles will tend to reach a greater number of students than teaching that does not. Active learning, as the concept is used in this book, finds students involved in small cooperative groups whose tasks are interesting and problem-oriented. Teachers organize and facilitate group activities by making use of a variety of active learning strategies—for example, cooperative learning groups, hands-on inquiry activities, and demonstrations. Underlying the active learning strategies is the idea that learning occurs in communities, and that new ideas are linked to previous knowledge and constructed by the learner himself or herself. Active learning is a metaphor for the constructivist model of learning as developed in Chapters 9 and 10.

Project-based Teaching

An outgrowth of active learning, project-based science teaching supports the idea that human beings construct knowledge through their actions and interactions with other humans. Such teaching also tends to support the notion that new knowledge is acquired in relation to previous knowledge, building on intuitive and informal

experiences. Projects have several advantages over traditional resources: they tend to create an environment that fosters informality and authentic learning; they typically are carried out by groups, which is consistent with the idea that learning is more powerfully facilitated in social groups than when students are left to work alone; they create a need on the part of students to expand their source of knowledge and information from a single textbook to more engaging types of learning, especially that available through the Internet; finally, they promote student conversation, cooperation, and collaboration.

Internet Resources

Emerging technologies have made possible a new way of thinking about science teaching. In this book, you'll find a model for using the Internet that is interactive and regards the Internet as a tool for facilitating communication and acquiring information. The students we are teaching today are growing up in a digital age. They are part of a new generation that uses computers and the Internet much like we used to use television. The big difference, of course, is that the Internet is an interactive medium, whereas TV is not. You'll discover many ways to harness the power of the Internet in your science teaching.

Assessment

This is a key dimension of science teaching. The approach taken in *Science as Inquiry* is that *active* learning must be assessed with *active* tools. You'll find presented here a model of assessment in which assessment occurs along a continuum of learning—one that begins with the ascertaining of students' prior knowledge and blends seamlessly into the integration of assessment strategies into instruction.

ORGANIZATION OF THIS BOOK

The materials in this book are intended to provide you with a framework for implementing inquiry strategies in your science class. The book is divided into five main sections.

---

[3] From *National Science Education Standards, pp. 92 and 95–96. Copyright © 1996 by the National Academy of Sciences. Reprinted by permission of the National Academy Press, Washington, D.C.*

Part I The Tools of Inquiry

Chapter 1 Cooperative Learning Strategies. This chapter presents several cooperative learning strategies and explains how to implement them in your classroom. Science activities accompany each cooperative strategy.

Chapter 2 EEEPs: Exciting Examples of Everyday Phenomena. This is a strategy this author developed several years ago that combines cooperative learning with discrepant events. Included are EEEPs in the Earth, life, and physical sciences, as well as guidelines for implementing them.

Chapter 3 Fuzzy Situations. These intriguing problems engage students in discussing the social implications of science.

Chapter 4 Active Learning Strategies. This is a collection of strategies, including pre-assessment, active reading, collaborative questioning, and games.

Part II Teaching Strategies and Assessment Tools

Chapter 5 Project-Based Teaching Ideas. This chapter presents a collection of projects for Earth, life, and physical sciences, as well as guidelines for implementing them in your classroom.

Chapter 6 The Online Science Classroom. A wealth of information is included on establishing an Internet-based classroom. There are interviews with teachers who are incorporating the Internet in their classroom, along with specific Internet structures and related Internet activities. Look here, too, for some important Internet sites in science teaching.

Chapter 7 Project Ozone: A Web-assisted Science Unit. This chapter provides you with a complete teaching package so that you can fully engage your students in an Internet project. A Web site was specially designed to support this project, and you will be able to make use of it with your students.

Chapter 8 Assessing Performance in Science. This chapter includes a variety of tools that you can use to assess your students. You'll find performance assessments, rubrics, student logs, portfolios, and a strategy for developing paper-and-pencil items that are active.

Part III Constructivism in the Bag: Active Science Lessons

Chapter 9 Earth Science and Environmental Science Lessons, and Chapter 10 Life Science and Physical Science Lessons.
These chapters contain thirty-one active science lessons in the areas of Earth science, environmental science, life science, and physical science. All lessons are based on the active learning model presented in this book, and all include links to the Internet.

Science Teaching Resources. This final section includes the names of active learning, professional, and Internet books, as well as information about Internet service providers and organizations.

Using Science as Inquiry
The materials in *Science as Inquiry* can be used in a variety of ways. They are meant to serve as a framework for planning inquiry activities that work for your students. Each chapter in this book can stand alone, so you can use the chapters and the materials in any order you wish. Here are just a few ways to use *Science as Inquiry*.

Implement Cooperative Learning

You'll find many cooperative learning strategies in the book, especially in Chapters 1 and 2, although all of the activities are based on a cooperative learning framework. Very specific approaches are included to help you successfully incorporate the strategies in your classroom.

Learn and Implement New Teaching Strategies

This book offers many new teaching strategies that you can easily implement in your class. Perhaps you'll find Chapter 2's EEEPs appealing because they focus on student motivation and inquiry. Take a look, too, at Chapter 3, "Fuzzy Situations"; "fuzzies" might be the perfect way to help your students discuss interesting, if not controversial, issues in science education. Chapters 6 and 7 will provide you with new ideas on how to use the Internet. And don't miss the 31 activities in Chapters 9 and 10 that pull together active learning, group projects, and the Internet.

Develop New Assessment Strategies

Chapter 8 offers a complete analysis of alternative assessment strategies. The approach here, and throughout the book, is practical. The assessment strategies are designed to be implemented and used in an active science class. Take a look, for example, at the very practical ways to use learning logs and portfolios with your students, as well as the guidelines for performance assessments. And, if you are looking to improve your tests and quizzes, you'll find suggestions for doing so in Chapter 8.

The Internet

The Internet strategies developed for this book should prove interesting and worthwhile, even if you have limited access to the Internet. You will find very practical ways to incorporate the Internet into your teaching no matter what your approach. In particular, take a look at Chapters 6, 7, and 9. The Internet project presented in Chapter 7, when used in conjunction with the *Minds On Science* Web site, gives you a complete Internet activity you can do with your students.

Enhance Your Science Program

Chapters 9 and 10 contain thirty-one active learning lessons that you can use to augment your current science program. There are enough activities for a full, integrated science program, and all activities have links to the Internet.

USING THE *MINDS ON SCIENCE* WEB SITE

This Web site (Figure I.1), specifically designed for this book, gives you access to additional resources that promote active learning, project-based teaching, Web-assisted activities, and active assessment. In Chapter 7 I have designed a complete Internet-based science project in which you will utilize the *Minds On Science* site and the Internet to collaborate with other schools. The URL is: http://www.gsu.edu/~mstjrh/mindsonscience.html/

Figure I.1
Minds On Science Web site

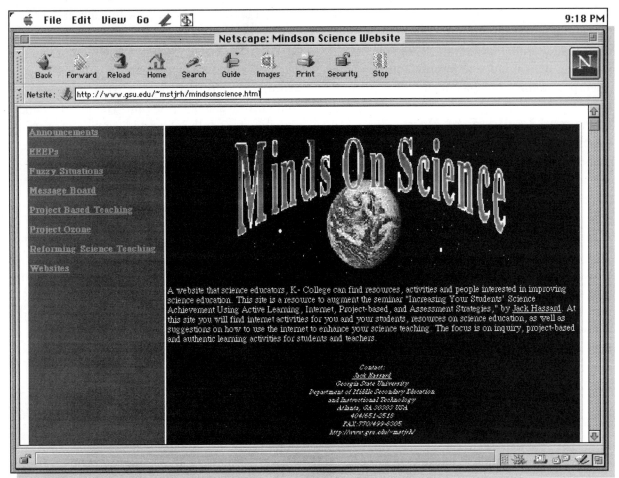

CHAPTER 1 COOPERATIVE LEARNING STRATEGIES

Figure 1.1
Cooperative learning is fundamental to learning and brings students together to work on important problems. Learning this way mirrors some of humanity's best efforts at solving real problems.

This chapter will introduce you to several cooperative learning strategies designed to enhance the way students work together in small groups. Science education research has shown that cooperative learning, when used effectively, can lead to greater cognitive gain, better (more positive) attitudes toward science, and a higher motivation to learn science. Moreover, the National Science Education Standards emphasize the importance of cooperative learning as a key strategy in fostering student inquiry in the science classroom.[1]

KEY CONCEPTS

Two concepts are fundamental to implementing cooperative learning strategies: positive interdependence and individual responsibility. The roles of each can best be understood by considering the examples in Figure 1.2. Engendering positive interdependence is the most important thing that we as teachers can do to help students work in small groups. Interdependence can be achieved in science activities by having students collaborate on an activity that requires a single

product, by dividing the labor, by assigning roles, or by rewarding all of the students in a group.

Individual responsibility is just as important as positive interdependence. In the activities that we plan, we can encourage individual responsibility by focusing on individual outcomes, by giving feedback on each student's progress, by having students work alone at first and then share their work with the group, or by using experts.

Figure 1.2
Two Key Cooperative Learning Concepts

Positive Interdependence	Individual Responsibility
• We sink or swim together.	• I must learn this material.
• None of us is as smart as all of us.	• I cannot "hitchhike."
• I win when you win.	• My teammates depend on me.
• The whole is greater than the sum of the parts.	

THE STRATEGIES

The strategies presented in this chapter will show that cooperative learning is much more than putting students in groups and telling them to work together. Discussed here are seven cooperative learning strategies that have been used successfully in teaching seminars over the past eight years. Each is a stand-alone strategy, which means you can use any strategy in this chapter in any order that you wish.

Collaborative Inquiry Strategy

This approach combines the principles of cooperative learning—individual responsibility and positive interdependence—with science inquiry. On the one hand, each student in the group has a specific role; on the other hand, all students in the group are involved in science inquiry.

---

[1] *National Research Council (1995).* National Science Education Standards. *Washington, DC: National Academy Press.*

Figure 1.3
Cooperative Inquiry Roles

Communicator	Tracker	Checker	Materials Manager
• Helps resolve problems • Can leave team to communicate • Sends and downloads Internet messages	• Helps track progress • Records data/information for the team • Collaborates with communicator on Internet activity	• Helps team understand the activity • Facilitates talk about the activity • Is not the leader; is a facilitator	• Picks up/returns materials • Facilitates cleanup • Checks to make sure equipment is in working order

SIDEBAR 1.1

Collaborative Inquiry[2]

• Students explore problems in natural world.

• Students "do" science.

• Knowledge about natural world is "constructed" through talk, activity, and interaction.

• Talk is focused through small-group activity.

Students engaged in collaborative inquiry play one of the four roles shown in Figure 1.3.

In science inquiry, students explore problems in the natural world. Students "do" science. In Collaborative Science inquiry, students construct knowledge about the natural world through small-group talk, hands-on activity, and discussion. Sidebar 1.1 lists the key characteristics of "collaborative (science) inquiry."

Thus, in the Collaborative Inquiry approach to cooperative learning, students are not only individually responsible for a part of the activity, they are also interdependent on each other because they have different tasks, all of which play a part in solving a science problem. As you get started with Collaborative Inquiry, it is helpful to provide students with a "role card" describ-

ing their collaborative responsibilities. To do this, make each group of students a copy of Figure 1.4, which describes the various roles in collaborative inquiry. Have students cut out the cards and distribute them so that each student receives the card describing his or her role. You might also want to make a poster identifying the four roles. By hanging it prominently in your classroom, you can quickly and effectively review the roles with your students.

LESSON PLAN: THE FOOTPRINT PUZZLE

Goals: To give students practice using the Collaborative Inquiry approach to cooperative learning; to generate alternative hypotheses to explain dinosaur footprints found in rocks dated to be 100 million years old; to encourage all group members to participate

Materials: Footprint Recording Sheet (Figure 1.5), Footprint puzzle(s) (Figures 1.6 and 1.7), photographs of dinosaurs

Web Site: Dino Russ' Lair: http://128.174.172.76/lsgsroot/dinos/dinos_home.html

Procedure: Organize your class into teams of three or four students each. Have students num-

2 *After Rosebery, A., Warren, B., and Conant, F. Appropriate Scientific Discourse: Findings from Language Minority Classrooms. Working paper 1–92, Cambridge, MA: TERC.*

Figure 1.4

COOPERATIVE INQUIRY ROLES

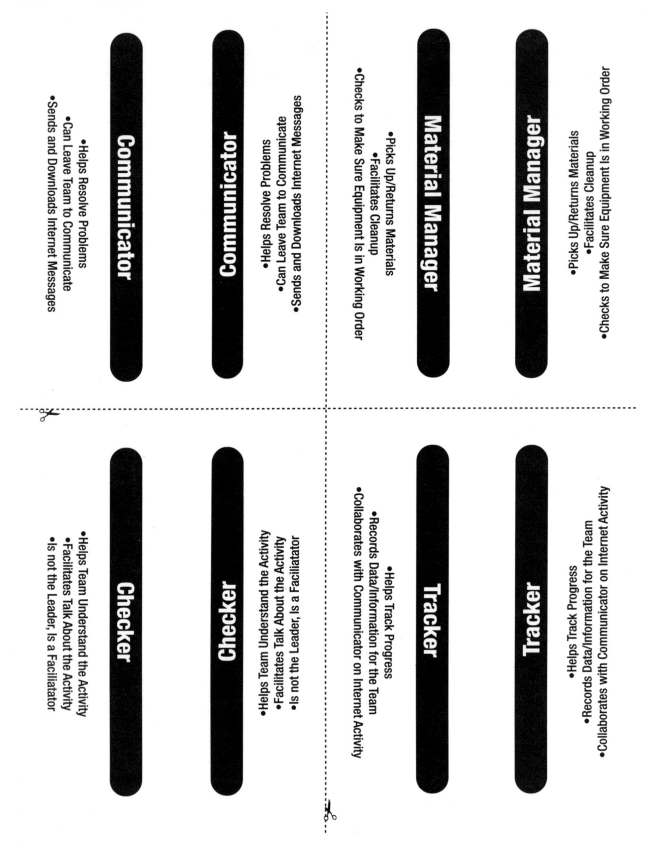

Communicator
- Helps Resolve Problems
- Can Leave Team to Communicate
- Sends and Downloads Internet Messages

Communicator
- Helps Resolve Problems
- Can Leave Team to Communicate
- Sends and Downloads Internet Messages

Material Manager
- Picks Up/Returns Materials
- Facilitates Cleanup
- Checks to Make Sure Equipment Is in Working Order

Material Manager
- Picks Up/Returns Materials
- Facilitates Cleanup
- Checks to Make Sure Equipment Is in Working Order

Checker
- Helps Team Understand the Activity
- Facilitates Talk About the Activity
- Is not the Leader, Is a Faciliatator

Checker
- Helps Team Understand the Activity
- Facilitates Talk About the Activity
- Is not the Leader, Is a Faciliatator

Tracker
- Helps Track Progress
- Records Data/Information for the Team
- Collaborates with Communicator on Internet Activity

Tracker
- Helps Track Progress
- Records Data/Information for the Team
- Collaborates with Communicator on Internet Activity

ber off within each group, and then assign each of the numbers one of the four Collaborative Inquiry roles. (If you decide to work with groups of three, have one of the students be the Communicator as well as the Materials Manager.) Give each team a copy of the Footprint Data Sheet and follow these steps:

1. Investigate the set of footprints with your teammates. Make a list of as many hypotheses to explain the pattern of the footprints as there are members of your team. Make sure that everyone contributes ideas and that you listen to each other's ideas.

2. Explain the task to the students. Tell them their job is to investigate, as a team, a set of footprints (show them Figure 1.6) found in rocks in central Connecticut. The rocks were dated to be about 100 million years old (which means they were deposited during the Cretaceous Period in the Mesozoic Era). Tell students they are to make a list of as many hypotheses as there are people in the group to explain the pattern of the footprints. Tell them to be sure that everyone participates. Give the students about five to eight minutes to generate their hypotheses.

3. At the end of this period, tell the students that you have some additional data from the footprint site—that is, scientists have sent you additional prints. Present Figure 1.7, using a bit of dramatic flair. Now have the students look over their hypotheses and, in light of the "new data," have them revise, discard, or accept their hypotheses. Have each team select one hypothesis to share with the class.

4. Select one student from each group to write the group's hypothesis on a chart or white posterboard. Divide the chart or board into four, so that each group has a space in which to write. Discuss the results, and ask students to defend their ideas with observations they made while working as a group.

5. Announce that the most likely explanation is that these are dinosaur prints, but that no one really knows for certain. Thus all the students' hypotheses can be considered plausible.

6. *Going Further.* You might visit the Museum of Natural History Web site and have students do research on one or more dinosaurs that they find online: http://www.amnh.org/

Text copyright © Jack Hassard. Illustration copyright © Good Year Books

SIDEBAR 1.2

Possible Hypotheses

- Two animals (birds) approached a water hole; one flew off, the other walked away.

- Two animals walked toward something; one spotted the other and tried to run; a fight ensued; one walked away.

- Two animals independently approached an area at different times.

- Two animals approached an area (mother, daughter); the daughter rode away on the mother's back.

Figure 1.5
Footprint Recording Sheet

FOOTPRINT PUZZLE
PRACTICING COLLABORATIVE INQUIRY

OBJECTIVES

1. Explore and investigate a problem from the natural world.
2. Generate alternative hypotheses to explain data in the form of footprints found in rocks that are 100 million years old.
3. Practice using Collaborative Inquiry roles.
4. Encourage everyone in the group to communicate ideas.

MATERIALS

1. One set of footprints per team
2. One data recording sheet per team

COLLABORATIVE INQUIRY ROLES

Role	Team Member
Communicator	_____
Materials Manager	_____
Tracker	_____
Checker	_____
Coach	_____

FOOTPRINT DATA SHEET

Tracker's Name: _____   Date: _____

List of Hypotheses

Modified Hypothesis

Figure 1.6
Footprint Puzzle, Part A

Two adaptations of Figure 19-10 from *Investigating the Earth: Earth Science Curriculum Project,* p. 416. Copyright © 1967 by American Geological Institute. All rights reserved. Reprinted by permission of McDougal Littell Inc.

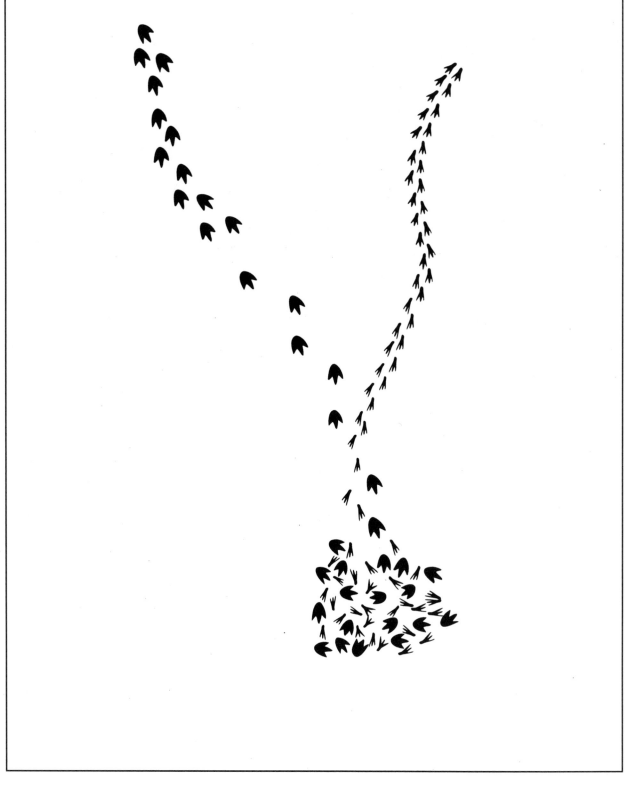

Figure 1.7

Footprint Puzzle, Part B

Two adaptations of Figure 19-10 from *Investigating the Earth: Earth Science Curriculum Project,* p. 416. Copyright © 1967 by American Geological Institute. All rights reserved. Reprinted by permission of McDougal Littell Inc.

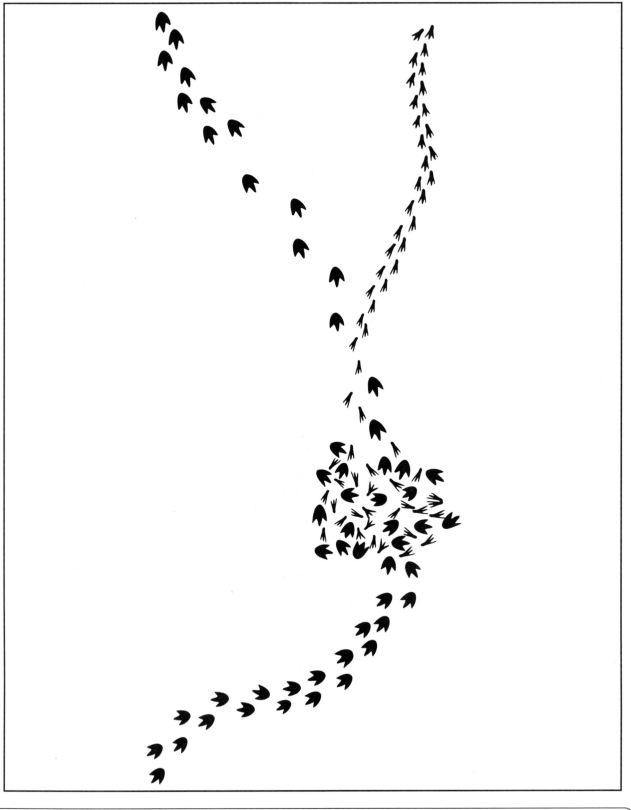

Figure 1.8
Abilities in Science Chart*

Verbal–Linguistic Word Smart	Visual–Spatial Picture Smart	Logical–Mathematical Minds-on-Smart	Bodily–Kinesthetic Hands-on-Smart
• Science word games • Use new science words in discussions • Create a science activities dictionary & pictionary • Word processing • Science writers, reporters	• Make diagrams of cells, atoms, Earth systems • Create video presentations • Mapping activities • Make 3-D models • Flowcharts, decision trees, concepts maps mind mapping • Multimedia presentation software • Draw and paint computer software	• Solve problems • Create problems; ask questions • Discuss and debate societal implications of science • Create data tables and spreadsheets • Find analogies • Work problems backward • Use science processes: observing, inferring, predicting, hypothesing, analyzing data, and drawing conclusions	• Build physical models • Express science concepts with bodily motion • Sensory awareness • Science probes plugged into computer (MBL, Science Toolkit)

*The abilities across the top of this chart are based on Howard Gardner's theory of multiple intelligences.

Multiple Abilities Strategy

Generally speaking, successful cooperative learning activities require multiple abilities among a team of students who work together to complete a task. Activities requiring only one or two abilities (especially if they are reading or mathematical calculations) tend to put many students at a disadvantage in cooperative groups. Thus, an activity that calls on students to make careful observations, to guess or make hypotheses, to record data, to manipulate hands-on materials, to construct a model, to role-play, and to write brief reports will tend to be more successful than one in which students read a section of the text and answer a set of questions.

Figure 1.8 identifies eight different abilities that students possess, in varying degrees, along with examples of activities that they might do in a science class to help them develop these abilities. Look it over, and use it as a checklist for the activities that you are assigning in your class.

When we use the Multiple Abilities approach to cooperative learning,[3] our goal is to convince students that many abilities are truly needed to successfully complete the activity or the task at hand. One way to do this is to make a list of all the abilities that will be required. In the case of the whirlybird activity, which follows, students will be doing the following:

- Designing helicopter-type vehicles
- Using trial and error
- Observing
- Predicting

[3] This approach is based on Cohen, E. (1994). Designing Groupwork: Strategies for the Heterogeneous Classroom. New York: Teachers College Press.

Figure 1.8
Abilities in Science Chart* (continued)

Musical Rhythm and Tone Smart	Interpersonal Cooperative Smart	Intrapersonal Reflective Smart	Naturalist Ecologically Smart
• Find and use science-related songs • Write and sing musical scores of science concepts • Play background music in class • Use natural music and sounds (birds, nature)	• Use cooperative groups, such as quality circles, tribes, and multiple abilities • Science board games • Computer games for pairs and groups • Teach active listening • Create a community of practice in class • From "I" to "W" • Networks • Join teacher discussion groups on computer networks • Link with others	• Journaling activities • Help students write goals and objectives • Portfolios • Provide time for reflection • Biographies • Motivational speakers	• Sensory awareness activities • Hikes and field trips into natural sites • Mini-field trips outside the classroom • Readings from nature magazines • Nature videos • Understanding, relating to, and functioning in the natural world

*The abilities across the top of this chart are based on Howard Gardner's theory of multiple intelligences.

- Testing a hypothesis
- Interpreting data
- Controlling variables
- Writing observations
- Making drawings of their designs
- Making a poster report

Having made the list of abilities, it is helpful to create an environment of "mixed expectations" for the class. For example, you might say the following: "Isn't it unlikely that any one member of the group will possess all of these abilities, but likely that each member will possess some of them?" Most students will agree. By posing this question, we help to close the gap between the high-ability student and low-ability student in each group. Typically, it is the low-ability student who is left out and not invited to participate. If we can convince the students that all students can contribute to the solution of the activity, then "permission" is given to every student to become involved. Further, by subtly focusing on the low-ability student in each group and by "catching" this student making intellectual contributions, the teacher can positively influence the group. Visit the groups frequently. When you hear something positive, clearly restate for the group what you heard. This reinforces not only the low-ability student, but the group as a whole.

LESSON PLAN: WHIRLYBIRDS

Goals: To test the Multiple Abilities approach; to build and fly whirlybirds; to investigate the effect of one variable on a whirlybird's speed of descent to the floor; to report results to the class

Materials: Scissors, Whirlybird Template (Figure 1.10), stopwatch, Group Mini-log (Figure 1.11), poster paper, markers

Procedure:

1. Show students a whirlybird that you have cut out and folded (see Figure 1.9). Ask students to brainstorm the factors (variables) that they think will affect the whirlybird's speed of descent to the floor. List students' ideas on chart paper. Students will likely suggest the following variables: wind, height from which the whirlybird is dropped, length of the wings, the length of the shaft, angle of the wings or blades, and weight of the whirlybird.

2. Have each group select one variable that it will investigate. Tell the students that they must conduct an experiment to find out how their variable affects the speed of the whirlybird. For example, groups that decide to study the length of the wings must keep the other variables constant. That is, when they build whirlybirds, they must be sure to keep the length of the shaft the same while they vary the length of the whirlybird wings. They will also need to consider the angle of the wings, the mass of the whirlybird, and the height from which the whirlybird is dropped.

3. Copy Figure 1.10 to use with the whirlybird activity. Students can use these strips to cut and make whirlybirds out of different materials (newspaper, construction paper, file folders). Each strip should be 2.5 cm × 21.5 cm.

4. Have the Materials Manager pick up the necessary materials (scissors, whirlybird template [Figure 1.11], group mini-log). Give students time to build and test their whirlybird designs. Point out that they should have the Tracker use the group mini-log to record the team's ideas as well as to make illustrations of its whirlybirds.

5. Have the Materials Manager obtain a large piece of chart paper and markers. Tell students that they should create a poster report of their research. The poster should contain the results of their work and include (at a minimum) the following:

- The variable they investigated
- The method they used
- The data they collected
- The results they obtained—a statement explaining how the factor they studied affected the flight of a whirlybird
- Their whirlybird models
- The group mini-log

6. Give each team copies of the Whirlybird Assessment, located on the last page of the mini-log. Have a representative from each group present its poster to the class. When a team completes its presentation, have the other teams

Figure 1.9
Completed Whirlybird

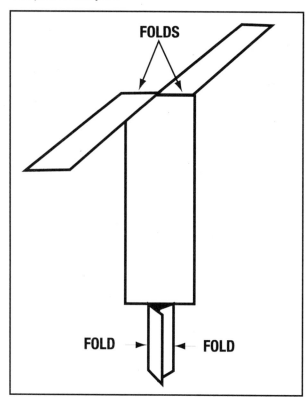

FOLDS

FOLD ► ◄ FOLD

Figure 1.10
Whirlybird Template

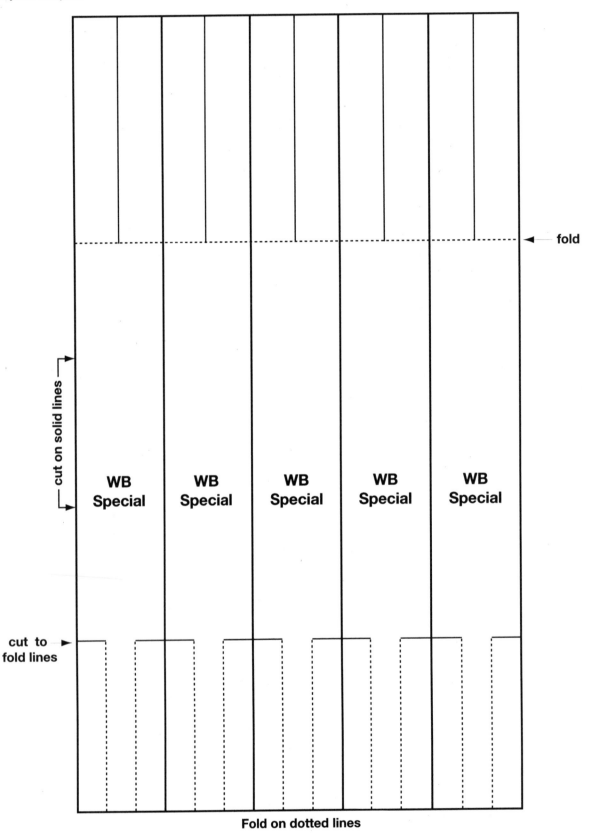

Fold on dotted lines

Figure 1.11
Whirlybird Group Mini-Log

THE WHIRLYBIRD PROJECT

GROUP MINI-LOG

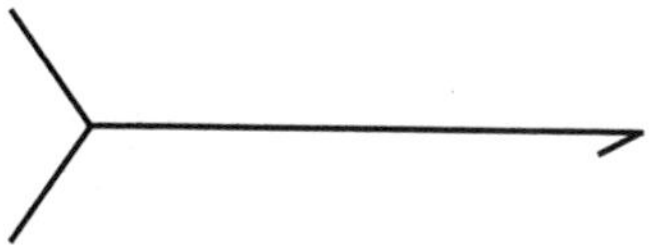

Rubric 1

Response	Criteria	Rating
Outstanding	Showed expanded thinking and clear understanding of task; showed evidence of testing models and cooperative effort	4
Very good	Completed task, reached acceptable conclusions, completed models; cooperative effort in evidence	3
Satisfactory	Task nearly completed; conclusion incomplete	2
Fails to Complete	Could not communicate understanding of the task; attempted the task	1
No Attempt	No whirlybird was constructed; little cooperation in evidence	0

Rubric 2

Response	Criteria	Rating
Cooperative	To what extent did the group cooperate with each other to help solve the problem?	0 1 2 3 4
Content	To what extent is there evidence that the team understood the physics concepts in the task?	0 1 2 3 4
Completion	To what extent did the team use the allocated time wisely?	0 1 2 3 4

Rubric 3 Design Your Own

Figure 1.11
Whirlybird Group Mini-Log (continued)

What abilities did your team use in this activity?

- •
- •
- •
- •
- •

What criteria would you use to assess other students' progress on the whirlybird project?

- •
- •
- •
- •

Have your team assess itself as a group by using one of the rubrics on the last page of this log.

Mini-record of your team's ideas, data, and exploration:

Illustration of your team's ideas:

Your team's hypothesis:

use the assessment rubrics to evaluate the team's project. Collect these and, after looking them over, present them to the team. Hang the finished posters in the class for observation.

Numbered Heads Together Strategy

The Numbered Heads Together approach to cooperative learning can be used by students to complete a small-group activity, answer a question, or complete a hands-on task. It can be a powerful way to encourage student inquiry and problem solving. Here is how it works.

1. Have students number off into cooperative learning groups of four students each. Make sure students remember their numbers, as they will come into play later.

2. A demonstration, question, or task is posed. For example, show two identical balloons, one filled with helium and the other that you blew up. Release them. One falls to the floor, the other rises to the ceiling. Or ask: How are reptiles different from amphibians? Or present this hands-on task: Using a bag of shells, create a chart showing how your team would classify the shells.

3. Students then put their heads together. Teams work together for a specified period of time to brainstorm, answer the question, or complete the task.

4. When the time has elapsed, the teacher tells the students to take a half-minute to review their work so that each group member understands the groups' results. Let students know that numbers will be randomly called and that they will be expected to respond.

5. Call a random number. The student in each group whose number is called stands and responds for the group, goes to a designated area on a board and records the team's findings, or holds up a drawing or chart of the group's work.

LESSON PLAN: EGG IN THE JAR

Goal: To have students work together as a problem-solving team to answer questions, make predictions, and explain a phenomenon

Materials: White boards, marking pens, hard-boiled eggs, glass jars with mouths smaller than the cooked eggs, matches, four index cards numbered 1, 2, 3, and 4

Procedure:

1. Organize the students in cooperative groups with three or four team members. Have the students number off from 1 to 3 or 4. Tell them that you will use the numbers as a way to ask questions of team members.

2. Show the students a glass jar and a cooked egg that you have peeled. Place the egg in the mouth of the jar. Ask the students how they could get the egg in the jar without damaging or breaking the egg. Tell the students to put their heads together. Give each group two or three minutes to discuss their ideas. They should record them on the white board.

3. Present the four numbered index cards to the class. Have one student in the class draw one card. Read the number aloud. Ask the student in each group with this number to stand near his or her group. Go around the room and ask each standing student to tell one idea that his or her group thought would enable the egg to get in the jar. Record these on paper.

4. One way to get the egg in the jar is to light a match and drop it into the jar and then immediately put the egg over the mouth. The egg will slowly be pulled into the jar. If the students did not suggest this idea, present it to them and conduct the demonstration for the class.

5. After the demonstration, have the students put their heads together a second time. This time, they should draw a diagram showing the bottle and the egg, and use it to what they think causes the egg to go into the bottle. Give the students five minutes to do this. Encourage them to illustrate their diagram and be ready to share their explanations with others in the class.

6. Tell the students to make sure that everyone in their group understands the explanation that their team generated. Tell them that you will call on one student from each group by drawing one of the index cards. Draw the card, and have the student whose number was drawn do one of the following:

  a. Stand near the group and briefly describe his or her team's explanation.
  b. Go to another group in the class and sit with this group and explain their team's explanation. The group should ask questions, and share the idea that their team created.
  c. Go to the board and briefly draw and write their team's explanation.

7. After the students have shared either by standing, visiting another group, or going to the board, discuss with the students the ideas that they generated to explain the egg in the bottle. What further questions do they have?

Round Table Strategy

In the Round Table approach to cooperative learning, each student completes an action and then passes on the responsibility for completing another action to a member of his or her group. Round Table is a good way to involve each and every student in a group activity because it gives students "permission" to participate; in so doing, it tends to increase low-ability student participation and reduce high-ability student domination.

LESSON PLAN: PROBLEM ON THE WAY TO MARS

Goals: To engage students in a problem-solving activity in which they practice the Round Table approach; to teach students how to take turns in a small-group activity; to solve a problem using group decision-making skills

Materials: Chart paper, markers, set of "Mooncards" (Figure 1.13), Mars Data Recording Sheet (Figure 1.15), NASA Scorecard (Figure 1.16)

Web site: http://www.nasa.gov/

Procedure:
1. Read the following scenario to your class:

You are members of an international space exploration team in the process of using a moonport in preparation for a human flight to the planet Mars. As astronauts, you frequently fly from a space station orbiting the moon to the surface of the moon, where the moonport is located. On your most recent flight to the moon, your space shuttle crashes to the moon's surface about 10 miles from the moonport (Figure 1.12). The rough landing ruins your shuttle and everything in it, except for the fifteen items you are about to see (Figure 1.13). Survival of your team depends on reaching the moonport as soon as possible. In order to do this, you must look over the fifteen items and rank them in order of importance from most important to least important, to getting back to the moonport.

2. Give each team an envelope containing the mooncards for the fifteen items and a sheet of

Figure 1.12
Moon Scene

chart paper with a line on it, labeled at one end "Most Important" and at the other end "Least Important," as in Figure 1.14.

After students in each group have numbered off from 1, tell the students to put the cards face-down on the table.

3. Astronaut 1 goes first by drawing a card from the deck and deciding where on the line the item should go. The decision as to the card's placement should be reached by group consensus. Astronaut 2 goes next by drawing a card, and so on. The process continues around the group until all cards have been drawn and placed on the line.

4. When all teams have completed the task, have one person in each group record the team's top five choices on a chart you have created on white posterboard or on a piece of chart paper. Meanwhile, give each team a copy of the Mars Data Recording Sheet (Figure 1.15) and the NASA Scorecard (Figure 1.16). Have teams

score their work by recording their team ranks on the Data Recording Sheet, then comparing their results with those shown on the NASA Scorecard. Students can obtain a score by finding the difference between each of their ranks and those proposed by NASA.

5. Have teams discuss their rationale for the top five items, and discuss how their rationales compare with NASA's.

6. Going Further. Have students investigate the training that astronauts undergo in preparation for a flight into space. Visit NASA on the Internet at: http://www.nasa.gov/

Circle of Knowledge Structure
The structure of this approach to cooperative learning is like that of the Round Table, except that the task requires the Tracker to record data for the team. Circle of Knowledge requires turn-taking and serves as a powerful strategy for hands-on lab activities by ensuring that all students participate. To help teams work more efficiently, you'll be distributing the Team Data

Figure 1.13
Mooncards

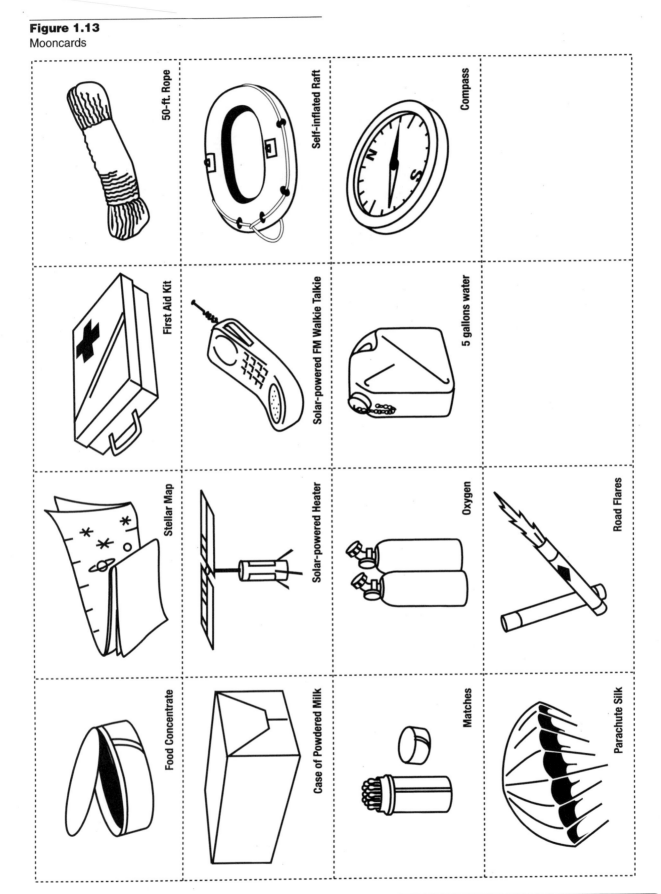

Figure 1.14
Arranging the Mooncards

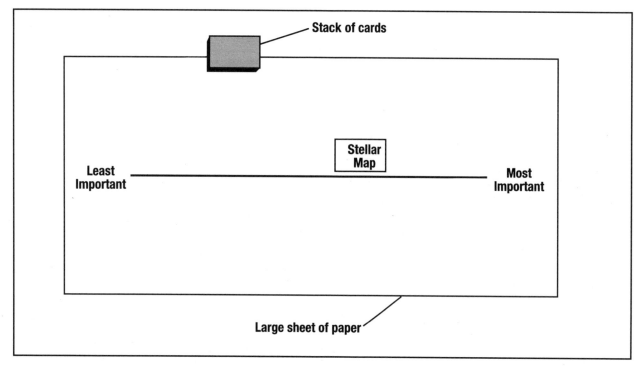

Stack of cards

Stellar
Map

Least
Important

Most
Important

Large sheet of paper

Figure 1.15 Mars Data Recording Sheet

PROBLEM ON THE WAY TO MARS

Item	NASA's Ranks	Your Ranks	Error Points	Group Ranks	Error Points
Box matches					
Food concentrate					
Fifty feet of nylon rope					
Parachute silk					
Solar-powered heater					
One case of powdered milk					
Two 100-pound tanks of oxygen					
Stellar map					
Self-inflating life raft					
Magnetic compass					
Five gallons of water in jug					
Signal flares					
First-aid kit					
Solar-powered FM walkie-talkie					
		Total			

Error points are the absolute difference between your ranks and NASA's.	Scoring for individuals: 0–25—excellent 26–32—good 33–45—average 46–55—fair	56–70—poor 71–112—very poor, suggests possible faking or use of Earth-bound logic

Figure 1.16 NASA Scorecard

Name	NASA's Reasoning	NASA's Ranks	Your Ranks	Error Points	Group Ranks	Error Points
Box matches	No oxygen on moon to sustain flame; virtually worthless	14				
Food concentrate	Efficient means of supplying energy requirements	4				
Fifty feet of nylon rope	Useful in scaling cliffs, tying injured together	6				
Parachute silk	Protection from sun's rays	8				
Solar-powered heater	Not needed unless on dark side	12				
One case of powdered milk	Bulkier duplication of food concentrate	11				
Two 100-pound tanks of oxygen	Most pressing survival need	1				
Stellar map of moon's constellations	Primary means of navigation	3				
Self-inflating life raft	CO_2 bottle in military raft may be used for propulsion	9				
Magnetic compass	Magnetic field on moon is not polarized; worthless for navigation	13				
Five gallons of water	Replacement for tremendous liquid loss on lighted side	2				
Signal flares	Distress signal when mother ship is sighted	10				
First-aid kit	Needles for vitamins, medicine, etc., will fit special aperture in NASA space suits	7				
Solar-powered FM walkie-talkie	For communication with mothership, but FM requires line-of-sight transmission and short ranges	5				

Organizer, which is used by the Tracker to collect team observations, measurements, and inferences (or whatever type of information the students are collecting).

LESSON PLAN: MYSTERY AT THE RINGGOLD[4] ROADCUT

Goals: To introduce students to Circle of Knowledge as a method for collecting group data on fossils (or any object); to help students understand that fossils are remains of organisms that lived in the past and can be used to reconstruct the history of life on Earth; to make observations and inferences; to predict the nature of the environment at the time these now-fossilized organisms were alive

Materials: Fossil crinoid stems (Figure 1.17) (put four to eight each in a small plastic bag),[5] hand lens, metric ruler, geological time scale, copy of Team Data Organizer (Figure 1.18)

Procedure:
1. Divide students into cooperative teams and distribute the materials. Explain the task to the teams—namely, that the teams should collect information on the objects in front of them (do not tell students what the objects are). Point out that some of the information gathered will be in the form of observations about the objects, while the other information will be inferences students make based on their observations.

---

[4] Ringgold is a small town located in Northwest Georgia in the folded Appalachian Mountains. During the early Paleozoic, this area was flooded with ocean water and was teeming with many varieties of marine life. Some of the remains of these living things were preserved as fossils. As one of my favorite fossil-hunting areas, I have used fossil remains as the main focus of this activity.

[5] Available from Two Guys Minerals & Fossils, 1087 Plymouth Street, East Bridgewater, MA 02333, or call 1-800-FOSSILS.

2. Explain that the Tracker collects data for the team. To begin, the Tracker asks each student, in order (from Student 1 to Student 4), to make and explain an observation. For example, it's brown; it's about 2 cm in diameter; it has grooves along the side; it's circular or cylindrical. The Tracker records each observation. Tell the Trackers to then go around again, asking each student for a second observation and recording it. To conclude, the Tracker asks each student to contribute an inference. For example, it is made of clay; it was once alive; it was a sea animal; it comes from the Earth's core. Again, the Tracker records each inference.

3. Circulate about the room and check on the groups, straightening out any problems you see developing. Notice that you can tell immediately from looking at the Team Data Organizer who is contributing and at what stage of the activity the group has arrived.

4. Have team members discuss the observations and inferences that were made. After a short discussion, have each team select what it thinks is the most important observation and inference, then record it on the data sheet. Collect this data and discuss the results.

5. Return the data sheets and let the groups know you will be presenting a series of questions that they should answer independently, using the Round Table method. Give the data sheet to Student 1. This person reads the question aloud, facilitates the discussion, and writes the answer on the data sheet. He or she then passes the sheet to Student 2, who repeats the process for question 2. This continues until each

Figure 1.17

Fossil crinoids. Students use the "circle of knowledge" structure to make observations and inferences.

question has been answered. When all the teams are finished, go over each question using the Numbered Heads Together approach. Read out the question, have a student draw a number from a deck of four cards, and ask students whose number was drawn to answer.

Questions:

- What kind of organism is this fossil? animal? plant? How do you know?
- How old do you think it is? Why?
- Of what kind of material is it composed?
- In what kind of environment did the organism live?

6. *Going Further*—Crinoid Task Cards. After students have completed their initial inquiry, they are ready for further activity. Distribute the Crinoid Task Cards (Figure 1.19), one to a

group. Each task focuses on a different aspect of research. The tasks are summarized below:

Tasks 1a. & b. Students perform as scientists and refine their observations.

Task 2. Students perform as mathematicians, measuring all crinoids and graphing their results.

Task 3. Students perform as paleogeologists and try to imagine what the crinoids looked like when alive.

Task 4. Students perform as poets and write short poems about the crinoids.

Task 5. Students perform as artists and make crinoid pendants using craft materials.

Task 6. (Create your own.)

Task 7. (Create your own.)

Figure 1.18
Team Data Organizer

MYSTERY AT THE RINGGOLD ROADCUT

TEAM DATA ORGANIZER

	Student 1	Student 2	Student 3	Student 4	Student 5
Observation 1					
Observation 2					
Inference					

Observation:

_____

Inference:

_____

Analysis Questions

1 _____

2 _____

3 _____

4 _____

Figure 1.19
Crinoid Task Cards

TASK 1A

Your group is composed of scientists. Make as long a list of observations of the crinoid as your group can. When your group has completed the list, make a second list of inferences. Note: Be sure to write your list on a large sheet of chart paper; you can use more than words!

TASK 1B

Classify each of the observations your group made according to the human sense it used to make it—for example, F=feel; S=smell; E=eyesight; H=hearing; and O=other senses. How is your list of observations different from the list of inferences? What thinking skills did you use to make the observations? the inferences? How are the thinking skills you used for the observations different from those you used for the inferences? Which do you think is more important—observations or inferences? Why?

TASK 2

Your group is composed of mathematicians. Measure the diameter (in centimeters) of at least 20 crinoids. You will have to visit other groups in order to get a total of 20 measurements. Send out four members of your group to measure five crinoids each; have the remaining members measure your crinoids. Make a population graph of the crinoids you measured. Set up the graph to look like the one shown on this card.

Note 1: Draw your graph on a piece of chart paper. Make it large and colorful.

Note 2: Seek out another group that did this task. Compare your graphs. Are your populations different? How do you know?

GRAPH

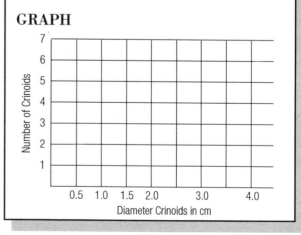

Figure 1.19
Crinoid Task Cards (continued)

TASK 3

Your group is composed of historians, anthropologists, and geologists. Use your imaginative side to draw a complete picture of what your team thinks the crinoid looks like. Remember, you are looking at only a piece of the animal. How do you think it looks as a complete creature? Does it have a head? Does it have feet? How does it move?

Note: When you draw your creature, place it in the context of an environment. Consider these questions: Where does this creature live? Does it live alone or are there others about? What does it eat? How does it get its food? What are its predators? its prey?

TASK 4

Your group is composed of writers . . . poets! Your task is to write several poems about the crinoid that your group will either publish or read aloud to your peers. Write several poems called Syntus, using the following formula:

Line 1: Single word or concept, such as fossil, crinoid, age, time, etc.

Line 2: An observation about line 1.

Line 3: An inference about line 1.

Line 4: A feeling or emotion about line 1.

Line 5: A synonym for line 1.

Note 1: Brainstorm as a group as many observations, inferences, and feelings about the crinoid as possible. Use the results of the brainstorming to create Syntus. Pair off and work on the poems together.

Note 2: Write your poems on sheets of chart paper. Make them colorful and easy to read from a distance.

Figure 1.19
Crinoid Task Cards (continued)

TASK 5

Your group is composed of artists. Your task is to make pendants using the crinoids, bell caps, gold or silver chain, and glue. After your group has made the pendants, show other groups how to do the same.

TASK 6

(Create your own.)

TASK 7

(Create your own.)

Think Aloud Pair Problem Solving

Thinking out loud about one's strategy for solving a problem can be an important aspect of learning. Think Aloud Pair Problem Solving is a cooperative learning strategy designed to help students acquire this skill. Students work in pairs. The teacher presents a problem in which Student 1 in the pair solves the problem by talking aloud, while Student 2 encourages and supports Student 1. Students alternate being "problem solver" and "encourager." Following are two lesson plans that make use of the Think Aloud strategy.

LESSON PLAN: FOREIGN LANGUAGE

Goal: To practice Think Aloud Problem Solving, which involves learning to talk aloud while thinking about a strategy for solving a problem and learning to listen and encourage

Materials: A sheet of paper with the following language problem printed on it:

> In a different language *luk eir lail* means "heavy little package," *bo lail* means "heavy man," and *luk jo* means "pretty package." How would you say "little man" in this language?[6]

Procedure:

1. Student 1 reads the problem out loud, then tries to solve the problem by talking aloud. Student 2 encourages Student 1. Encouragement does not mean giving away the answer; it does mean suggesting a method or telling one's partner to continue with a line of reasoning.

2. Discuss the results as a class. Ask a few students who were problem solvers to describe the method they used. Have the encouragers comment as well.

---

[6] *This strategy and this problem is based on Whimbley and Lockhead, as cited in B. Pestel, 1992, "Teaching Problem Solving Without Modeling Through 'Think Aloud Pair Problem Solving,'" Science Education, 77 (1) 83–94.*

LESSON PLAN: BOSTON HARBOR

Goal: To use the Think Aloud Problem Solving strategy to analyze an environmental science problem and suggest a solution to it.

Materials: A sheet of paper with the following language problem printed on it:

I'm going to tell you a true story; it's sort of a mystery. It's about the Boston Harbor. In the last few years, people have noticed that there is something wrong with the water in the Harbor, but no one knows exactly what is wrong. Fishermen have noticed that there are fewer fish in the Harbor. And they have seen a lot more algae. People who spend time near the Harbor have noticed that the water looks dirty; it is brown and foamy. It also has garbage in it. Tin cans, paper, and old food float in the water. Sometimes you can even see dead fish floating on the waves. You are a famous scientist. The Mayor of Boston asks you to find out what is wrong with the water.[7]

Questions:
- What is the first thing you do?
- What do you think might be wrong with the water?
- How will you find out if you are right?
- Do you have any ideas about how you could make the water clean again?

Procedure:
1. Student 1 reads the problem out loud, then tries to solve the problem by talking aloud. Student 2 encourages Student 1. Encouragement does not mean giving away the answer; it does mean suggesting a method or telling one's partner to continue with a line of reasoning.

---

[7] *Figure 2, Problem 1: Boston Harbor from* Appropriating Scientific Discourse: Findings from Language Minority Classrooms, *Working Paper 1-92, January 1992 by Ann S. Rosebery, Beth Warren, and Faith R. Conant, p. 14. Reprinted by permission of TERC.*

2. Discuss the results as a class. Ask a few students who were problem solvers to describe the method they used. Have the encouragers comment as well.

Jigsaw

Jigsaw is a cooperative learning strategy in which students become experts in some aspect of the material under investigation. By becoming an expert and then teaching other members of their team or working together with them to solve a problem, students become responsible for their own learning. The Jigsaw model has the advantage of encouraging students of all abilities to take equal responsibility for the subject matter; of course, the depth and quality of students' work may vary.

The overall strategy is depicted in Figure 1.20. Phase I of Jigsaw is to divide the content to be learned into chunks based on the number of students in each learning team. The sample lesson that follows divides the content into three sections—igneous, sedimentary, and metamorphic rocks. Thus each learning team will consist of three students. And each student will become an expert on one of the rock types.

In Phase II pairs of experts-to-be meet for about one class period to investigate and learn about the rock type to which they have been assigned. An expert sheet (see Figures 1.21, 1.22 and 1.23) guides their work. In addition, students receive hands-on materials and can consult a text. Students complete the expert sheet, perform the investigation, summarize their work, and prepare to return to their "home" team.

In Phase III the experts report back to their home teams. At this point, students do one of two things. They may give an informal report to the team, teaching their teammates about their "chunk" of content. (This can be viewed as direct teaching.) You may wish to provide the home team with a set of problems (see page 42) that the team must solve as a group. (In this case, the expertise of each team member is called on to help solve the problems.)

Figure 1.20
Jigsaw Strategy

JIGSAW II Robert Slavin (1978)

- **Groups:**
  - Expert groups are heterogeneous and made up of four to five students who represent a balance of academic ability, gender, and ethnicity.
  - Learning teams may be heterogeneous or homogeneous groups.
  - Each student has a task which contributes to the group objectives.
  - Student is a member of an expert group and a learning team.

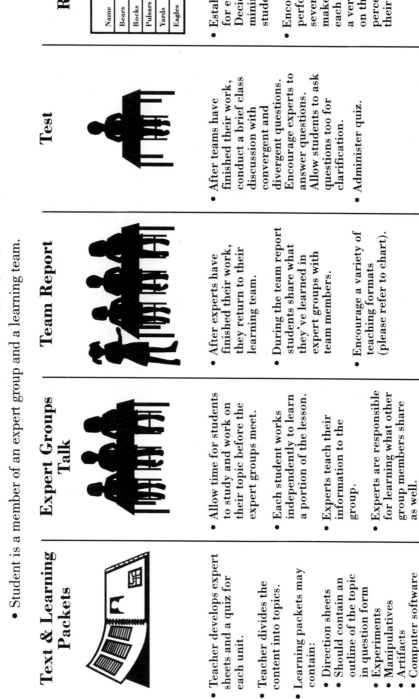

Text & Learning Packets	Expert Groups Talk	Team Report	Test	Team Recognition
- Teacher develops expert sheets and a quiz for each unit. - Teacher divides the content into topics. - Learning packets may contain: - Direction sheets - Should contain an outline of the topic in question form - Experiments - Manipulatives - Artifacts - Computer software	- Allow time for students to study and work on their topic before the expert groups meet. - Each student works independently to learn a portion of the lesson. - Experts teach their information to the group. - Experts are responsible for learning what other group members share as well.	- After experts have finished their work, they return to their learning team. - During the team report students share what they've learned in expert groups with team members. - Encourage a variety of teaching formats (please refer to chart).	- After teams have finished their work, conduct a brief class discussion with convergent and divergent questions. Encourage experts to answer questions. Allow students to ask questions too for clarification. - Administer quiz.	- Establish a baseline score for each student. Decide on what minimum score each student must receive. - Encourage academic performance. Identify several students who make improvement each week. Praise has a very positive effect on the way they perceive themselves & their achievements.

Weekly Chart

Name	1	2	3	4	5	6	7	8
Bears								
Rocks								
Pulsars								
Yards								
Eagles								

In Phase IV a test is given. It can be a written test or it can be more of a performance test, in which students have to apply what they have learned about the subject matter.

Phase V is a recognition and reward phase in which teams are presented a certificate for successful work.

LESSON PLAN: JIGSAW ROCKS

Purpose: To learn how to implement the Jigsaw learning strategy; to differentiate between igneous, sedimentary, and metamorphic rocks; to solve problems about rocks
Materials: Enough learning packets for pairs of students as follows:

> Igneous Experts: granite, pumice, obsidian, basalt, hand lens, bottle of vinegar
> Sedimentary Experts: sandstone, shale, conglomerate, limestone, any fossilized rock, hand lens, bottle of vinegar
> Metamorphic Experts: gneiss, schist, slate, marble, hand lens, bottle of vinegar; also Expert Sheets (Figures 1.21, 1.22, and 1.23)

Procedure:
1. Divide the students into pairs based on the three expert areas. Student pairs should sit together on the same side of the table or push their desks together. Have one student obtain the set of materials (learning packet) for the pair. At the same time, the student should obtain an Expert Sheet for their team. Copy the expert sheets that are described below for the pair.

2. Students use the materials and work together as a pair to answer the questions on the Expert Sheet. They can also use references and the Internet to help complete the questions.

3. At the end of the allotted period, students return to their home teams. Give each team a Problem Sheet (Figure 1.24) that it must answer together as a team.

4. Discuss each problem one at a time by using the Numbered Heads Together strategy (see page 23).

5. Test students on their knowledge of rocks. You might use this approach: Give each student a rock (such as sandstone with fossils in it if possible, or granite), and a hand lens. Ask the students to write on a sheet of paper how they could make a rock from scratch that looked like the one that they have been given. Tell them to describe their procedures very carefully.

6. Design a certificate that you can present to each member of the class.

SUMMARY

Cooperative learning is a key strategy for bringing inquiry into the science classroom. It's more than simply putting students into groups and asking them to complete a task. It involves making decisions that will lead to increased interdependence among team members so that their work together is greater than the individual efforts of team members. Creating teams that work together as a unit to solve problems not only can be a wonderful experience for your students, but also mirrors some of humanity's best efforts at working together to solve real problems.

Figure 1.21 Igneous Rock Expert Sheet

Rock	Color	Shape and Color of Crystals	Arrangement of Crystals (Even or Banded)	Effect of Vinegar (Acid)	Presence of Fossils	Use of the Rock
A						
B						
C						
D						

1. How were these rocks formed?
2. Under what environmental conditions were they formed?
3. Observe each rock and record your observations on the chart provided.
4. What, if any, minerals are contained in these rocks?
5. Where would you find these rocks?
6. Would you find these rocks in, on, or under your school grounds?
7. What can you tell from the size of the crystals: (a) rock cooled slowly, (b) rock cooled rapidly, or (c) rock cooled in water?
8. What is the difference between a rock that cooled above ground and one that cooled underground?
9. If you wanted to demonstrate how an igneous rock is formed, what would you do?
10. Do you think there are igneous rocks on other planets? Explain.

Figure 1.22 Sedimentary Rock Expert Sheet

Rock	Color	Shape and Color of Crystals	Arrangement of Crystals (Even or Banded)	Effect of Vinegar (Acid)	Presence of Fossils	Use of the Rock
A						
B						
C						
D						

1. How were these rocks formed?
2. Under what environmental conditions were they formed?
3. Observe each rock and record your observations on the chart provided.
4. What, if any, minerals are contained in these rocks?
5. Where would you find these rocks?
6. Would you find these rocks in, on, or under your school grounds?

7. Why might you expect to find fossils in sedimentary rocks?
8. Does shaking a jar of mixed-size sand and water, and observing the results demonstrate part of the sedimentary process? Explain by using a diagram and words.
9. Do you think there are sedimentary rocks on other planets? Explain.

Figure 1.23 Metamorphic Rock Expert Sheet

Rock	Color	Shape and Color of Crystals	Arrangement of Crystals (Even or Banded)	Effect of Vinegar (Acid)	Presence of Fossils	Use of the Rock
A						
B						
C						
D						

1. How were these rocks formed?
2. Under what environmental conditions were they formed?
3. Observe each rock and record your observations on the chart provided.
4. What, if any, minerals are contained in these rocks?
5. Where would you find these rocks?

6. Would you find these rocks in, on, or under your school grounds?
7. If you wanted to demonstrate how a metamorphic rock is formed, what would you do? Illustrate and explain.
8. Do you think there are metamorphic rocks on other planets? Explain.

Figure 1.24

PROBLEM SHEET FOR HOME TEAMS

1. Consider the following rocks: sandstone, granite, and marble. (a) Under what conditions is each formed? (b) Would they be found on other planets? (c) Where would you find these rocks in your state?

_____

_____

_____

2. What are the differences among sedimentary, igneous, and metamorphic rocks?

_____

_____

_____

3. Name some rocks that can be identified by an acid test. What does this tell you about the rock's composition?

_____

_____

_____

4. Complete these sentences:

a. Metamorphic rocks form when. . . .

_____

b. The southern part of our state contains rocks such as. . . .

_____

c. In a county next to ours, you'll find these rocks. . . .

_____

d. Fossils can be found in these rocks. . . .

_____

CHAPTER 2 EEEPs: EXCITING EXAMPLES OF EVERYDAY PHENOMENA

WHAT IS AN EEEP?

An EEEP is an exciting example of an everyday phenomenon. It is a science demonstration. It is an active learning tool designed to gain the attention and pique the curiosity of students. I coined the term several years ago after reading an article about the importance of linking science concepts to students' everyday experiences. Since that time, I have used EEEPs as a teaching tool in numerous classes and seminars. You'll find many examples of EEEPs—in the Earth, life, and physical sciences—later in this chapter. But first, let's look at the potential value of EEEPs in science teaching.

HOW CAN EEEPs ENHANCE MY SCIENCE LESSONS?

Most of us would agree that science inquiry is an important goal of science teaching—or, put another way, that helping students inquire into questions, phenomena, and ideas is fundamental to the science curriculum. EEEPs are designed to help us meet this goal.

A good EEEP, first and foremost, creates a look of surprise and fosters an environment in which students might be heard to say such things as, "How did that happen?" or "What caused that?" or "My prediction wasn't even close to what happened!"

For this reason, EEEPs work especially well as the opener for a short cooperative learning activity. By combining them with one of the cooperative learning strategies presented in Chapter 1 (Numbered Heads Together, in the following example), an inquiry environment is established in the context of small cooperative groups. Figure 2.1 is one of my favorite EEEPs.

AN EEEP EXAMPLE: WHERE DID THE WATER GO?

Materials: A small bottle of waterlock, also called sodium polyacrylate (this white, powdery substance absorbs a lot of water)[1]; 3 large polystyrene foam cups (large coffee cups work well); a large box (that you will place upside-down on the desk on which you perform the EEEP); bottled water

Procedure:

1. Prior to students entering the classroom, pour about 1 teaspoon of waterlock into *one* of the large cups. Put the cups on the box (Figure 2.2). Now you are ready to begin.

2. Arrange students in groups of three or four. Tell the students that you are going to conduct an EEEP.

3. Open the bottled water and let the students know that you are going to pour some water into

Figure 2.1
Sample EEEP Poster

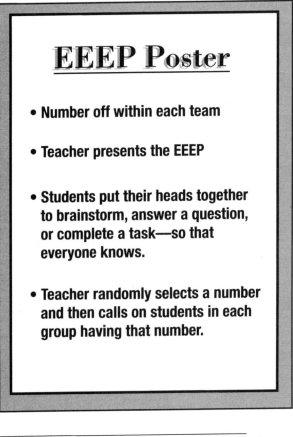

EEEP Poster

- **Number off within each team**

- **Teacher presents the EEEP**

- **Students put their heads together to brainstorm, answer a question, or complete a task—so that everyone knows.**

- **Teacher randomly selects a number and then calls on students in each group having that number.**

[1] *Order Waterlock from Flinn Scientific, Inc., P.O. Box 219, 131 Flinn St., Batavia, IL 60510. 630-879-6900.*

Figure 2.2
Where Did the Water Go?

one of the cups. Take the cup containing the waterlock, and pour a small amount of water into it. Immediately put the cup back on the box, returning it to its original location.

4. Now, start moving the cups around on the top of the box. As you do so, tell the students to keep their eyes on the cup with the water in it. Move the cups so that you exchange their places one or two times.

5. Now ask students: "Where is the cup with the water?" As students point to a cup, take it and turn it over in front of them (but do not let them look up into the cup). Because the waterlock absorbs water quickly, even the cup with the water in it will appear to be empty when you turn it over. Continue turning the cups over until all three are shown to be empty.

6. Without any class discussion (this is important), tell the students that they have a problem, and the problem is: Where did the water go? Tell the students that they have three minutes to write down, as a group, as many different answers as

there are people in their group. (I like to provide small white boards, one for each group, and a dry-erase marker for this activity.) When the three minutes are up, tell the students to take another thirty seconds to review their work and to make sure that everyone in the group knows all of the answers their team generated.

7. Now you are ready to call on students. Do so using the Numbered Heads Together technique. Have the students number off within each group from 1. Then have one student in the class draw a card from a deck of cards numbered the same way. Tell the students that if their number is drawn, they should stand and be ready to represent their group, providing one explanation for the big question (Where did the water go?).

8. Move around the room quickly, asking one student at a time to give one answer. Jot down student replies. When all the students have provided answers, write their replies on chart paper for all to see. You might ask for further opinions at this time.

Typical Answers

- It evaporated.
- There was a third cup.
- Something absorbed the water.
- A small bug drank the water.
- There was a hole in the cup.
- It went down your sleeve.
- It's a trick!

9. Finally, ask one student to come up to the box holding the large cups. Let the student turn over each cup, one at a time, noting the contents. A look of surprise and delight will emerge when he or she inspects the cup with the mush in it (the water has turned the powder to a gel).

WHEN SHOULD I USE EEEPs?

There are a number of situations in science teaching in which you might want to use EEEPs. Here are a few:

- As an introduction to a new chapter or unit of teaching. An EEEP is a wonderful way to begin something new. It helps establish interest and gives the students some idea of what is to come. If you use EEEPs this way, you won't need to use too many more during the course of a year.
- As a pre-assessment activity to ascertain students' prior knowledge. This is a really good use of EEEPs. It lets students hear each other's views, and lets you hear what ideas they bring to the topic.
- As a test of students' ability to:
  - Predict
  - Brainstorm alternative ideas
  - Make observations
  - Hypothesize
  - Work cooperatively
- As a performance assessment

USING THE EEEP ACTIVITY SHEET

A specially designed (generic) EEEP Activity Sheet (Figure 2.3) helps students consolidate their ideas. Distribute one EEEP sheet to each group. Here, students can make predictions, record their observations, think visually by drawing pictures of their explanations, summarize their findings, and jot down any questions they may have. If you choose, collect the sheets and assess them using the categories on the form as a rubric. They become a powerful learning tool linking instruction and assessment.

EARTH SCIENCE EEEPs

A Cool Experiment

Wrap a piece of wet cotton around the bulb of one thermometer. Hold another thermometer (with nothing on the bulb) next to the wet-bulb thermometer. Fan both thermometers with a piece of cardboard until there is no further change in their readings. Invite students to explain why the thermometer with the cotton on the bulb has a lower reading than the one without. *Concepts:* evaporation, heat, relative humidity.

Water Evaporation

Pour equal amounts of water into a shallow dish and a test tube. Set the dish and the test tube next to one another and have students observe over a period of several days. Invite students to explain why the water in the dish evaporated faster than the water in the test tube. *Concepts:* surface area, evaporation, heat.

Hot Water Freeze

Put equal amounts of water (about 500 mL) in two metal canisters (labeled 1 and 2). Heat the water in canister 1 to a temperature of about 70 °C. Put both canisters in a refrigerator, and have the students monitor them for the next several hours. Invite students to explain why the water in canister 1 froze before the water in canister 2. *Concepts:* molecular motion, heat energy, freezing point.

Figure 2.3

EEEP ACTIVITY SHEET
EXCITING EXAMPLES OF EVERYDAY PHENOMENA

Prediction: What do you think will happen?

_____

_____

_____

Observations and Data: What did you observe?

_____

_____

_____

Explanation of the EEEP

    Explain Your Idea in Words

_____

_____

_____

    Illustrate Your Idea

_____

_____

_____

Further Questions

_____

_____

_____

Team Sign-off

_____

_____

_____

The Punctured Can

Puncture three holes at different heights in an empty large juice can or a 2-liter plastic bottle. Set the container in a large pan. Cover each hole with a piece of plastic tape. Now fill the container with water. Ask the students to predict what will happen when the plastic tape is removed from each hole. Students should be encouraged to draw a diagram illustrating their predictions. Now remove the pieces of tape very quickly, one at a time, and have the students observe. Invite students to explain why the water coming from the hole at the bottom of the can streamed out further than the one near the top, comparing their predictions to what they actually observed. *Concepts:* pressure, water pressure.

The Foggy Cloud

Fill a flask with hot water. Pour out most of the water, leaving about an inch of it at the bottom. Sit the bottle in bright light. Hold an ice cube over the opening. Ask students to predict what they think will happen. After water vapor becomes visible, invite students to explain what happened. *Some questions:* Where did the water vapor come from? What cooled the water vapor? What is water vapor? *Concepts:* evaporation, condensation, cloud.

Breaking Rocks

Show students several pieces of sandstone that you have soaked in water overnight. Tell the students you are going to do something to the rocks before the next class. That night, put the rocks in resealable plastic bags and place them in the freezer. Show the bagged rocks to the students the next day. Invite them to explain what you might have done to cause the change in the rocks. Can they explain why some of the rocks have cracked? Have them make diagrams showing how they think the change may have occurred. *Concepts:* physical weathering, expansion, freezing.

The Mini-Telescope

Show students two lenses (hand lenses will work just fine) (Figure 2.4). Invite students to use the

Figure 2.4
Mini-telescope

Figure 2.5
The Case of the Mealworms

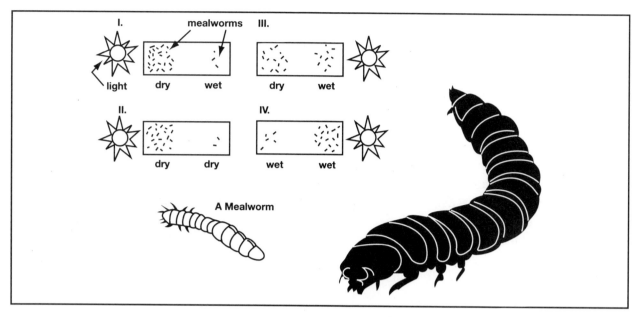

A Mealworm

lenses in combination to enable them to see a distant object (a picture or chart on a wall of the classroom, for example). The first challenge is for students to figure out how to hold the lenses in relationship to each other. (Hint: Hold one lens up to one of your eyes; hold the other lens at arm's length out in front of the first lens. Move the lens at arm's length toward and away from the "eyepiece" until objects are focused.) The second challenge is for students to explain why the image they see is upside-down. Invite them to illustrate their explanation of this phenomenon. *Concepts:* refracting telescope, magnification, image.

LIFE SCIENCE EEEPs

Earthworm Investigation

Show students a few earthworms. Invite students to speculate on the interaction of earthworms and changing environmental conditions (e.g., light, temperature, smell, gravity, sound, etc.). Have them formulate their ideas in the form of "If . . . , then . . ." questions. Then have students design simple investigations to answer

their questions. *Concepts:* animal behavior, reflexes.

Gravity and Plant Growth

In preparation for this EEEP, begin growing plants in various situations—for example, in a pot on its side, in a pot hanging upside-down, and so on. When the plants have taken hold, show them to students. Invite students to speculate on the relationship between plant growth and the force of gravity. Does gravity affect plant growth? Have students talk about designing an experiment to answer this question. *Concepts:* experimental design, factors affecting plant growth.

The Case of the Mealworms

Show students the diagram of the mealworms (Figure 2.5) As you do so, read them this scenario:

An experimenter wanted to test the response of mealworms to light and moisture. To do this, she set up four boxes as shown here. She used lamps for light sources and constantly watered pieces of paper in the boxes for moisture. In the center of each box she placed twenty mealworms. One day she returned to count the number of mealworms that had crawled to the different ends of the boxes.

Invite students to consider the following proposal: The diagrams show that mealworms respond to (*respond to* means "to move away or toward"): (a) light but not moisture; (b) moisture but not light; (c) both light and moisture; or (d) neither light nor moisture. Please explain your choice.

Have students work in groups of two, but have them write their responses in their own science log. Here is one student's response: "Boxes I and II show they prefer dry and light to wet and dark. Box IV eliminates dryness as a factor, so they do respond to light only. Box III shows that wetness cancels the effect of the light, so it seems they prefer dry. It would be clearer if one of the boxes were wet-dry with no light." *Concepts:* animal responses to environment, reflexes.

PHYSICAL SCIENCE EEEPs

The Penny and a Glass of Water
Present a full glass of water to the class. Ask them to predict how many pennies can be dropped, if done carefully, into the full glass of

Figure 2.6
The Penny and a Glass of Water

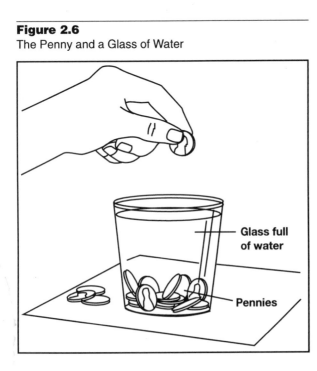

Glass full of water

Pennies

water without causing it to overflow. Note students' predictions. (If you want to take some extra time, have teams of students work together to talk through their predictions.) In full view, begin dropping one penny at a time into the glass of water (Figure 2.6).

(NOTE: If you hold the penny so that it slides into the water vertically, as opposed to on one of its flat sides, then you should be able to drop between 20 and 50 pennies into a full glass of water.) Invite students to work in small teams to illustrate and describe in their own words what happened on an EEEP Activity Sheet. Figure 2.7 is a sample activity sheet of a student who might have participated in this EEEP. *Concepts:* surface tension, properties of water.

The sample EEEP activity sheet is based on "The Penny and a Glass of Water" EEEP that was performed in Alma James's high school science class at the Benjamin Mays High School, Atlanta, Georgia.

Electric Balloons
You'll need a few balloons, some string, and a piece of wool for this EEEP. Inflate two balloons and tie about 50 cm of string to each. Rub one balloon briskly against a piece of wool fabric. Bring the balloon up to a wall in the room and let go. The balloon should stick to the wall. Now, take the second balloon and rub it briskly with the piece of wool. Hold the second balloon close to the first balloon. The balloons should move apart from each other. Have students work in teams to explain both demonstrations. Give each team an EEEP Activity Sheet. On it, students can draw diagrams and use words to help express their ideas. *Concepts:* static electricity, charged particles.

Why Does the Water Rise?
Stand a candle (use clay for support) in a pan of water. Light the candle, and then place a small glass jar over the candle (Figure 2.8). The flame will go out very soon after the jar is introduced, and the water will rise into the jar. Invite students to develop explanations that will answer

Figure 2.7
Sample EEEP Activity Sheet

Prediction: What Do You Think Will Happen?

We think that the glass of water will hold 5 pennies.

Observation: What Did You Observe?

After 30 pennies, the water overflowed.

Explanation of the EEEP

Drawing (Visual Pictural)

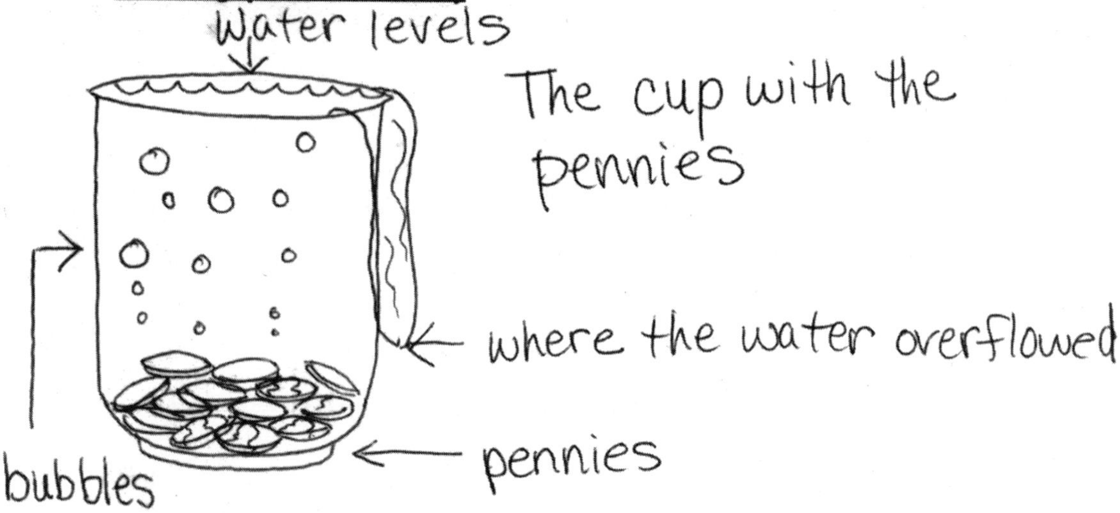

water levels

The cup with the pennies

where the water overflowed

pennies

bubbles

Team Explanation (words)

We think the weight of the pennies caused the water to rise.

Team Sign Off

Andrew   Carlos

Melissa   Melinda

Figure 2.8
Why Does the Water Rise?

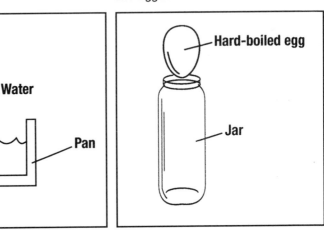

Figure 2.9
The Egg in the Bottle

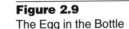

the following two questions: (1) Why did the flame go out? (2) Why did the water rise? *Concepts:* heat, air pressure, molecular model of matter.

The Egg and the Bottle

Have plenty of hard-boiled eggs on hand for this activity, along with several glass bottles or jugs and matches. Place a peeled hard-boiled egg in the mouth of a bottle (Figure 2.9) and present students with the following problem: How can you get the peeled hard-boiled egg in the bottle without touching the egg? Have students work in teams and propose a methodology for solving the problem. Each team should present you with written details of the proposed procedure before going ahead. Once students have a methodology, they can obtain the material to test out their idea. *Concepts:* air pressure, molecular model of matter.

Fill the Beaker!

Provide students with rubber tubing, a syringe, a beaker, and a pan of water. Tell them to invert the beaker in the pan of water. Challenge them to find a way to fill the beaker with water while leaving it in that position. Have students talk through possible methods. When they have an idea constructed, tell them they can go ahead

Figure 2.10
The Coin Drop and Throw

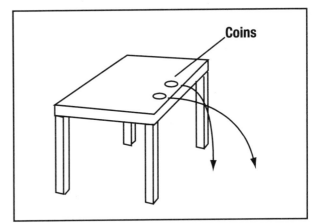

and test their method. NOTE: Students will discover that removing air, not trying to force water in, will help! *Concepts:* air pressure, molecular model of matter.

The Coin Drop and Throw

Place one coin (a quarter) on the edge of a table; hold another quarter in your hand at the edge of the table. Tell students that, at the same instant, you will flick the coin on the table outward horizontally with your finger while you drop the other coin straight down (Figure 2.10). Invite students to speculate on which coin will hit the floor first. After groups of students come up with their ideas, provide coins for students' use in testing their ideas. Invite students to explain the result. NOTE: In most cases, both coins will hit the floor at the same time. *Concepts:* gravity, Newton's laws of motion.

SUMMARY

EEEPs are science inquiry experiences in which teams of students work together to solve a problem that you have presented. EEEPs from Earth, life, and physical science have been presented in the chapter. An effective EEEP will be one that fosters student inquiry and teamwork. As you try them, think about the many demonstrations that you currently are using, and modify them to reflect the EEEP strategy. How can you use the method presented here to engage your students in inquiry?

CHAPTER 3   FUZZY SITUATIONS

Oftentimes, science teachers ask students to use their writing skills to answer an essay question about a specific concept in science, at which point students generally slip into a tried-and-true format for answering the question:[1]

- State the question.
- State the answer.
- Give a few explanations or supporting points.
- Summarize the answer.

For this reason, the essay question can become a decidedly tunnel-visioned endeavor. One answer is being sought. The student regurgitates the information presented in class or in the text in direct response to the question.

Writing in science can be more imaginative and constructive than this. Research has shown that creative writing in a subject area can build a sense of discovery, a yearning for explanation, and a need to conceptualize in order to verbally "paint the picture."

Storytelling has been a valid avenue for relaying information and attitudes throughout the ages and across all cultures. In his book *Tell Me a Story*, Roger Schank (1990) explains that "there are two aspects of intelligence [that] are critical for humans. One is to have something to say, to know something worth telling, and the other is to be able to determine others' needs and abilities well enough to know what is worth telling them. To put this another way, our interest in telling and hearing stories is strongly related to the nature of intelligence." Schank goes further, describing the dilemma of every teacher:

When people seem to truly understand what we have said, we give them high marks. But how can we determine that they have, in fact, understood us? We cannot really believe that intermittent head nodding and sage um-hums indicate real understanding. What else is there to go by? Our only recourse, outside of administering intelligence tests, is to listen to what our listeners say in response to what we have told them. The more they say back that seems to relate in a significant way to what we have said, the more they seem to have understood. In order to respond effectively, a listener must have something to say. We have a memory full of experiences that we can tell to others. Finding the right ones, having the right ones come to mind, having created accounts of the right ones in anticipation of their eventual use in this way, are all significant aspects of intelligent behavior.[2]

WHAT IS A FUZZY SITUATION?

Fuzzy situations are questions that allow teachers of science to tap into the creative writing abilities of their students, as well as probe their content knowledge and conceptual understanding. Fuzzy situations differ from essay questions in the following ways:

- They are told in story form.
- They contain a minimum of facts—the only facts given are the ones needed to set the stage for the story; details are fuzzy.
- There can be as many answers as there are students who answer the fuzzy situation.
- They require a prediction; the student must respond to the fuzzy situation by continuing the storyline and predicting an outcome.
- They ask students to defend their prediction by linking the creative answer they design to facts and terminology from the subject content underlying the situation.
- They address situations in which the self and society are linked to science and technology such that the student can construct a concept of the subject content under study based on personal understanding of the interface of science and society.

---

[1] *Introductory material prepared by Dr. Nydia Hanna, Assistant Professor of Science Education, Georgia State University. Used with permission.*

[2] *Roger C. Schank, Tell Me a Story: A New Look at Real and Artificial Memory. New York, NY: Charles Scribner's Sons, 1990, pp. xi–xii.*

Fuzzy situations can take many forms. They may appear in the form of a question, a challenge, a letter to a member of a hypothetical committee, a real or hypothetical activity, or even a news bulletin (Figure 3.1).

USING FUZZY SITUATIONS

Fuzzies lend themselves to many instructional uses in the classroom. Following are four distinct ways to employ them.

Assessing Prior Knowledge

Use fuzzies at the beginning of a unit to assess prior knowledge of a subject area. With a fuzzy, students are engaged in a creative writing assignment centered on the content area, but without the pressure to deliver the "correct" answer. In this manner, students are free to describe their concept of the situation, define terms, and offer their thoughts on the subject. The resulting fuzzy situation answer is authen-

tic, original, conceptual, and delineated by the student's prior knowledge.

From the answer, teachers can determine the depth of students' knowledge, how they conceptualize the topic, what terms they can define, how they associate ideas, how they process and describe scientific explanations, and how they perceive the interface of science and society. The prior knowledge assessment aspect of fuzzies makes them a powerful tool for teachers. Knowledge of "where students are" can assist the teacher in developing lesson plans that will be appropriate, effective, and challenging.

Ongoing Challenge

Try using a fuzzy situation as an ongoing project, a challenge to be met as the unit progresses. Typically, students identify their initial predictions and then adjust or alter them according to new knowledge they are constructing in the classroom. The ongoing fuzzy project thus documents learning and showcases conceptual con-

Figure 3.1
Headlines

struction. Students may keep a "Fuzzy Log" of their thoughts and ideas about their prediction.

By using fuzzies as ongoing projects, teachers foster an understanding of the scientific process of collecting data, the construction of knowledge, the reality of science and society interactions, and the power of prediction. Students' "Fuzzy Logs" will be evidence of their learning.

Final Assessment

A fuzzy situation also lends itself to a final assessment. The fuzzy story may be carefully written so as to incorporate all topics covered in the unit. The students make their (unique) predictions and then back them up with the knowledge they have constructed throughout the unit. You may wish to share with students criteria for

a successful fuzzy response. This helps to ensure a higher caliber of student response and to clarify your expectations. Criteria may include specifics or broader concepts.

Fuzzy situations used as final assessments require assessment tools that examine the depth, breadth, and creativity of the response. This type of assessment can be achieved by using a rubric. Figure 3.2 is an example of a rubric you may want to use to assess fuzzy situations.

Taking Action on STS Issues

Use fuzzy situations to empower students to take action on a science/technology/society (STS) issue. As the culminating experience in a unit, a fuzzy situation provides opportunities for students to brainstorm possible solutions to or

Figure 3.2 Rubric

Criteria	Possible Points	Points
Identified social relevance in one area of impact	1	
Identified social relevance in two areas of impact	2	
Identified social relevance in three or more areas of impact	3	
Predicted/discussed pros and cons of one outcome	1	
Predicted/discussed pros and cons of two outcomes	2	
Predicted/discussed pros and cons of three or more outcomes	3	
Creativity	1–3	
Level of logical progression	1–3	
Level and accuracy of science facts to support the positions stated	1–3	
Application to disciplines other than science	2	
Clarity of expression	1	
Suggested action to take	2	
Total	20–26	

resolutions of societal issues that require scientific understanding. Students might, for example, propose actions to be implemented in their school or community.

In this application, the fuzzy situation becomes a tool used by the teacher to open a window between the classroom and the outside world. It functions as a catalyst, converting theory and book knowledge into practice.

ADDITIONAL APPLICATIONS

1. If fuzzy situations are written by an interdisciplinary team of teachers, responses can be geared toward assessing knowledge in a variety of disciplines—perhaps science, math, history, or even art.

2. Fuzzy situations have been described here as tools the teacher uses. Alternatively, students can design fuzzy situations and "test" their peers. The process of designing a fuzzy situation may bolster creative writing skills and link writing in science to conceptualization of the big ideas in science.

3. A well-written fuzzy situation works for a wide range of age groups. It is not fact-laden; rather, it requires the students to supply facts based on their level of understanding. It would be interesting to track an individual student's answers to one fuzzy situation over the course of several years. What type of learning would have occurred? Would it be conceptual? relational? concrete? abstract?

LIFE SCIENCE FUZZIES

No Insects[3]

Wheat and barley farmers in the United States have been experiencing crop failure due to an overpopulation of hungry locusts. Concurrently, scientists from a private European firm have

Figure 3.3
No Insects

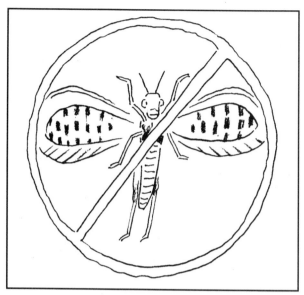

been working on an experimental pesticide that they believe will have the power to eliminate entire populations of locusts and other insect pests. The farmers are desperate to save their crops, so they talk the reluctant scientists into allowing their farms to be the first testing grounds for the experimental pesticide. The European firm prepares the pesticide to be shipped overseas by air. Unfortunately, the plane never reaches the United States. The plane mysteriously explodes mid-flight, releasing all of the pesticide into the atmosphere and contaminating the whole planet. It seems the scientists from the European firm were not aware of how powerful their pesticide was—it not only killed the locusts of the world, but every other insect as well (Figure 3.3).

- How will the world be different without insects?
- How great an impact do insects have on the day-to-day functioning of the Earth?
- Should the farmers have used the experimental pesticide before it had been fully tested?
- How else might the farmers have eliminated their locust problem?

---

[3] *Written by Julie Jasper while an Intern in the TEEMS Science Education program at Georgia State University. Used with permission.*

Human Population Growth[4]

In two years, an International Conference on Human Population Control will be held in India, a country in which mass human suffering has resulted from human overpopulation. Due to the gravity of the topic, leaders from every nation will be encouraged to attend this conference. At the conference, leaders will vote on a new International Law. It is to be called the "International Application to Give Birth" (IAGB).

If this vote passes, people all over the world will be required to fill out this application and have it approved according to international standards before having a baby. On the application, prospective parents will have to state how the child's medical, educational, nutritional, child care, and emotional needs will be covered. Parents will also have to reveal whether they have any drug, alcohol, or psychological problems that might interfere with the care of their child. Other information will be asked for on the application, as well, which will help the international committee decide whether the prospective parents are "fit" to reproduce. If parents do not fulfill the requirements, their application will be denied and they will be given three years to change their lifestyle so as to enable them to have a baby and raise it in a healthy manner. The conference points out that as the human population continues to grow exponentially, the effects are felt worldwide.

- Activity 1. Try to think of ten to fifteen problems that our world faces today that you think are caused or worsened by an increasing human population.
- Activity 2. Many countries have tried to implement programs to help curb human population growth. The most famous is China's One Child Law. This law is very controversial; many people think that it is a violation of human rights to impose a ruling of this type. Try to think of at least five possible programs

countries could develop to help curb human population growth.

- Activity 3. How do you think the world at large would feel and react if the "International Application to Give Birth" were enforced? Do you think it is a good or bad idea? Do you think it would help curb human population growth? Why or why not?
- Activity 4. Hold a debate. Randomly divide the class into four groups, two pro and two con groups. Provide an environment in which the students can express their opinions in a structured manner. After the debate, have the students (as a class) share their favorite alternative Human Population Control programs. Send these ideas to local, state, and federal politicians. Or, if possible, have the students develop a Web site that presents the results of their research (Figure 3.4).

GENES Committee[5]

You receive a letter today. In it you are asked to be prepared to discuss the implications of an incredible scientific discovery and breakthrough. Here is the letter (Figure 3.5).

Crazy Virus[6]

A horrible virus has been spreading throughout the world. It is similar to AIDS, but it is spread through in other ways than through bodily fluids. At present, it seems to be spreading by floating through the air. It will surely be the end of mankind as we know it, unless something is done quickly.

A biochemist who has been working long hours for many years on AIDS research finds a cure for AIDS that also seems to work on this new virus. But the drug she has discovered requires two chemicals: one from the tiger and one from the humpback whale, both endangered species. The process for retrieving these chemicals

---

[4] *Written by Sarah Bexell while an Intern in the TEEMS Science Education program at Georgia State University. Used with permission.*

[5] *Written by Kelli Schuyler while an Intern in the TEEMS Science Education program at Georgia State University. Used with permission.*

[6] *Written by Maggie Hewes while an Intern in the TEEMS Science Education program at Georgia State University. Used with permission.*

Figure 3.4
Debating the Human Population Growth Fuzzy Situation

Figure 3.5
GENES Letter

Dear Colleague,

As the esteemed head of the Global Ethics for New and Experimental Science (GENES), you must contact and meet with the other members of the GENES committee in one week in Helsinki, Finland, to discuss the incredible scientific discovery and application proposed by our revered colleague Dr. Wendell Lipshaw. It is essential that all members of the GENES committee be present, including the scientific, social, cultural, religious, environmental, and economic attachés from the various nations.

Dr. Lipshaw seems to have unlocked the mystery of aging. By using gene therapy, not only is he able to expand the average life expectancy to three times the current average of 76 years of age, but his anti-aging therapy seems to rejuvenate cells, tissues, and organs such that individuals can expect to live well into their second century with smooth skin, firm muscles, clear vision, high energy, and vigorous reproductive capabilities.

It is the job of the GENES committee to discuss when and if we should accept this gene therapy for widespread use. Please predict the outcome of projected widespread use of Dr. Lipshaw's therapy over the next two generations—both its advantages and its disadvantages—and make any recommendations you may have to the committee for implementing the use of this therapy.

Respectfully Yours,
Kelli Schuyler
Chairperson of the Projects for the Advancement of the Human Race
Global Awareness Committee

requires that the animals be killed. Although the biochemist is sure her fellow organic chemists, if given the time, could make the same compounds in the lab and end this crazy virus, it may take too long. In the meantime, the current process would wipe out the populations of tigers and humpback whales, two wonderful animals. The biochemist must act quickly.

- What should she do? What are her alternatives?
- To whom must she talk in order to solve the problem?
- Do you see humans as the most important species in this world?

PHYSICAL SCIENCE FUZZIES

Icy Situation[7]

A young scientist, tired of always having to drink around the ice cubes in a glass, devises a solution that, if added to water, would cause the ice to sink to the bottom of the glass. This neat invention is about to go on the market. You, as part of the U. S. Food and Drug Administration, have to either approve or disapprove the manufacturing of this special solution (Figure 3.6).

- What are some questions you would ask the scientist about the special solution?
- How would you explain how the process might work?
- Should we be worried about what implications this invention could have on the world?

Anonymous Letter[8]

You have been contacted by the United Nations on the basis of your world-renowned problem-solving abilities in the realms of science and society. You will be one of five members of an ad

---

[7] *Written by Robert Pike while an Intern in the TEEMS Science Education program at Georgia State University. Used with permission.*

[8] *Written by Daniel Whitehair while an Intern in the TEEMS Science Education program at Georgia State University. Used with permission.*

Figure 3.6
Icy Situation

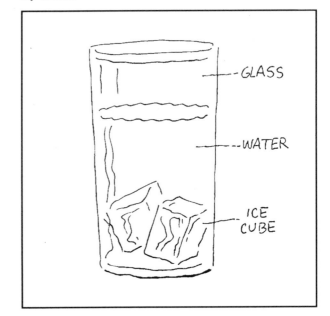

hoc committee that will review an anonymous letter (Figure 3.7) that was received by the United Nations. Your committee will meet according to the following schedule:

- First Meeting: The committee will hold a brainstorming session in which members will discuss all the issues that could be involved in the crisis situation as described in the letter. (Each member of the committee should keep a written copy of the issues discussed in the brainstorming. Each member should research and develop a proposed plan of action for the UN.)
- Second Meeting (one week later): The committee will review and discuss each of the five proposed plans of action. It will then create one Official Plan of Action that will be the committee's recommendation to the UN as to what should be done.
- Third Meeting (two to three days later): In this brief meeting, the committee will finalize its Official Plan of Action and prepare an oral presentation of its plan. (Every committee member should participate in some manner in the presentation.)

Figure 3.7
Anonymous Letter

Dear United Nations,

I write this letter anonymously for my own safety. There is a good chance I may disappear as a result of the enclosed information . . . please look after my cats.

As you are all aware, in 1998, trendy self-made media millionaire Mr. Ed Trunter donated $150 billion to NASA. As you are most likely not aware, the donation contract contained a secret provision that gives Mr. Trunter the right to do private research on 50% of any discoveries made by NASA projects funded by his donation.

Two years after Mr. Trunter's donation, the NASA Sherpa Mission to Venus brought back 120 kg of an unknown substance now known as "CJ" (named for its resemblance to Cracker Jacks™). NASA wasted its 60 kg of CJ on researching space laser weaponry.

Mr. Trunter, however, poured billions into covert research and reached astonishing results. Moreover, he utilized only 20 kg of his 60 kg on research, and thus currently possesses the only 40 kg of CJ that exists!

First, Mr. Trunter developed a cure for AIDS from CJ. The cure, which was tested on mammals and then on third-world humans with only a few casualties resulting, is now 100 percent effective in removing the AIDS virus from a human. The cure, which is a pink liquid that is ingested, has been labeled "PC" or "Pink Cure." One liquid gram of PC is enough to cure one human!

Second, the CJ can also be easily manipulated into a stable gas that could serve as a "patch" over the hole in our ozone layer. For every 10 kg of CJ that is converted to gaseous CJ, one-fourth of the ozone layer could be patched up!

And lastly, the CJ can be converted into a powder known as "NTN" that would be the most explosive substance on Earth. One gram of this powder equals the blast of an atomic bomb.

As you can see, this is powerful, powerful information. As an insider, I can assure you it is still uncertain what exactly Mr. Trunter plans to do with the remaining 40 kg of CJ. It could be used for any one of the above-mentioned possibilities, or it could be used in further research, which could lead to more breakthroughs. You should be aware that Mr. Trunter has spoken with several countries that have made offers to purchase his CJ.

Nevertheless, CJ is in the hands of a commercial omnivore, which can only be DEVASTATING for humanity. You must act for the sake of our existence.

—Anonymous

• Last Meeting (one to two days later): The committee will present its Official Plan of Action before the entire UN (the class) and submit a copy of the plan in written form to the Visiting Observer (teacher).

EARTH SCIENCE FUZZIES

Water or Gas[9]

The largest oil and water pipeline in the United States runs from Texas to New Jersey. The route takes it through your county. The government

[9] *Written by Karen Stewart-Tolmich while an Intern in the TEEMS Science Education program at Georgia State University. Used with permission.*

has just released a report on the status of the pipeline. The walls are deteriorating and there is an 85 percent chance that the contents of the pipeline will begin leaking into the ground. Since the pipeline crosses major rivers in the area, there is a 90 percent chance that it will begin leaking into the water that your city uses as its drinking water. The company that owns the pipeline says that if it rebuilds the pipeline to meet government standards, the company will have to quadruple the price it charges for transporting the oil and gas. That will result in the price of gas at the pump rising from $1.00 to $4.00 a gallon.

- Should the government force the pipeline company to repair the pipeline?
- If so, what effects will that have on the city and the people in it?
- What will happen if the company is not forced to repair the pipeline?

Aqua City[10]

It's the year 2150. Scientists and architects have designed an undersea city in response to a constantly increasing population on Earth. The construction of Aqua City may, however, cause unnatural changes in the ocean's environment. The prototype, built five years earlier, has been a success in the sense that humans can safely inhabit the city without complications. However, the number of waste products in the water has increased. There also have been reports of an increased number of shark attacks and whales beaching within 10 miles of the prototype city. Because of the growing need for inhabitable spaces, the actual city would have to be ten to twenty times larger than the prototype. Researchers cannot say for certain what will happen to the ocean's ability to support life in the next ten years if the project is approved.

- Should the city be built? Why or why not?
- Where should it be built?
- What are some alternatives to an undersea city?

A Smelly Dilemma[11]

Following are the minutes from a local town meeting:

The local citizens are totally opposed to the proposed landfill. The site would serve as a dumping ground at least until the year 2005, at which time other sites will be available to serve as landfills. The citizens insist that the government should find alternative methods for the disposal of trash. Moreover, the homes in the neighborhood are at most five years old, and the city council has just approved the construction of 500 additional single-family-home units.

You are a member of a task force that has been commissioned by the city to examine the way in which garbage disposal can be handled. During this examination, you are to consider the accumulation of solid waste due to the growth of the community, the cost and feasibility of potential handling plans, and the effectiveness of past initiatives (Figure 3.8).

- Part One: Brainstorming Possible Problems. Do not begin this section until you have carefully considered the above situation and thought about it or discussed it. When you feel you understand the situation, brainstorm as many problems associated with the disposal of solid waste as you can. List only your five best ideas and number each one.
- Part Two: Identifying the Underlying Problem. Select one of the problems you have just listed and write it below. It should begin with the words "In what ways might . . ." or "How might. . . ." Your problem should be written as clearly and specifically as possible.

---

[10] *Written by Nedeidre Smith while an Intern in the TEEMS Science Education program at Georgia State University. Used with permission.*

[11] *Written by Arlethea Williams while an Intern in the TEEMS Science Education program at Georgia State University.*

Figure 3.8
A Smelly Dilemma

- Part Three: Alternative Solutions. Brainstorm as many possible solutions as you can to the problem as you have defined it above. Record only ten of your solutions below, numbering them in order of feasibility.
- Part Four: Scenario. If Solutions Are Enacted. Each member of your group should choose a different solution and describe how it would be implemented, along with any possible drawbacks.

ENVIRONMENTAL SCIENCE FUZZIES

Should We Make the Plunge?[12]

You live in a lovely country setting, with a forest surrounding your house and a beautiful crystal-clear river running near your home. You've always enjoyed having the river nearby as a resource for swimming and fishing in the sum-

mer months and for watching the wild animals drink and play by the water year-round.

To make a public lake and social meeting place, the local government is suggesting damming the river about a mile upriver from your house. They plan to create a wonderful play-ground and picnic area for the surrounding community. The town developers doing research on the dam report that little or no change should occur to the river community. They believe they can build the new lake and allow much of the riv-er to continue flowing. A private citizens' group also has been doing some research on this topic and does not believe the developers' findings. The group's findings suggest that diverting the river flow will greatly alter the surrounding neighborhoods.

As a concerned citizen yourself, you want to do some research on the topic of water diversion and dams. Discuss the situation with your peers and brainstorm some questions or issues that you would raise with the developers and/or the citi-zens' group. Consider the following:

---

[12] *Written by Kirsten Mixter while an Intern in the TEEMS Science Education program at Georgia State University.*

- What do you think would be the effect of changing the flow of water?
- Construct a list of pros and cons for and against the construction of the dam and lake.
- Would you support the construction of the dam and lake? Why?
- What could you do to support or protest its construction?

SUMMARY

Fuzzy Situations are a way to engage your students in discussions in which they have to make decisions and consider the consequences of human actions. They enable your students to explore science-related social issues, ethical situations in science, the role of writing and discussion in an inquiry approach to science teaching. Once you start using the Fuzzy Situations presented here, you will be in a good position to write and create your own. For more Fuzzy Situations, check out the *Minds On Science* Web site at http://www.gsu.edu/~mstjrh/mindsonscience. html/

CHAPTER 4   **ACTIVE LEARNING STRATEGIES**

This chapter focuses on a collection of six active learning strategies that build on the cooperative learning strategies, EEEPs, and Fuzzy Situations presented in Chapters 1, 2, and 3. In each case, the strategies have been shown to improve students' motivation, attitudes, and conceptual learning in science.

- Pre-Assessment Strategies
- The Collaborative Questioning Strategy
- The Q-M-S Strategy
- The Active Reading Strategy
- Visualization: Guided Imagery
- Games

PRE-ASSESSMENT STRATEGIES

The goal of a pre-assessment strategy is to assess students' prior knowledge, ideas, beliefs, and attitudes. Research studies in science education have linked the use of pre-assessment strategies with improved student concept learning. By having students participate in an activity designed to identify their existing ideas about a topic, we add a powerful active learning strategy to our lesson planning. Following are five strategies you can use to identify students' prior knowledge.

T-charts

In this strategy, teams of students answer two questions about a science topic:

(1) What have you heard about . . . ozone (or dinosaur extinction, or the Big Bang Theory, The Laws of Motion, etc.)?

(2) What questions do you have about this topic?

The T-chart on ozone (Figure 4.1) is an example of the type of work created by four seventh-grade students working together as a small team. As you read the listings under the "What we have heard about ozone" column, note the misconceptions that are included. These should not be corrected immediately; rather, they should be revisited later in the unit of study and reconsidered by the students.

Figure 4.1
Sample T-chart—what we might expect from middle-school students

Ozone	
What we have heard about ozone	What questions do we have about ozone?
• It makes us burn up. • It's smog and it's harmful to us. • Makes the earth heat up. • Air pollution can cause ozone. • It's caused by chemicals in the air. • It can be dangerous to people with breathing problems. • There is good and bad ozone.	• What causes ozone? • How can we tell if there is ozone in the air? • Is it different in the center of a city compared to the suburbs? • What effect does it have on humans? • Is it caused by cars? • What will happen if the ozone in the air is all gone?

Procedure: Provide sheets of chart paper and pens, and instruct the student teams to make a T-chart similar to the one shown in Figure 4.2, which happens to be about rocks.

1. Tell the students they will have about 6 minutes to brainstorm and write their ideas on the chart. At the end of 6 minutes, tell the students to finish the thought they are currently writing.

2. Then tell the students to look over their lists and select one very interesting idea and question and to be ready to share it. At this stage, you should have a master T-chart on a piece of chart paper.

3. Have one student from each group write the group's idea and question on the class chart.

4. Hang the student-produced T-charts and the master T-chart in the classroom. As students study the topic further, have them evaluate their ideas, crossing off those they can refute and discussing the questions they posed.

Surveys

This strategy can help you identify any "alternative views" students might have on a particular science concept or topic. Cards with pictures and diagrams on them, classroom demonstrations, open-ended questions, and even multiple-choice questions can be used. The goal is to find out *what students really think* about a topic.[1]

Procedure: Give each student a copy of a survey such as the one that appears in Figure 4.3. This Living Things Survey is designed to help determine students' understanding of the statement "An animal is a living thing." Tell students to look over the list and place a check mark next to those items they consider to be animals, and another check mark alongside those they consider to be living. Have the students total the number of check marks in each column. By a

show of hands, you can see the range of responses in your class. The important point here is that we all construct meanings for the words we see and hear.

Interviews

Although interviewing students is a time-consuming process, it, like surveying, can help us find out what students really think about the concepts we are teaching. When interviewing, you might use pictures, cards, and other props that will help students express their ideas.[2]

Procedure: Interview students individually. Following is a set of interview questions for the word *animal*. Use it as a basis for constructing your own interviews about key topics you are introducing to your students.

1. **Introduction.** "I would like to talk to you about your understanding of the word *animal*. First, I'll show you some drawings and then we'll have a little talk about them."

2. **Question for each card.** "Given your understanding of the word animal, would you consider this to be an animal?"

3. **Follow-up for each card (choose one).** "Why did you say that?" or "Can you explain to me why you think that?" or "Can you tell me more about that?"

4. **A final question.** "Thank you for telling me about your understanding of the word *animal*. Just to finish, I wonder if you could describe to me, in your own words, what you think an animal is."

NOTE: A good set of interview cards can be created from the survey example on animals.

---

[1] *The following idea comes from Roger Osborne and Peter Freyberg in* Learning in Science *(Portsmouth, NH: Heinemann, 1985).*

[2] *Adaptation of Appendix D2: Interview questions from* Learning In Science: the Implications of Children's Science *by Roger Osborne and Peter Freyberg, with Beverley Bell et al., p. 177. Copyright © 1985 by Roger Osborne and Peter Freyberg. Reprinted by permission of Reed Publishing Ltd.*

Figure 4.2
T-chart Template

ROCKS

What have you heard about rocks?	What questions do you have about rocks?
Most interesting idea	**Most interesting question**

Figure 4.3
Living Things Survey

Adaptation of Figure 12.2: Exploring teachers' meanings for 'animal' and 'living' from *Learning in Science: The Implication of Children's Science* by Roger Osborne and Peter Freyberg, with Beverley Bell et al., p. 140.
Copyright © by Roger Osborne and Peter Freyberg.
Reprinted by permission of Reed Publishing Ltd.

	ANIMAL	LIVING
ELEPHANT		
FISH		
SNAKE		
SPIDER		
TREE		
FLY		
BOY		
MUSHROOM		
BIRD		
FIRE		
COW		
GRASS		
LION		
CAR		
FROG		
CAT		
WORM		
SLUG		
WHALE		

Cushioning/Underexplaining

In *Inspiring Active Learning*, Merrill Harmin points out that cushioning and/or underexplaining a new idea will tend to create a climate of openness and thus increase the chances that students will talk about the idea. This, in turn, will help teachers find out what students really believe, and, in the case of a skill, what they are able to do.

Procedure:

Cushioning. When we introduce new material, it is often a good idea to minimize anxiety and maximize a relaxed, open-minded focus. So we might start off by saying, "We will talk about something new today. Do not assume you need to understand it completely right now. We will review and help each other later, so relax, and let's just see what happens today."

Underexplaining, using learning pairs: Present the concept or principle to be learned—for example, using a balance (Figure 4.4). You might begin by saying something like this: "There are lots of ways to get a scale like this to balance. You can move this center point or the position of the weights, as I am doing here. You can invent your own system, but one general rule to follow is. . . ." Continue your brief, cursory explanation, so perhaps only half the class understands it. Then say: "Now get together in pairs. Help each other figure out how to do this. When you both get it, work some practice problems. If you're both stuck, ask another pair for help."

Attentive lecture/discussion. Ask the class: "How did we do? What did you figure out? What questions remain?" Continue discussion or explanation as appropriate, but no longer than whole-class involvement and attention are maintained.

Ask a friend/individual work. Have students complete their worksheets. Tell them: "Practice good thinking. If you get stuck, ask a friend for help."

Concept Mapping

Concept mapping is a strategy aimed at getting at the connections our brains make between the

Figure 4.4
Swing Balance

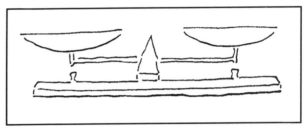

ideas that we think about and use. As such, it is a powerful tool for pre-assessing knowledge (or, naturally, for assessing learners at any stage of the learning cycle). (See Figure 4.5.)[3]

Procedure: Begin by giving students marking pens, small index cards or self-stick writing pads, and chart paper. Choose a key word or topic for the concept map—e.g., food chain, plate tectonics. Then lead students through these steps:

1. Think of as many words as you can that relate to the key word. Write these words on scratch paper. (Encourage brainstorming, with little discussion.)

2. Look over the words on your scratch paper and throw out any words that remain.

3. Write each of the words, including the key word, on individual index cards or self-stick removable notes.

4. Rank the concepts from most inclusive to most specific.

5. Group the concepts into clusters. Add more specific concepts (on cards) if necessary.

6. Arrange concepts (using the cards or self-stick writing pads) in a two-dimensional array.

---

[3] *The ideas presented here are based on the work of Joseph D. Novak and D. Bob Gowin,* Learning to Learn. *Cambridge, England: Cambridge University Press, 1984, pp. 32–33.*

Figure 4.5
Concept Map for Rocks

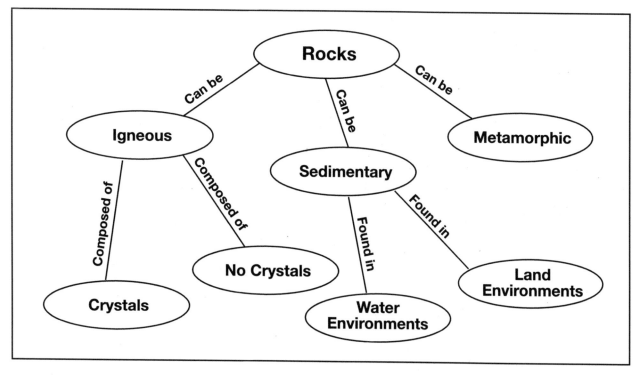

7. Write the concepts on the sheet of chart paper exactly as they appear in the two-dimensional array, or simply attach the cards to the chart paper.

8. Link the concepts and label each link.

COLLABORATIVE QUESTIONING

When we ask students questions in the course of our lessons, quite often the question is presented to the whole class, and then we use one of several methods to get ONE student to reply. What about the rest of the class? Collaborative questioning is a strategy designed to involve the entire class in discussing the questions we pose. This is important, because there is evidence that the more students have an opportunity to talk about science, the more they will learn.

Collaborative questioning can be used in a number of different contexts and for a variety of purposes, including:

- As a pre-assessment tool
- As a brainstorming tool
- As an inquiry session strategy
- As a way to encourage talking aloud within the safety of small groups
- As a cooperative group review strategy

Procedure:

1. **Students number off into cooperative groups.** Organize your class into cooperative learning groups of four students each. Although your goal is to have equal numbers of students within each group, this may not be possible if your class is not divisible by four. In that case, organize one or two groups of three students each. Have students number off within their groups from one to three or four.

2. **Teacher poses an inquiry question.** Inquiry questions can be either convergent or divergent. Low inquiry questions tend to be closed or convergent, whereas high inquiry questions tend to be open and divergent. Each

Figure 4.6
Collaborative questioning engages cooperative teams of students in answering important questions, as well as completing challenging problems as a team.

type is appropriate, depending on your objective(s). Suggestions for both types of questions appear in Figure 4.7.

3. **Students put their heads together to collaborate on and discuss the question.** Try allotting students just a few minutes to discuss the question; that way, they will immediately focus their attention on the task. Give each team either a small white board and dry-erase pens, or a sheet of newsprint, to record their answers. Appoint one student to be the team recorder.

4. **Teacher randomly calls a number.** If you wish, in lieu of calling a number, try using numbered cards and typically asking a student to draw the card. (Refer to Numbered Heads Together strategy in Chapter 1.) The student whose number is called "represents" the team by standing and answering the question, by

Figure 4.7 Inquiry Chart

LOW AND HIGH INQUIRY QUESTIONS CHART

Type of Question	Student Responses	Type of Response	Examples
Low inquiry (convergent)	• Recall, memorize • Describe in own words • Summarize • Classify on basis of known criteria • Give an example of something	Closed	How many . . . Define . . . In your own words . . . state similarities and differences. . . What is the evidence . . . ? What is an example . . . ?
High inquiry (divergent)	• Create unique or original design, report, inference, prediction • Judge scientific credibility • Give an opinion or state an attitude • Make value judgments about issues	Open	Design an experiment . . . What do you predict . . . ? What do you think about . . . ? Design a plan that would solve. . . . What evidence can you cite to support . . . ?

going to a designated space on a class board to write the team's answer, or by holding up the small white board presenting the team's work.

THE Q-M-S STRATEGY

The Q-M-S strategy is designed to help us rethink how we structure hands-on laboratory activities and reorient them so that they emphasize problem solving and inquiry, both of which are central to the reform of science education. Whenever students are faced with experiments or activities in the lab or on the classroom table-top, they should be presented with challenging situations that encourage them to use inquiry and problem-solving approaches. In the Q-M-S strategy:[4]

Q stands for **Question** or problem situation
M stands for the possible **Means** to finding the solution or alternative solutions
S stands for the **Solution**

In classroom situations (laboratory, small-group discussion, assessment), one or more of the three components of the strategy can be left "open." The table in Figure 4.8 shows many variations on the Q-M-S strategy. The engaging science classroom will generally make use of different variations at different times, depending on teaching objectives, student abilities, subject matter, and the like.

Q question given   **"Q"** question not given
M means given   **"M"** means not given
S solution given   **"S"** solution not given

Following are some activities that you can use with your students that make use of the Q-M-S strategy.

[4] From the Do-It-Yourself Curriculum Guide *published by the Education Department of South Australia, by Roger Cross, La Trobe University, Melbourne, Australia.*

Task 1. The Onion Lab

Examine the following activity (Figure 4.9) and classify it in terms of the Q-M-S strategy. Then modify the activity to satisfy one of the other inquiry and problem-solving types.

Activity: Looking at Onions

Onion cells are easy to see through a microscope. Following are the materials you will need for this investigation and the procedure you should follow.

Materials: Part of an onion, microscope, one slide with coverslip, one toothpick, one dropper with water, transparencies of onion skin cells, methylene blue solution, blotting paper or filter paper

Procedure:
1. Squeeze a drop of water onto the center of the slide.

2. Peel off a small piece of the thin onion skin.

3. Float the skin on the drop of water on the slide.

4. Cover with the coverslip. Put your slide in a safe place.

5. Look at the transparency of onion skin cells. You will see something like this when you look at your slide.

6. When you know what you are looking for, examine your slide through the microscope. Use the lowest magnification first. Later, you may be able to view the cells by using a higher magnification. Draw some of the onion cells in your science log.

7. Stain the cells. Look at them through the microscope again, and check what you see.

8. Draw some of the stained onion cells in your science log.

Figure 4.8 Q-M-S Chart

Variation	Example	Type of Activity
"Q" "M" "S"	Students are asked to think of new questions to ask, to investigate them, and to arrive at conclusions. This may be appropriate as a follow-up exercise after a project or laboratory investigation. You might also elect to work from student questions, in which case, you might say, "Work out and do an investigation to find possible solutions to that question."	Asking question, inquiry
Q M S	A complete presentation of a scientific explanation or an historical account of a scientific investigation (e.g., Rutherford Gold Foil Investigation) is given.	Historical
Q "M" "S"	Given a question or hypothesis, students are asked to design their own investigation. This works very nicely after doing a demonstration or an EEEP. Students might also generate a hypothesis based upon the observation of the EEEP and then design an investigation.	Given this . . . then . . .
Q M "S"	In this standard laboratory exercise, the question is stated and a method is suggested that the students then follow to arrive at a solution. This variation has often been called the "cookbook" approach to lab activities.	Cookbook lab
"Q" M "S"	Students are given a means or technique (e.g., measuring water loss in plants) and are asked to think of questions and then use the means to answer them.	Using techniques to solve problems
Q "M" S	You might begin this way: "The text says that molds grow best in dark, warm conditions. What kinds of experiments could scientists do or have they done to show that?"	Investigating a method
"Q" M S	Students are given an account of an experimental procedure, with data collected and results obtained, and are asked: "What hypothesis was being tested?"	Working backward

Figure 4.9
The Onion Lab

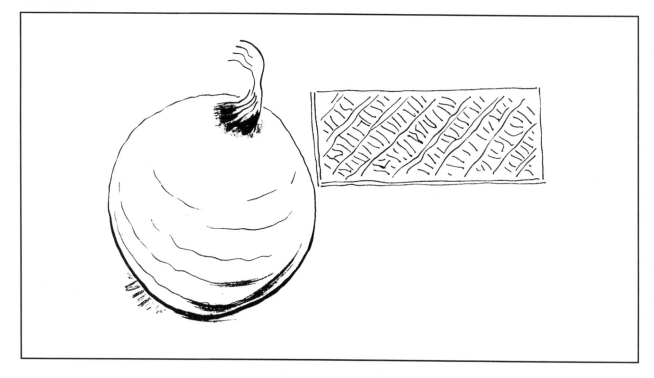

Task 2. The Drifting Continents

Examine the maps of the Earth (Figure 4.10) showing the movement of continents over the past 210 million years. Using the Q-M-S strategy, design two inquiry activities that make use of the cards in Figure 4.10.

Task 3. The Geoblock

The Geoblock is a technique designed to help students understand the structures in rocks such as the folds shown in Figure 4.11. The students can cut out the block, fold the edges, and examine it from different angles. Using the Q-M-S strategy, design as many variations as you can using the Geoblock to help students understand ideas related to rock formations and geological maps.

THE K-W-L STRATEGY

One active reading strategy that is worth exploring is the K-W-L strategy. An active reading strategy prepares students to make predictions about what they will be reading, as well as engaging them with other students in a discussion of the content of the topic. The procedure consists of three steps:

K = Assessing what we know or have heard
W = Determining what we want to learn
L = Recalling and discussing what we did learn

In step K, students do two things. First, they brainstorm what they know or what they have heard about a topic. Using the K-W-L Strategy Data Sheet (Figure 4.12), students work in small groups and begin to record their ideas. The focus should be specific. In the sample lesson plan that follows, for example, students would talk about what they know or have heard about earthquakes, not what they know about natural disasters. The second part of step K is to categorize the information students have generated. In the sample case that follows, the teacher might suggest these categories: causes of earthquakes, how earthquakes are measured, and damage caused by earthquakes.

Figure 4.10

The Continents

National Association of Geology Teachers. *Journal of Geological Education,* Vol. 23, No. 5, pp. 169–170 in *Continental Drift,* by Scotese and Baker. Copyright © 1962 by C. Scotese.

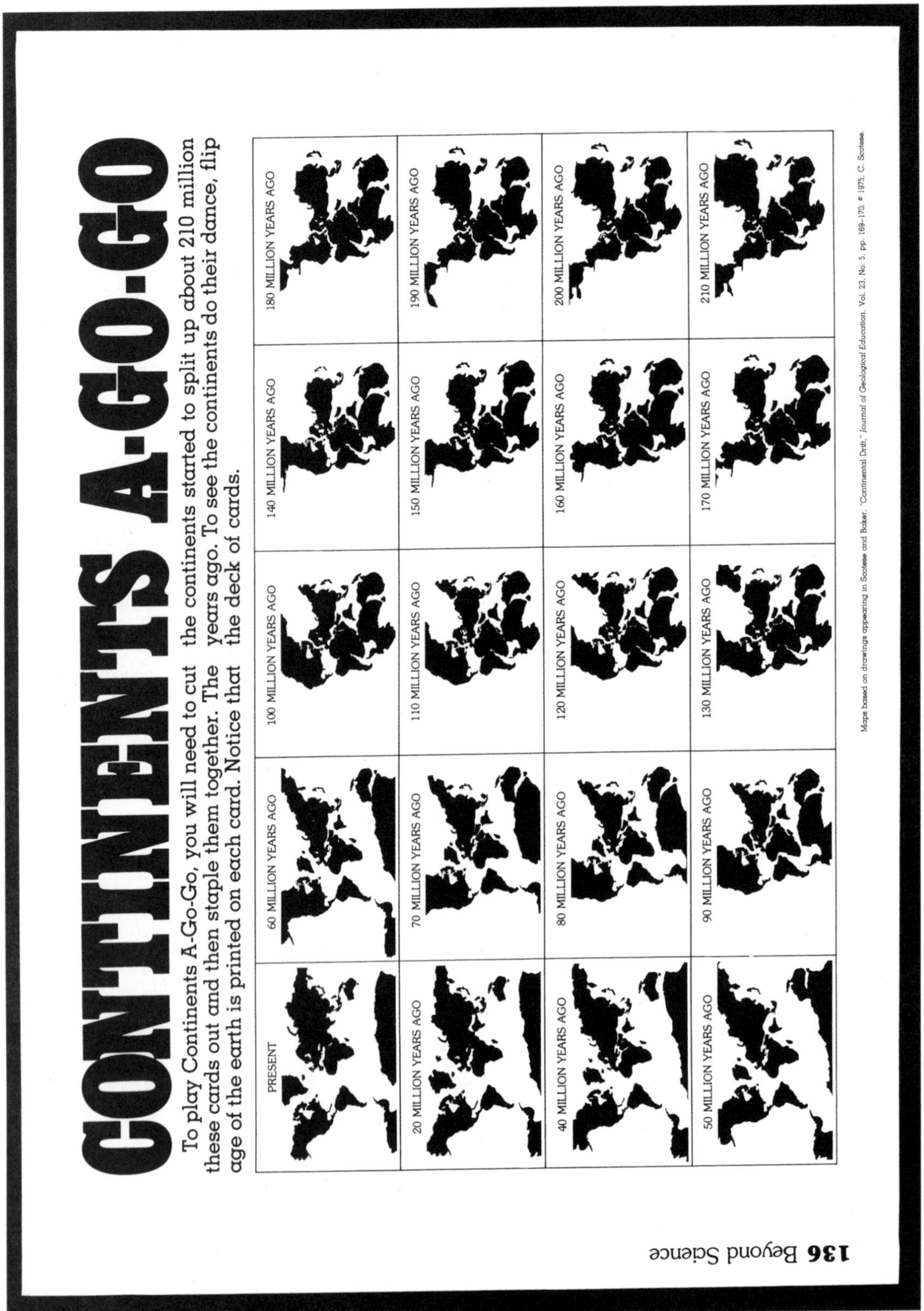

CONTINENTS A-GO-GO

To play Continents A-Go-Go, you will need to cut these cards out and then staple them together. The age of the earth is printed on each card. Notice that the continents started to split up about 210 million years ago. To see the continents do their dance, flip the deck of cards.

PRESENT	60 MILLION YEARS AGO	100 MILLION YEARS AGO	140 MILLION YEARS AGO	180 MILLION YEARS AGO
20 MILLION YEARS AGO	70 MILLION YEARS AGO	110 MILLION YEARS AGO	150 MILLION YEARS AGO	190 MILLION YEARS AGO
40 MILLION YEARS AGO	80 MILLION YEARS AGO	120 MILLION YEARS AGO	160 MILLION YEARS AGO	200 MILLION YEARS AGO
50 MILLION YEARS AGO	90 MILLION YEARS AGO	130 MILLION YEARS AGO	170 MILLION YEARS AGO	210 MILLION YEARS AGO

Maps based on drawings appearing in Scotese and Baker. "Continental Drift." *Journal of Geological Education,* Vol. 23, No. 5, pp. 169–170. © 1975. C. Scotese.

Figure 4.11
Geoblock

From *Adventures in Geology* by Jack Hassard. © 1989
American Geological Institute.

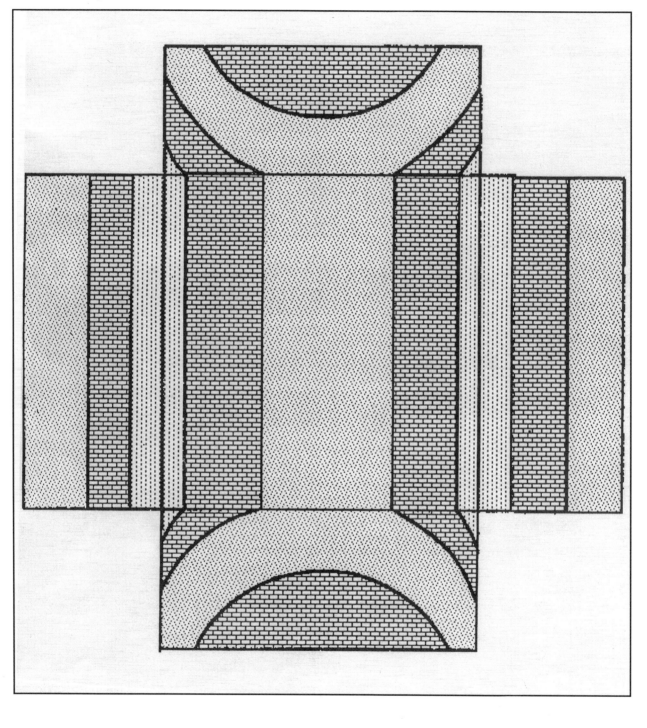

Figure 4.12

"K-W-L Strategy Sheet" from *Minds-on Science* for Figure
8.14, "K-W-L: A Teaching Model That Develops Active
Reading of Expository Text" by Donna M. Ogle from *The
Reading Teacher,* February 1986, pp. 564–570.
Reprinted with permission of the author.

K-W-L STRATEGY DATA SHEET

K—What we know	W—What we want to find out	L—What we learned and questions we still have

Categories of information we expect to use:

   (Categorize the information from the K step.)

A. _____   E. _____

B. _____   F. _____

C. _____   G. _____

D. _____   H. _____

Step W helps students anticipate the reading that is to come and helps the students focus on what they want to learn from the reading. The teacher directs the groups to write on the data sheet several questions they are most interested in having answered, based on their prior discussion and brainstorming.

Step L, which follows the reading of the text passages, focuses the students on recalling what they learned from the reading. As a group they should brainstorm a list of ideas representing things they learned in the reading. They can also try and answer the questions they posed.

LESSON PLAN: EARTHQUAKES

This lesson plan is appropriate for any chapter on earthquakes in a middle-level science textbook.

Objectives:
- To describe how earthquakes are caused
- To predict the effects of an earthquake

K: What do students already know about the topic?
NOTE: This is a brainstorming session in which students describe what they know about earthquakes—your role is to pose a specific problem or task in order to help students focus on the reading yet to come.

1. Pose the question: "What do you know about earthquakes?" Pairs of students brainstorm and record what they know about earthquakes.
2. Pairs of pairs (groups of four) share lists and prepare composite list.
3. Groups of four share with the whole class by taping composite lists on the walls of the classroom. Focus on the lists, and ask groups of four to categorize the information—topics might include causes of earthquakes, damage caused by earthquakes, earthquake waves, and how earthquakes are measured.

4. Ask students how they got their information about earthquakes. This final substep personalizes student knowledge and recognizes the sources of students' prior knowledge.

W: What do students want to know about the topic?
NOTE: This step helps students anticipate the reading that is to come, and helps the students focus on what they want to learn from the reading. This step should be carried out as a group activity.

1. Each group of four develops four questions about the topic.
2. Teacher records these questions on the board. Teacher can elaborate on the questions, perhaps selecting two or more that seem especially interesting to the students.

L: What did students learn about the topic?
NOTE: Students read the assigned text material. Students write what they learned on the K-W-L Strategy Data Sheet. They also check to see if their questions were answered, and if some of their prior knowledge was confirmed. Students work in small groups to discuss their questions.

1. Group circles information on the master list that was taped to the wall that the text confirmed.
2. Group crosses off information that the text refuted.
3. Students contribute to the final column of the list: What we learned!
4. Teacher goes around the class and asks each student to indicate (by thumbs-up or thumbs-down) if his of her question(s) was(were) answered.
5. Teacher asks each group to make a concept map of the main ideas and supporting secondary categories of what they learned from the reading.

VISUALIZATIONS: GUIDED IMAGERY

Close your eyes and try to recreate the most beautiful rock you have ever seen in the natural world . . . .

The teacher who gave her students these instructions was using an active learning strategy called *guided imagery,* which is a visualization technique. Some cite guided imagery as an example of a right-brain activity.

Guided imagery is a powerful tool well worth incorporating into science lessons. Some science teachers see the power of guided imagery as giving students insight into concepts by drawing on the students' own experiences, thereby personalizing the learning of science. Science has many recorded instances of reverie, insight, and/or dream experiences leading to the central insight in a scientist's theory.

In science teaching, guided imagery functions much like a story; the teacher guides the students on a journey, encouraging them to create images and form ideas. Imagery experiences should take place in a quiet, relaxed atmosphere. Some teachers dim the lights or play music and have students sit quietly at their desks. Follow-up activities after the guided imagery are an important part of the experience. These can include making something (perhaps with clay or other manipulatives), writing in a journal, or pairing off and discussing the experience.

Using Guided Imagery in Science Teaching

The following exercise helps to show how guided imagery can enhance science learning. The example is based on a mini-unit focusing on rocks.[5]

Objectives:
- To describe how rocks are formed
- To use imagery to explore the processes that affect rocks

---

[5] *Adapted from* 4Mat And Science Toward Wholeness in Science Education *by Bob Samples, Bill Hammond, and Bernice McCarthy, pp. 86–87. Reprinted by permission of Excel, Inc.*

- To classify rocks
- To invent a rock

Materials: Index cards, marking pens, large samples of granite, sandstone, and marble, collection of rocks for each group that should include granite, sandstone, shale, marble, limestone, gneiss, slate, and obsidian

Procedure:

Phase I. Introduction/Prior Knowledge/Personal Meaning

1. **Guided Imagery Experience.** "Close your eyes and try to re-create the most beautiful rock you have ever seen in the natural world. . . . Try to remember everything you can about the setting. . . . Note the colors and smells. . . . Imagine what the rock feels like. . . . Pretend the rock can talk and tell you about its history. . . . Listen carefully to its story so you can remember it. . . . You will have two full minutes, starting now."

2. **Cooperative Group Activity.** Have students form groups of four students each and have them tell each other all they can about their rocks and the stories of their rocks. After the discussion have them write their description of their rock on a 3" × 5" card. Remind them that the descriptions should include color, shape, weight (heavy or light), and texture (bumpy, smooth, jagged, etc.). Have them save the descriptions for later.

Phase II. Some Information, Please!

3. **Guided Imagery Experience.** "We are going to use guided imagery again to continue our exploration of rocks. This time we will explore some of the ways rocks are formed. Close your eyes and relax. . . . Some rocks form in the waters of oceans or lakes. . . . Most often they are made of particles of mud or sand that drift to the bottom of the water. . . . Try to visualize this process. After long periods of time, they may become crushed and fastened together by

Figure 4.13
Granite, Sandstone, and Gneiss

different materials. . . . Think back and see if this is how you think your rock formed.

"Other rocks formed deep within the Earth and were once melted or molten. . . . Sometimes these rocks come to the surface in volcanoes. . . . Try to imagine rocks pouring out of the Earth. . . . Some never make it to the surface and end up cooling down deep in the Earth. These rocks often have crystals and large grains of different materials. . . . Try to imagine them forming.

"Some rocks lie near the deep heat sources of the volcanoes. These rocks are baked and even remelted by the heat. . . . Try to visualize rocks being melted and twisted by other molten rocks flowing by.

"Keep your eyes closed and review the three kinds of rocks: those formed in the water . . . those formed by molten rock inside the Earth and at its surface . . . and those formed by being crushed, twisted, and melted by other rocks. . . ."

At the end of the visualization, have your students open their eyes, and then show them a video on the origin of rocks. (A variety of videos are available. You might want to try focusing on volcanic rocks or sedimentary rocks.)

4. **Mini-Lecture (10/5) Strategy.** Prepare a mini-lecture (about 10 minutes long) on the origin of rocks. Show students examples of igneous, metamorphic, and sedimentary rocks. You might try giving formal definitions of the types of rocks, and then (for about 5 minutes) have students work in small groups to write out their own definitions on index cards while they handle and observe rock samples.

Phase III. Analysis

5. **Quiz/Worksheet.** Provide a quiz or worksheet on rock formations and how they are classified. Have students work in small groups to complete them. Also, have the groups refer back to the descriptions they wrote on 3" × 5" cards (Phase 1) and use the cards to reclassify their original rock descriptions based on the classification system they have now learned.

6. **Laboratory Activity.** Give groups of students a collection of rock specimens and have them classify the rocks according to origin. Have the students try to match up the rocks with the descriptions of rocks on their cards. For a homework assignment, you might give each student a small plastic bag of sand and have students try to make a synthetic rock at home (Figure 4.14). Allow at least 2 days for this activity. Tell the students the "fake" rock is intended to approximate some of the same processes that are involved in the formation of rocks in nature.

Phase IV. Synthesis and Application

7. **Synthesize.** In this phase, students present their "fake" rocks to the class in the form of a display and discuss the effort that went into making the "fake" rock. Connections should be drawn between what the students did to make "fake" rocks and processes in nature that make "real" rocks.

8. **To the Field.** The final activity in this guided imagery example is a short field trip into

Figure 4.14
Recipe for a fake rock: 1/2 cup sand, 1/4 cup gravel, 1/2 cup water, 1/2 cup plaster of Paris. Mix ingredients in a quart-size milk carton and let the mix harden. Remove the carton to reveal the "fake" rock.

nature, which can be anywhere in nature or in the community. The goal is to look for and identify real and fake rocks, and discuss the way in which they were formed.

Creating Your Own Visualizations

Visualizations are easy to create, which is nice since you'll find many opportunities for their use during the course of the year. Some teachers make up visualizations and record them on audiocassette tapes for future use by individual students or small groups of students. Figure 4.15 provides suggestions for creating visualizations.

GAMES

Not only do games promote active learning in the science classroom, but they serve as powerful motivators for your students. Games can be used to introduce new science concepts, to help students apply concepts already explored, and, in many cases, to review for quizzes and tests. Finally, games can be used as an alternative form of assessment.

Included here is a complete description of one game, the Disaster Game, followed by descriptions of several other games.[6]

The Disaster Game

Objective: To get each system on your disaster board to balance by placing exactly 200 Earth balance points in each space.

Materials: One set of cards (disaster cards, response cards, Earth balance point cards), 1 Disaster game board (Figures 4.16 and 4.17)

Number of players: 2

Game Rules: One player deals the disaster cards, one at a time, until each player has seven cards. The dealer puts the next card face up between the players to form a discard pile. The other player starts by picking a card from the top of the discard pile. After drawing one card, the player can do one of the following:

- Place a disaster card on any earth system on the opponent's game board, draw another card, and then discard one card.
- Place an Earth balance points card on any Earth system on the player's own game board, draw as many cards as were placed on the game board, and then discard one card.
- Discard one card.

A player who has a disaster occurring in any system cannot continue to play until the correct response card is placed on top of the disaster. Thus the only move open to this player is to draw and discard cards.

Exactly 200 Earth balance points secure a system from disaster. Any value on the system less than 200 does not. If a disaster card is placed on a system that has less than 200 points, the player loses whatever earth points are on that system.

[6] All of the games can be obtained from Carolina Biological Supply Company, 2700 York Road, Burlington, NC 27215. 800-334-4451.

Figure 4.15
Visualization chart. What visualizations do these images help you create for your students?

Paleontology

Idea: Living with dinosaurs

Question: *Which one is the largest?*
Which one do you fear the most?
Do dinosaurs live in families?
How do dinosaurs eat?

Glaciers

Idea: Being a piece of frozen water in a moving glacier

Question: *What sounds might you hear?*
What effect might you and the rest of the glacier have on the rocks and land you pass over?
What might you leave behind?

Hurricanes

Idea: Being a cloud traveling near the eye of a hurricane

Question: *How fast are you going?*
In what direction do you move?
How predictable are you?
What damage do you do?

Rocks

Idea: Being a rock tossed along a streambed

Question: *How might this experience change your appearance?*
Where might you end up?
What sights might you see along the way?

Figure 4.16

Disaster Game

"Disaster Game" from *Earthpeople Activity Book* by Joe
Abruscato and Jack Hassard, pp. 158–162. Copyright ©
1978 by Goodyear Publishing Company, Inc.

Figure 4.17

Disaster Game Cards

"Disaster Game" from *Earthpeople Activity Book* by Joe Abruscato and Jack Hassard, pp. 158–162. Copyright © 1978 by Goodyear Publishing Company, Inc.

How to Play	Rock Slide	Lightning	Evacuation	Tornado Alert
Objective: To get each system on your disaster board in balance by placing exactly 200 earth balance points in each space. *Materials:* One set of Disaster cards. 1 disaster gameboard (each player to use half). *Number of players:* two. *Game rules:* One player deals the Disaster cards, one at a time, until each player has seven cards. The dealer puts the next card face up between the players to form a discard pile. The other player starts by picking a card from the top of the face-down stack or from the top of the discard pile. After drawing one card, the player can then do one of the following: 1. Place a disaster card on any earth system on the opponent's gameboard, draw another card, and then discard one card. 2. Place an Earth Balance Points card on any of his or her earth systems, draw as many cards as were placed on the gameboard, and then discard one card. 3. Discard one card. A player who has a disaster occurring in any system cannot continue play until the correct Response card is placed on top of the disaster. The only move open to this player is to draw and discard cards. Exactly 200 Earth Balance points secure a system from disaster. Any value on the system less than 200 does not. If a Disaster card is placed on a system that has less than 200 points, the player loses whatever eath balance points are on that system. *End of Game:* Play ends when one player has exactly 200 earth balance points on four systems on his or her gameboard.	Wet earth, soil, and rocks slide down a hillside, destroying vegetation and buildings. Place over a *Gravity* card to stop. Respond with a *Zoning Laws* card to continue.	Severe thunderstorm hits home. Potential fire and electrical damage. Place over *Storm System* card to stop. Respond with a *Lightning Rod* card to continue.	This is the best response if a volcano erupts. This action will keep you alive! Place over a *Volcano* card before continuing.	Open windows, go to center of building, and take cover. This card will protect you and tell you what to do in case of a tornado. Place over a *Tornado* card before continuing.
	Rock Slide	Lightning	Evacuation	Tornado Alert
	Wet earth, soil, and rocks slide down a hillside, destroying vegetation and buildings. Place over a *Gravity* card to stop. Respond with a *Zoning Laws* card to continue.	Severe thunderstorm hits home. Potential fire and electrical damage. Place over *Storm System* card to stop. Respond with a *Lightning Rod* card to continue.	This is the best response if a volcano erupts. This action will keep you alive! Place over a *Volcano* card before continuing.	Open windows, go to center of building, and take cover. This card will protect you and tell you what to do in case of a tornado. Place over a *Tornado* card before continuing.
	Rock Slide	Lightning	Evacuation	Tornado Alert
	Wet earth, soil, and rocks slide down a hillside, destroying vegetation and buildings. Place over a *Gravity* card to stop. Respond with a *Zoning Laws* card to continue.	Severe thunderstorm hits home. Potential fire and electrical damage. Place over *Storm System* card to stop. Respond with a *Lightning Rod* card to continue.	This is the best response if a volcano erupts. This action will keep you alive! Place over a *Volcano* card before continuing.	Open windows, go to center of building, and take cover. This card will protect you and tell you what to do in case of a tornado. Place over a *Tornado* card before continuing.

Volcano	Flood	Tornado	Earthquake	Conservation	Zoning Laws
A volcano has erupted, spilling hot lava on the earth's surface. Place above a *Volcanic Rock System* card to stop. Respond with an *Evacuation* card to continue.	A river has flooded beyond its flood plain. Erosion increases: buildings and homes are destroyed. Place above a *River System* card to stop. Respond with a *Conservation* card to continue.	A tornado has been sighted and reported by the weather bureau. Place over a *Wind System* card to stop. Respond with *Tornado Alert* card to continue.	The earth begins to shake and roll: buildings begin to collapse. Place over a *Tectonic System* card to stop. Respond with *Building Codes* card to continue.	Conservation techniques such as terracing, building higher levees, and revegetation can help control erosion by flooding. Place over a *Flood* card before continuing.	Better zoning laws would prohibit construction in areas of weak rocks. Place over a *Rock Slide* card before continuing.
A volcano has erupted, spilling hot lava on the earth's surface. Place above a *Volcanic Rock System* card to stop. Respond with an *Evacuation* card to continue.	A river has flooded beyond its flood plain. Erosion increases: buildings and homes are destroyed. Place above a *River System* card to stop. Respond with a *Conservation* card to continue.	A tornado has been sighted and reported by the weather bureau. Place over a *Wind System* card to stop. Respond with *Tornado Alert* card to continue.	The earth begins to shake and roll: buildings begin to collapse. Place over a *Tectonic System* card to stop. Respond with *Building Codes* card to continue.	Conservation techniques such as terracing, building higher levees, and revegetation can help control erosion by flooding. Place over a *Flood* card before continuing.	Better zoning laws would prohibit construction in areas of weak rocks. Place over a *Rock Slide* card before continuing.
A volcano has erupted, spilling hot lava on the earth's surface. Place above a *Volcanic Rock System* card to stop. Respond with an *Evacuation* card to continue.	A river has flooded beyond its flood plain. Erosion increases: buildings and homes are destroyed. Place above a *River System* card to stop. Respond with a *Conservation* card to continue.	A tornado has been sighted and reported by the weather bureau. Place over a *Wind System* card to stop. Respond with *Tornado Alert* card to continue.	The earth begins to shake and roll: buildings begin to collapse. Place over a *Tectonic System* card to stop. Respond with *Building Codes* card to continue.	Conservation techniques such as terracing, building higher levees, and revegetation can help control erosion by flooding. Place over a *Flood* card before continuing.	Better zoning laws would prohibit construction in areas of weak rocks. Place over a *Rock Slide* card before continuing.

Figure 4.17
Disaster Game Cards

"Disaster Game" from *Earthpeople Activity Book* by Joe Abruscato and Jack Hassard, pp. 158–162. Copyright © 1978 by Goodyear Publishing Company, Inc.

Lightning Rod This card will ground you and the structure you are in. It will save your life. Place over a *Lightning* card before continuing.	**50** Earth Balance Points	**50** Earth Balance Points	**100** Earth Balance Points	**100** Earth Balance Points
Lightning Rod This card will ground you and the structure you are in. It will save your life. Place over a *Lightning* card before continuing.	**50** Earth Balance Points	**50** Earth Balance Points	**100** Earth Balance Points	**100** Earth Balance Points
Lightning Rod This card will ground you and the structure you are in. It will save your life. Place over a *Lightning* card before continuing.	**50** Earth Balance Points	**50** Earth Balance Points	**100** Earth Balance Points	**100** Earth Balance Points
Building Codes Designing and locating buildings to withstand earthquakes is possible. This card will do it. Place over an *Earthquake* card before continuing.	**50** Earth Balance Points	**50** Earth Balance Points	**100** Earth Balance Points	**100** Earth Balance Points
Building Codes Designing and locating buildings to withstand earthquakes is possible. This card will do it. Place over an *Earthquake* card before continuing.	**50** Earth Balance Points	**100** Earth Balance Points	**100** Earth Balance Points	**100** Earth Balance Points
Building Codes Designing and locating buildings to withstand earthquakes is possible. This card will do it. Place over an *Earthquake* card before continuing.	**50** Earth Balance Points	**100** Earth Balance Points	**100** Earth Balance Points	**100** Earth Balance Points

Additional column (fifth card in each row):

- Row 1: **100** Earth Balance Points
- Row 2: **150** Earth Balance Points
- Row 3: **150** Earth Balance Points
- Row 4: **150** Earth Balance Points
- Row 5: **150** Earth Balance Points
- Row 6: **150** Earth Balance Points

End of Game: Play ends when one player has exactly 200 earth balance points on four of the six systems on his or her game board.

Earth Science Games

The Disaster Game. A challenge game in which students learn about various natural disasters and ways to protect themselves. (See preceding description.)

Geological Time Chart Game. Players learn eras and periods of geologic time and how populations survive or disappear.

Environmental Science Games

The Dead River. A role-playing game in which players learn the complexities of water resource and problem-solving methods.

Endangered Species. An introduction to animal conservation. Players attempt to save five rare and exotic animals.

Extinction: The Game of Ecology. A very popular game designed to entertain as well as to illustrate key principles of population ecology.

Food Web Game. Introduces basic ecological and wildlife topics. Players choose an animal—predator or prey—and try to survive in the American North.

Pollution. A simulation of environmental pollution and the measures taken to control it.

Life Science Games

The Cell Game. Players explore either a plant or an animal cell, carrying out such processes as synthesis, parasitism, respiration, and photosynthesis.

Human Body Bingo. An easy way to learn to identify specific areas of the circulatory, muscular, nervous, and skeletal systems.

Insect Quiz. A deck of forty cards with a color photograph of a different insect or spider on each. More than four hundred questions explore insects.

Monarch. A card game of butterflies and moths.

The Pollination Game. Students study the pollination of flowers.

Shello. A bingo-like game about seashells. Contains twenty-five real shells mounted on cards.

Physical Science Games

Chem Cubes: Elements. Teaches the names and chemical symbols of common metallic and non-metallic elements, use of the periodic table, and writing of simple chemical equations.

The Electric Circuit Game. Teaches basic electrical circuitry. Players try to be the first to complete a circuit without being shocked or shorted out.

Element-O. Introduces many basic chemistry concepts, such as the configuration of the periodic table and physical characteristics of elements.

In-Quest. Students learn about the scientific method and how to prepare for research and science fair projects.

SUMMARY

This chapter brought together several strategies that expand our notion of science inquiry. Exploring students' initial ideas on a topic, as was presented in the section on pre-assessment strategies, honors student ideas. It is important to recognize the value of student ideas and beginning instruction by soliciting their views. Questioning and active reading strategies explore the importance of language and writing in science and show how students can be encouraged to talk about their ideas and to express them in writing as well. Finally, we saw the value of visualization in helping students explore, in their mind's eye, the nature of science.

CHAPTER 5   **PROJECT-BASED TEACHING**

One of the goals for science teaching reported in the National Science Education Standards is to provide a learning environment in which students "experience the richness and excitement of knowing about and understanding the natural world."[1] A compelling way to achieve this goal is to use project-based activities. The purpose of this chapter is to provide ideas and resources for implementing project-based activities in science teaching.

WHAT IS A SCIENCE PROJECT?

Greg Lockett, a science teacher from Cottonwood, California, provides this conception of a science project:

Children learn by doing. If you want students to learn physics, they must "do" physics. From this view, the goal of the teacher is to re-create the process and experience of working in a physics laboratory. As experimenting is central in physics, experimenting takes a central role in the project classroom. Several features are important in this approach. Students are free to choose a research problem. They do not know the solution to their problem at the outset of their project. While students must work within the constraints of time, resources, and their current knowledge, they are given considerable time and freedom to attack their problem as they see fit. Collaboration is acceptable and desirable. The end product of student work can vary widely (reports, papers, equipment, experiments, constructions, models, etc.). Student success is not easily measured by objective tests.

In this process, the goal of the teacher is not the efficient transfer of large amounts of information and mathematical problem-solving skills. The goal is to give the student an immediate and compelling "inside" view of science (physics). The teacher functions primarily as a facilitator. In many respects, she or he is

Figure 5.1
Students working on a project

like a research director in a laboratory. She or he familiarizes new researchers with the laboratory, obtains needed resources or suggests alternatives, resolves disputes—from equipment scheduling to squabbling among the researchers, and in general attempts to maximize the creation of new ideas and technology within the laboratory. At all points, the teacher is guided by the current practice of physics and the goal of re-creating that practice within the classroom.

The goals of the project paradigm are broader and deeper than those of the basal-text paradigm. At the highest level, they include firsthand knowledge of what science is, how it works, and its limits. Mathematical problem-solving skills are encompassed within a broader structure that includes research skills (using libraries), motor skills (building apparatus

---

[1] National Science Education Standards, 1996. *National Committee on Science Education Standards and Assessment. Washington, DC: National Academy Press.*

and operating it), cooperative social skills (collaborating on projects), communication skills (oral reports during informal lab meetings, writing science papers), and thinking skills (logic, induction, deduction, analysis, synthesis). Skills are learned as needed. Motivation is rarely a problem since the context makes the need for the skill obvious to the student.[2]

RATIONALE FOR USING PROJECTS

Project-based teaching supports the active learning paradigm developed in this book. Project-based science teaching, although not a new concept, has enjoyed something of a renaissance during the past 10 years. The merger of new technologies, especially microcomputer-based labs (MBLs) and the Internet, with reform efforts in science education that emphasize science as inquiry, have led to greater interest in project-based teaching. Four shifts in perspective (Figure 5.2) provide a rationale for using project-based teaching in science.

TYPES OF PROJECTS

Although projects can be done individually, those completed by teams of students generally prove more valuable. Not only do group projects reduce the workload for the teacher, but, more significantly, they emphasize the importance of group work in the learning, understanding, and doing of science. To help you decide what projects to use in a unit of science teaching and when to use them, consider the three categories of projects that follow. Note that it is quite possible to combine the categories in the development of a project. For example, you might have students build something (an airplane) and then design an experiment to study the effects of one or more variables on its motion.

Construction or Engineering Projects

Students build something (a cell, volcano, racing car, musical instrument). They focus on what they learned, demonstrate how the product works, and explain how they would improve on their product the next time.

Experimental/Research/Measurement Projects

Students design an experiment to study the effects of one or more variables on an object. Students model scientific procedures by presenting their results in a group report that should include these headings: "Problem Studied," "Purpose of the Study," "Method Used," "Results Obtained," and "Conclusion Reached."

Search and Find Projects

Students select a topic (global warming, mission to planet Mars, the FLU) or a scientist, and use primary and secondary resources to build a presentation board summarizing their findings. Students make use of a variety of resources, including the Internet.

USING THE GROUP INVESTIGATION METHOD

Projects can be carried out by student teams in a variety of ways. One approach that you might want to consider using is the Group Investigation Method developed by Yael and Shlomo Sharan. By means of a series of steps, students work through the various stages of their project as shown in Figure 5.3. This method places more responsibility on the student (rather than the teacher) for thinking through what has to be learned, and then figuring out how to gather the information, analyze and interpret it, and share it with others.

EVALUATING PROJECTS AND PRESENTATIONS

The best method for evaluating projects combines peer review, self-evaluation, and teacher evalua-

---

[2] *From Labnet: Toward a Community of Practice by Richard Ruopp et al., p. 35. Copyright © 1993 by Lawrence Erlbaum Associates, Inc. Reprinted by permission of Lawrence Erlbaum Associates, Inc.*

Figure 5.2
Project-Based Teaching: Shifting Paradigms

From an Older View	Perspective	To a Contemporary View
• Information is learned by listening to lectures from teachers, reading from texts, and answering questions.	• Nature of learning and learner	• The development of intelligence, in general, and subject matter understanding in science, in particular, is actively constructed by the individual. New knowledge is acquired in relation to previous knowledge, building on intuitive, informal experiences.
• Learning occurs individually, with little regard to context or communities.	• How learning occurs	• Learning occurs in communities of practice wherein students engage in authentic tasks in which real meaning is derived from immersion in, and conversation about, the task.
• Textbook-oriented curricula	• Materials for learning	• Subject matter presented in texts is not an end in itself but rather a means to engaging in authentic tasks and solving real problems.
• Teachers transmit subject matter through well-crafted lectures, demonstrations and other presentations.	• Role of teacher	• Teachers provide leadership in building a short-term community of learning. They promote meaningful conversation, encourage talking aloud on problems, and invite students to work collaboratively on problems and issues in science.

Richard Ruopp et al., *LabNet: Toward a Community of Practice.* Hillsdale, New Jersey:
Lawrence Erlbaum Associates, Inc., 1993, pp. 55–56.

Figure 5.3
Steps for Projects

Stage	Teacher's Role	Student's Role
• Determine subtopics to be investigated and organize into groups.	• Introduce general topic of investigation; lead groups in discussion of topic and subtopics.	• Generate questions of interest for an environmental project; sort questions into categories; form project groups.
• Plan project.	• Help groups formulate plans; meet with groups; help find resources; and provide equipment and materials.	• Plan what to study; choose resources; assign roles; send e-mail report describing plans.
• Carry out project.	• Help with study and research skills; check with groups to monitor progress.	• Seek answers to questions; locate information; collect data; interview people; integrate findings; and summarize.
• Plan presentation.	• Discuss with class plans for presentations; organize the process.	• Determine the main thrust of the presentation; plan how to make presentation; and prepare materials for presentation (poster, video, etc.).
• Make presentation.	• Coordinate presentations.	• Present project; offer feedback to classmates.
• Evaluate.	• Evaluate learning and summarize the project findings.	• Reflect on work as group members; reflect on impact of project on understanding of science.

Adaptation of Table 4.1 from *Expanding Cooperative Learning Through Group Investigation* by Yael Sharan and Shlomo Sharan, p. 95. Copyright © 1992 by Teachers College, Columbia University. All rights reserved. Reprinted by permission of Teachers College Press.

Figure 5.4 Rubric for the Paper Tower Project

Response	Criteria	Rating
Outstanding	Complete freestanding tower; clearly demonstrated need for base and support	4
Competent	Complete freestanding tower	3
Nearly Satisfactory	Tower has inadequate base/support	2
Assignment Not Completed	Concepts unclear; work attempted	1
Off Task	Tower not constructed	0

Figure 5.5 Holistic Rubric

Response	Criteria	Rating
Outstanding	Shows expanded thinking and clear understanding of task; clear evidence of testing models and cooperative effort	4
Very good	Completed task; acceptable conclusions; completed models; cooperative effort apparent	3
Satisfactory	Task nearly completed; conclusion incomplete	2
Fails to Complete	Failure to communicate understanding of task; task attempted	1
No Attempt	No project constructed; little cooperation	0

tion. Projects can be effectively assessed by means of rubrics, devices that identify evaluation criteria. Take, for example, one of the projects described in the physical science section of this chapter, called The Paper Tower. Students build a freestanding tower out of one sheet of paper. The teacher and/or other students assess the tower using the rubric shown in Figure 5.4.

See, too, the Whirlybird project described in Chapter 1, in which two rubrics were presented for use in assessing student work. The rubric shown in Figure 5.5 is a holistic rubric. This means that a single score is given for the project. The rubric shown in Figure 5.6, by contrast, is an analytic rubric, meaning that several specific criteria are developed for the project and each criterion is scored.

Figure 5.6 Analytic Rubric

Response	Criteria	Rating
Cooperative	To what extent did group members cooperate with each other to help solve the problem?	0 1 2 3 4
Content	To what extent is there evidence that the team understands the (physics) concepts behind the task?	0 1 2 3 4
Completion	To what extent did the team use the allocated time wisely?	0 1 2 3 4

PROJECTS FOR THE ACTIVE SCIENCE CLASS

The projects that follow have been organized into three categories—Earth science, life science, and physical science. These should help you to incorporate the projects into your course curriculum. In addition, detailed project descriptions have been provided so that you can present the projects clearly to your students, who can then tailor them to their own goals and learning interests. As you look over the projects, keep in mind that they are intended for small teams of "student scientists." The emphasis here is on "doing science" and on "student-directed learning." Be aware, too, that projects lend themselves to final presentations, which can take many forms in the classroom. It's best to think about the form(s) you want the presentations to take, and discuss these with students in advance. Here are some options to consider:

- Commercials
- Plays
- Puppet shows
- Sculptures
- Reports
- Mobiles
- Videos
- Computer simulations

Earth Science Projects

The Mars Egg Drop

The goal of this project is to design a cargo system that can safely transport an egg dropped from a high place. A drop of 3 meters to 10 meters is recommended. Provide a variety of materials, such as aluminum foil, string, polystyrene foam packing peanuts, cereal boxes, cups, tape, cardboard, and paper. Encourage students to bring in and share additional materials. Use either raw eggs or hard-boiled eggs. Students' responsibilities: Record their ideas in a journal or log; make drawings of their designs and, as they test them out, record the results; and provide explanations of the results. Be sure to establish a time period for the construction of the containers, as well as for the day of competition.

On the day of competition, each team will drop their cargo system. Assemble the students at the site from which the systems will be dropped. You should have only one team at a time present their system. They should explain their system, and why they constructed it as they did. After they drop their cargo system, they should open it in front of everyone for inspection. The egg systems that survive should compete in a second round of drops from a slightly higher elevation.

You may want to relate this project to NASA's Mars *Pathfinder* Mission. *Sojourner*, NASA's Mars rover (Figure 5.7a), withstood a crash landing on Mars. Packed inside a protective shield of bal-

Figure 5.7a

The Mars rover, *Sojourner,* which roamed the planet Mars for several months, made a safe landing on Mars after crashing to the surface, then bouncing more than ten times before coming to a rest.

loons, the vehicle bounced more than ten times after a free-fall landing on the planet. Despite the rough beginning, *Sojourner* was able to navigate the surface of the planet for several months, sending to Earth valuable data from and dramatic images of Mars. Have students visit NASA's Mars Web site (Figure 5.7b) at http://www.gpl.nasa.gov/mars/, and the *Pathfinder* site at http://nssde.nasa. gov/planetary/mesur.html.

The Erathosthenes Project

This project is named for the Greek astronomer (Figure 5.8) who accurately estimated the circumference of the Earth. It is described in

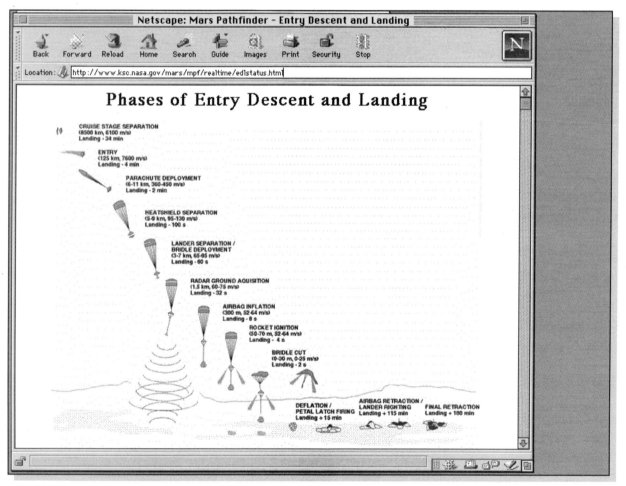

Figure 5.7b

Trajectory of *Pathfinder*

"Phases of Entry Descent and Landing" screen from www.ksc.nasa.gov/mars/mpf/realtime/ed/status.html Web page. Reprinted by permission of NASA and the Jet Propulsion Lab.

LabNet: Toward a Community of Practice as a telecommunications project shared by several science classes across the country.[3]

By measuring the length of an object's shadow and comparing this to the actual length of the object, students can determine the angle at which the sun's rays strike the Earth in their particular area of the world at a given time of the year. Data collected in places that are separated by at least 10° latitude can be used to calculate the circumference of the Earth. The idea is to contact, via the Internet, other science classes and then collaborate with them to try to solve this problem.

In the original experiment, conducted in 200 B.C., Erathosthenes assumed that the Earth was round and that the sun's rays were parallel. He set up a stick in Alexandria, Egypt, and measured the angle of the sun's shadow when a well at Syene (a city many miles away from Alexandria) was completely sunlit. He knew from geometry that this angle represented the angle of the Earth's center between Alexandria and Syene. He also knew that the distance between the two cities was 5,000 sta-

dia (1 stadium = about 200 meters). From the distance and the angle he measured, Erathosthenes calculated the Earth's circumference to be 250,000 stadia, which is equal to about 46,250 km (the actual circumference is about 40,000 km).

Shadows

Another interesting telecommunications-type project is to have classes from different locations across the globe measure the length of the shadow cast by a meter stick on specified days of the year (Figure 5.9). For a long-term project, students might measure shadow lengths at 12:00 noon on September 21, December 21, March 21, and June 21. Courtesy of the Internet, schools in

Figure 5.8
Erathosthenes

Figure 5.9
Shadows

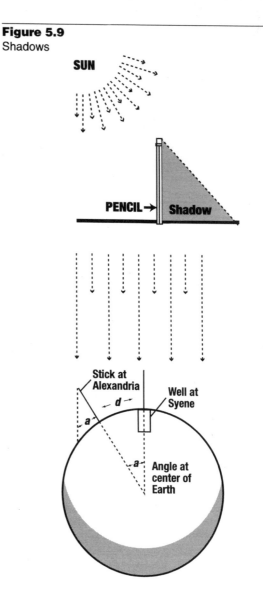

[3] *From* LabNet: Toward a Community of Practice by Richard Ruopp et al., pp. 116–118. Copyright © 1993 by *Lawrence Erlbaum Associates, Inc. Reprinted by permission of Laurence Erlbaum Associates, Inc.*

the Northern Hemisphere can collaborate with those in the Southern Hemisphere to compare results.

Lunar Settlement

Students design a lunar settlement out of cardboard, pipe cleaners, cotton, sand, construction paper, plastic, tape, and paint. Students need to consider the environment of the Moon and what alterations need to be made to sustain a human colony on the Moon.

Planetary Travel Brochure

Using both fact and fantasy, students design a travel brochure about one of the planets of our solar system. Students also design a transportation system used to shuttle people back and forth between the destination planet and Earth.

National Park Project

Students design a national park to demonstrate their knowledge of the environmental impact of these natural treasures. Their project should include a topographic map of the park and a description of how the park impacts the area in and around the park. Finally, students design a brochure for the park, describing its general operation.

Testing the Waters

Combining local monitoring and telecommunications, students set up a project where they investigate the quality of the water in a stream or river close to their home or school, then communicate with another group of students carrying out the same investigation elsewhere. Using simple monitoring equipment, students monitor the water for temperature, flow, pH, and dissolved oxygen. Students should also make qualitative observations of land use near the stream, surrounding ground cover, the odor of the stream, the color of the bed bottom, and any erosion near the stream. Students then organize their information in chart or map form. Using the Internet, students locate at least one group of students

from another school (in another town, state, or country) and compare findings.

Life Science Projects

The Biodrama Project

Students write a play about the parts of a cell and the life process of a cell. The "director" selects a cast of students, who rehearse and then present the play to other groups in the school. Students might wish to explore such cell-related topics as cancer, sickle-cell anemia, or cell division.

The Dirty Water Project

In this project, students are challenged to design a method to clean up dirty water (Figure 5.10). Provide students with small samples of the following materials, which they will use to make a large container of water dirty: wood chips, sand, grass, shells, potting soil, baking soda, vinegar, pieces of newspaper, polystyrene foam. Have student teams place these materials in a large container of tap water. This done, challenge students to come up with a method to clean up the water. Provide the following materials and tell

Figure 5.10
Water Filter System

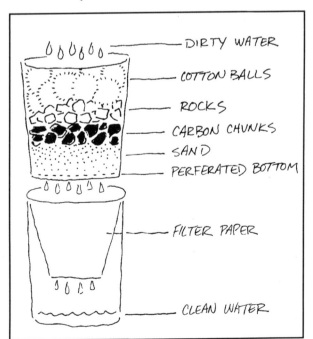

students they can use any of them to design a water treatment system: small plastic cups, beakers, sand, activated charcoal, cotton balls, filter paper. Allow students to add other materials pending your approval. Be sure students understand that they must document their work by recording their ideas in a journal.

The Insect Project

Student teams select an insect that they would like to study. Next, the students search for information about the insect, including its characteristics and habitat, traits beneficial and harmful to man, and literature about the insect. Students then create a model of their insect using any materials they wish. The model can be scaled up in size, but the various parts of the insect must remain proportional. Finally students present the results of their research to the class or another group (Figure 5.11).

The Design-an-Organism Project

Students use any materials they wish to design an organism that they think would be able to survive in a specified environment. You specify an actual environment, such as a forest or wooded area near your school, a meadow, a city park, a playground. Be sure students understand that they should be prepared to explain why they think their organism will survive. What characteristics does it have to protect it from predators, for example? What will it find to eat?

Project Feederwatch

Backyard or schoolyard birding provides a powerful way for students to investigate the behavior

Figure 5.12
Project Feederwatch

and characteristics of birds in their region (Figure 5.12.) To begin, have students build a birdfeeder by consulting references on professional feeder designs. Set the feeder in an area that is convenient for observation and study. Using their observation skills, students study the characteristics and behavior of the birds at the feeder, and the environmental factors that may affect them. Students then design research questions to investigate various aspects of what they've observed. Students may wish to consult an online project called Classroom FeederWatch at http://teaparty.terc.edu/comweb/bird/bird.html/. This project involves students in monitoring and data analysis of birds in North America.

Physical Science Projects

The Paper Tower

This project challenges collaborative teams to construct the tallest possible structure using one sheet of paper (8 1/2" × 11") and 50 cm of cellophane tape (see Figure 5.13). (Each team will also need a pair of scissors.) Allow students one or two days to complete the project. If a one-day project, give the students about 20 minutes to experiment with various designs, testing them out as they talk aloud. Then provide fresh mate-

Figure 5.11
The Insect Project

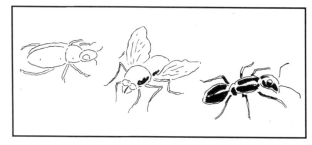

Figure 5.13
The Paper Tower. Students use a single sheet of paper to
construct a freestanding paper tower.

rials and give the students 30 minutes to build
the paper tower. If a two-day project, use the
first day for talking aloud and testing out
designs, and the second day for the challenge
contest.

Wind-Powered Vehicles

In this project, students design and build (using
household materials) a vehicle that harnesses
wind energy. The entire vehicle must fit inside a
1-cubic-foot space. Any common household
materials may be used, including aluminum foil,
plastic wrap, milk containers, tin cans, paper
bags, cardboard, toothpicks, string, paper clips,
shoe boxes, cereal boxes, and straws. Parts from
dismantled toys are not allowed. Materials not
listed here require teacher's approval. Each
team member keeps a log documenting his or
her team's ideas and designs. As students work
together and talk, they record and illustrate
their ideas. On the actual day of construction,
team members bring in all their materials. Give

them 30 minutes to build their vehicle. On the
next day, arrange for head-to-head matches to
determine the fastest vehicle to traverse 3 feet.
During the matches, each team has 30 seconds
to place its vehicle in the starting block before
the fan is turned on. Use rounds of single (or
double) elimination to determine the winners.
Award teams for neatest construction, most innovative design, and honorable mention, in addition. All entries should receive a certificate of
merit.

Clay Boats

Students' challenge in this project is to design a
boat that will float in water and hold the greatest
number of paper clips (or any other weight you
decide upon). Give students a measured amount
of clay (50 grams), a container of water, and
paper clips. Allow students 30 minutes to work
with the clay and test out their designs. Tell students to record their ideas and designs in their
logs, and to be ready to re-create their design

Figure 5.14
Spaghetti Car

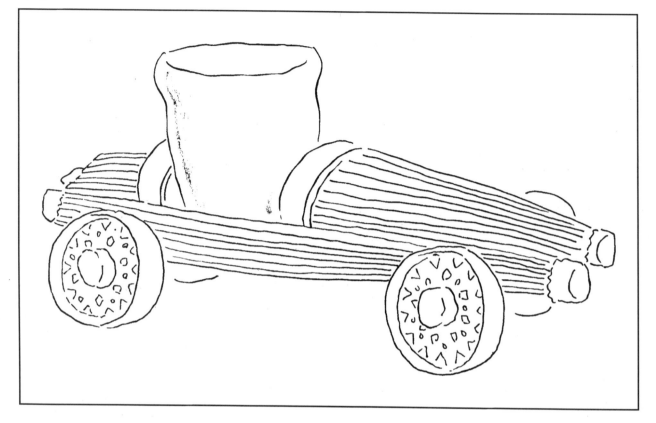

during the next class session. On the appointed day, give students 10 minutes to build the boat and then demonstrate in front of the class the number of "weights" the boat can hold. As with the Wind-powered Vehicles project, give out awards for a variety of "bests," such as longest boat, most innovative design, etc. Note: If you prefer, substitute aluminum foil for the clay. Give each team an equal amount of foil.

Spaghetti Cars

Students build cars out of spaghetti and small marshmallows (Figure 5.14). They then calculate how fast the car rolls down an incline. Give students 6 pasta wheels, 25 spaghetti strands, and 10 small marshmallows with which to work. Students' goal is to build a car that rolls and can hold one large marshmallow. Set up a "downhill track" and have students test and measure how fast their cars roll.

SUMMARY

This chapter underscores the importance of "learning by doing." Project-based learning is a compelling strategy that engages teams of students to solve real problems. There are many projects in the chapter from which to choose, and you should experiment with the ones included here. Start with one that relates directly to the content of the topic that you are currently teaching. Make use of the information in Chapter 1 on cooperative learning and help your students work together as a team on the project or projects that you assign. Projects can help you attain a variety of goals and objectives. Some of them can be used to help students build models (of a cell or an atom). Others can help them learn how to design scientific investigations and make use of the Internet by assigning projects that require students to find information on current topics.

CHAPTER 6 THE ONLINE SCIENCE CLASSROOM

This chapter will show you exactly how you can use the Internet as an active learning tool in your science classroom. It begins with responses to interview questions of a number of teachers who have been using the Internet as part of their science program. Their experience with the Internet should prove valuable in getting your classroom online. The chapter offers specific guidelines for creating the online classroom, including the tools you will be using once you enter the world of the Net! Finally, the chapter includes a collection of practical Internet activities and Internet sites geared to the online science classroom.

Figure 6.1
An online classroom

INTERVIEWS WITH TEACHERS: TIPS AND THINGS TO EXPECT[1]

Responding to the interview questions on incorporating Internet resources in the science classroom were three teachers and a principal. Sara Crim is a science teacher at Chattanooga Valley Middle School, which is located in Flintstone, a small rural town in northwest Georgia. Ken Royal is a teacher at Whisconier Middle School, Brookfield, Connecticut. Charles Eich is a former middle school teacher in Marietta, Georgia. Salyon Johnson is a school principal, in Savannah, Georgia. These people responded to five questions. Here is what the respondents had to say:

Interview Question 1: Why did you decide to use the Internet?

Teachers report that using the Internet is motivational and is an example of authentic learning. Charles Eich says that "telecommunications allows my science students to receive timely scientific data to study. Also, telecommunications allows my students to participate in scientific studies outside of the classroom. Finally, my students can communicate directly with experts in a field of study about questions that arise in our

classroom studies and projects." Sara Crim sees telecommunications as a way to really bring technology into her classroom. She puts it this way: "At the time that I began the use of computer-mediated telecommunications, it was such an innovative idea. Very few teachers were using this in their classes and I wanted to try something new with my students." Salyon Johnson believes that "the key to learning is wanting to learn." She says that "if students came to school with the desire to learn, then our jobs as teachers would be relatively easy. It is unfortunate, but since most of our students do not come to school ready to learn, then one of the roles of teachers is to encourage students to want to learn so that they can learn. Using computers in the classroom for any reason is an automatic motivator for students."

Interview Question 2: How do the students use telecommunications in their work?

(NOTE: As you will see as you read on, there are many ways that teachers can use the Internet in the classroom. Here we focus on the students and how they use the Internet in their work.) Charles Eich's students use e-mail to send off the data they gather as part of joint area and national studies, such as the Swoope Acid Rain

---

[1] *Excerpts of interviews with Sarah Crim, Ken Royal, Charles Eich, and Salyon Johnson used with permission.*

Project. His students rely on the Internet to receive timely information on earthquakes, weather, and other Earth science phenomena that they study. In the spring, his classes use e-mail to send their questions to and communicate with an agricultural expert about a garden project. Charles reports that "just recently, my students began taking part in an Internet weather project called Kids as Global Scientists, out of the University of Colorado at Boulder. We will be studying weather with teams of students, compiling portfolios of learning and gathering real data. Information will be communicated to Colorado and other schools in our cluster. Some of these schools include those in Israel, Australia, and Hong Kong as well as various states in the USA. My kids and I are excited about being a part of this project!"

Sara Crim indicates that her students are part of a group of students working on The Global Thinking Project, an environmental project that lets students share their findings on local environmental studies with students from other countries as well as with those within their state. Sara reports that "the students share this information via e-mail. Students are able to find out, through their messages, about other countries and have developed friendships; some have even had pen pals that they have met through e-mail."

Interview Question 3: What have been some of the benefits of using telecommunications with your students?

Charles Eich makes a powerful statement when he says that "my students feel like real scientists and investigators by using the computer and telecommunications. Science comes alive as they talk with experts, receive real-time data to study, and participate in actual scientific studies. As one student said, 'You mean these are actual earthquakes that occurred this month?!?' Also, their self-respect and respect for me as a teacher has increased with our use of telecommunications—science is no longer 'out of the textbook' for my students." Note two

themes that emerge here: kids feel like they are doing real science, and they develop a new respect for the teacher.

Sara Crim hits on another important benefit of telecommunications. She states that "my students have learned to appreciate other people and realize that we are all alike in so many ways, even though we are separated by thousands of miles. We have developed compassion for people and their problems. Somehow it is getting through to my students that we are not superior in everything and everything doesn't have to be done our way. There is instant gratification using telecommunications and, in this day and time, students and teachers appreciate this."

Interview Question 4: How have telecommunications been of value to you professionally?

Charles Eich indicates that since being on the Internet, he has linked up to numerous sources of information for his professional development, not just for the kids. Not only does he receive mailings and have access to up-to-the-minute data and information, but he also corresponds with other teachers and experts in order to become more proficient in his field, making him a better classroom teacher. He concludes by saying that "my self-esteem as a professional has improved because of this new tool that puts my students and me in touch with the world outside of our four walls."

As a life sciences teacher, Sara Crim reports that the Internet "has really helped me to get across to students both how different areas of the world are and how alike they are. We try to teach, for example, how seasons do not occur at the same time all over the world. It is taught instantly when an e-mail message arrives from Australia saying that they are getting out for summer break—while we are getting ready for our Christmas break! It has added a new dimension to my teaching. It is a tool that has brought to me new interest and has helped to make teaching fun, because I know that my students are learning and are eager to learn more. In what other classes do you have students who do not want to give up a class and are willing to come in after school to get to be part of a group learning through telecommunications!?"

Interview Question 5: Are there any tips you would give teachers who are just beginning to use telecommunications in their science class?

Charles Eich advises: "Internet access is costly on an ongoing basis. Once a line and modem are available, which is very difficult to do at times, there are monthly costs. University assistance through an Internet account for a classroom teacher is wonderful. The only drawback is a text format and not a Windows™ 'user-friendly' format. However, with some training the text format is not impossible to navigate. Inservices and workshops to assist teachers in their use of the Internet help a great deal—more needed. I see this new tool as more revolutionary than all previous technologies. Students can truly venture out of their small world to become part of a global classroom. Sharing ideas is a great way to bring down barriers that divide and separate us locally and globally."

Sara Crim and Salyon Johnson make the following recommendations:

- Know that there will be problems. They are not life-threatening and you will learn from them.
- Relax and let your students enjoy this new technology. Let them teach you something.
- Find telecommunications software that is easy for you and your students to use.
- Realize that you can be overwhelmed by all the information that is available. Choose only what will benefit you.
- Know how much money is available for you to use to be online. This will help you choose more carefully what you can and cannot participate in.
- Try to be part of a group that is doing something that will help you and your students.

- Be persistent!
- Send messages often—even brief hello messages.

CREATING THE ONLINE CLASSROOM

Why Go Online?
There are many good reasons for linking your classroom to the Internet. One very powerful reason is that Internet access will support your existing activities and enable you to implement new, even more authentic learning activities in your classroom. For example, your students will be able to ask experts in the field questions about science, they will be able to search university sites for current information on most any topic you might teach, and they will be able to carry out collaborative projects with students in other schools—schools in other states and other countries. Another good reason for going online is finding colleagues out there on the Net who will support and encourage you professionally. This becomes a two-way street, enabling you not only to get support but to lend your expertise to others. There is a vast array of information—databases, libraries, people—that you can bring into your classroom at the speed of light when you hook up to the Internet.

What Do I Need to Get Started?
There are a number of things that you will need to get in order to go online. Here's a brief rundown:

1. A Computer
It really doesn't matter what kind of computer you use. It is recommended that you have either a Mac with a hard drive with at least 32 to 64 megabytes of RAM or a PC with Windows. Note: If you're going to want to run software with easy-to-use graphical screens, then older computers such as Apple IIes or IBM 286s won't work. However, these older models will still connect you to the Internet. (The first time I got started on the Internet, I was using an Apple II!)

2. A Modem

A modem is a device that converts signals that computers use into a form that can be sent over telephone lines. The word *modem* is short for "modulator/demodulator." If possible, purchase a fax/modem and one that is fast—at least 28,000 bps (bits per second). You will find them available at 33,000 or 56,000 bps as well. Higher-speed modems will enable you to download graphic software and image files from the Internet in relatively short periods of time.

3. A Telephone Line

A regular telephone line will work. If there is no phone line in your classroom at present, your best bet is to have one installed. Alternatively, if there is a phone jack near your classroom (perhaps in the science department office), it is possible to run a line off of that line into your classroom. In this case, you would be sharing the line. If you are going to set up a telecommunications system at home, as well as the classroom, consider getting a separate fax/data telephone line. If not, you can use your existing phone line.

4. Telecommunications (Dial-Up) Software

Telecommunications software enables your modem and computer to "talk" to each other, and then interact with the Internet. You probably have telecommunications software in your school's computer and don't know it. Programs such as Claris Works, for example, have a telecommunications component that you could use. Moreover, many Internet service providers either give you or sell (typically at low cost) specially designed software enabling you to connect to the Internet. The software generally includes an e-mail program and a browser.

5. An Internet Provider

You need a phone number, supplied by your Internet provider, that your modem dials to connect you to the provider and, through the provider, to the Internet. First, check with your county or district Office of Education, and ask what options or plans there are for Internet connections. In some states, such as Florida (FIRN), Georgia (PeachNet & EduNet), and Texas (Tenet), Internet access is provided via a statewide network. Also, there are a number of commercial and not-for-profit telecommunication providers. For example, you might want to consider MindSpring (1-888-677-7464), NETCOM (1-800-382-4633), or the Institute for Global Communications (IGC) (415-442-0220). Each of these providers has Internet-accessible software, and each supports science education projects. You might also check with a local university or college to see if they provide Internet access to local teachers. (See Figure 6.2.)

6. Further Suggestions

Identify someone in your school who has been using telecommunications in the classroom and seek out his or her support. Most such people are more than willing to help. Many teachers who use the Internet have discovered that accessibility to the Internet at home increases the success of using telecommunications in the classroom. If you can't get a phone line into your classroom at first, do get started at home. You can use your computer at home to do a few start-up projects with your class, or you can use it to learn about the Internet and to begin to make contact with other science teachers. (This is the way I began.)

Anticipating Problems in the Online Classroom

One of the biggest problems facing teachers using the Internet is the problem of access. Can a teacher who has only one computer successfully use the Internet in his or her science teaching? The answer is yes. To help make this point, I contacted Ken Royal, a science teacher at Whisconier Middle School in Brookfield, Connecticut. Ken and other science teachers in his school are currently incorporating the Internet into their science curriculum. In fact, you can visit their Web page at: http://travel.to/wms/

Figure 6.2
Home page from *www.mindspring.com* Web site.
Reprinted by permission of MindSpring Enterprises, Inc.

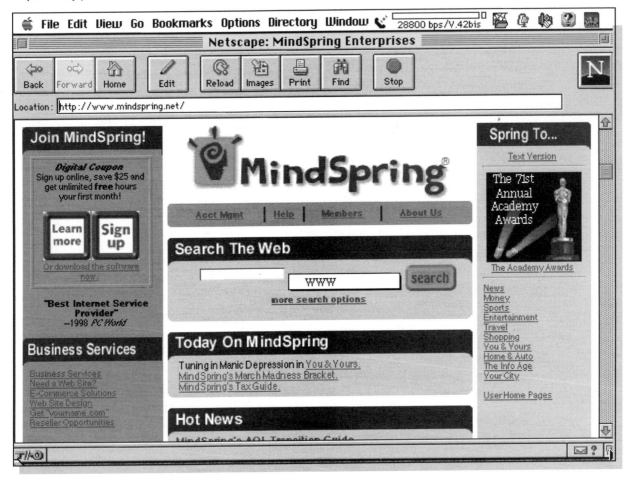

Here are Ken Royal's solutions to some potential problems.

Problem 1: How can I do Internet activities with only one computer in my classroom?

This is a problem I don't have, but one that most of my contact schools around the world and in the United States deal with daily. (My partner teacher and I wrote a grant and received four computers and two printers. I also ran a marathon to obtain an additional computer, which we use for overflow, weather, and our Web site.) Consequently, I've thought about the one-computer dilemma plenty. It is the most-asked question when trying to interest other schools in joining some of our projects.

To make the one-computer connection work, the computer must be one of many centers of activity in the classroom at any given time. Somewhat like a circus with many rings, the teacher acts as Ringmaster while small cooperative learning groups of students move from center to center, with one of those centers being the computer. In my own classroom, for example, these centers were available to students: Mealworms Lab, Lake/Pond Samples Lab, Green Tank Lab (this is a tank that truly is green and full of water specimens), Bone /Animal Anatomy Lab, and Internet Research and E-mailing Lab (Key Pals, Experts, and Projects, all of which are ongoing). Set up this way, groups are able to access the computer to do very specific kinds of online work, such as send e-mail letters, search specific sites

Figure 6.3
The Internet-based classroom enables teachers and students to use the tools of the Net to collaborate with others as well as access data bases of information in the form of Web pages. It is one of the most compelling innovations in the history of education.

previously identified, and/or use a search tool to research a question. The key concept here is that the group using the computer at any given time has a specific task and knows how much time it will have to complete it.

Problem 2: What do I do if the only Internet access is in the Media Center?

For schools in which the only Internet access is in the Media Center, Internet research can be a problem since the computer has to be shared with an entire school. If, however, the classroom has access to a computer for word processing, e-mailing can still be done, with the e-mails being saved on a floppy disk, later to be copied and pasted (by teacher, students, or media tech person) to e-mails at the Internet-connected machine. As I've discovered, the teachers who are doing this successfully are using their own machines at home to make everything work. I even know some who have taken laptops to school and back home, daily. The importance of being part of this new style of telecommunications teaching outweighs any monies or time covered in the teaching contract. That has been the way of teachers since the beginning.

Problem 3: With only one computer, how can all my students still benefit from the Internet?

Although we can't afford an expensive LCD Projector, we have an adapter (AverKey) attached to a 25" TV. This device connects to the computer and projects the computer screen's image onto the TV. The resolution is not great, and some of the letters may look a little funny, but it gets the job done. We do large-group presentations this way. In fact, we recently finished our Open House for parents using this equipment. We did a Powerpoint® presentation for them, featuring pictures of students and experiments. In addition to an adapter, a printer is a great device. We print out the pages and tack them up around the room so all students can see what's being done.

TOOLS OF THE INTERNET: NAVIGATING THE NET

We can make sense of Internet tools if we classify them into two categories:

- Interpersonal Tools: These tools let you connect with other people—for example, via an e-mail program, a video conference, or a chat room.
- Informational Tools: These tools let you harvest information from the Internet via a tool such as a browser. Netscape Communicator and Microsoft Explorer are the two most popular browsers.

Interpersonal Tools

E-mail—Wired to the World!

As you will see, you and your students will be able to do many things with electronic mail (e-mail), and it may prove to be the most important service that you have on the Internet. E-mail enables you to send and receive messages to anyone else who is connected to the Internet. You can use e-mail for professional contacts, to do collaborative science projects with another class, and (for students) to develop

Figure 6.4
Sample E-mail Letter

Topic 173   gtp   4 responses
jserent2.........................Global Thinking Project Teachers   2:14 PM Dec 9, 1997
(at pie.xtec.es)

>Date: Sun, 23 Nov 1997 09:28:58
>To: wenona1@abc.com.au
>From: josep serentill <jserent2@abc.com.es>
>Subject: gtp

>Hello Carol
>I'm writing from Joviat School in Manresa, Barcelona, Spain. We love receiving messages from different countries around the world. My pupils want to send messages to everybody. They find it difficult to write in English, they make a great effort.
>See you soon.
>Jose

"keypals," the electronic equivalent of "pen pals."

E-mail is to the computer what a written letter (which many of us now call "snail mail") is to the U.S. Postal System. A typical e-mail letter looks like Figure 6.4.

Everyone on the Internet has an e-mail "address," just like they have a postal address. All Internet addresses are in the user@host format. For example, my e-mail address is jhassard@gsu.edu. The "jhassard" is my e-mail name; the "gsu.edu" is the name of the host computer that I use. E-mail messages should always be signed by you or the students who are the authors of the message. In many e-mail programs, you can set up a signature that is automatically printed at the end of an e-mail message.

Here are some other things to keep in mind when sending e-mail messages:

1. Be conscious of the fact that for many readers of your messages, English is not the primary language. Keep your messages brief, and be aware of the complexity of words and phrases that you use in composing your messages.

2. Remind your students that you and they are trying to build relationships among teachers and students from around the world. Part of this relationship-building is responding to e-mail. Try not to delay in replying to any e-mail that you receive. To avoid problems, you might designate groups of students to be responsible for e-mail correspondence on a daily or weekly basis.

Internet E-groups

E-groups are Internet mailing lists that send messages automatically to everyone on the list. E-mail sent this way enables a group of individuals to have an online discussion. You might think of this as an E-group. Lists are powerful ways to make contacts and participate in discussions of interest to you and your students. Discussion topics will depend upon the list you join. You will find discussion groups on just about any topic you can think of. For teachers, discussion groups can be a valuable means to communicate with colleagues, to find answers to questions, and to ask questions that colleagues may be able to answer. To set up a discussion group for your

Figure 6.5
This is a screen image of a video conference among several schools in the United States, Japan, Finland, and New Zealand. Sample CU-SeeMe® Screen from *CU-SeeMe® User Guide, Version 2.1 for Windows.* © Copyright White Pine Software, Inc. Reprinted by permission of White Pine Software, Inc.

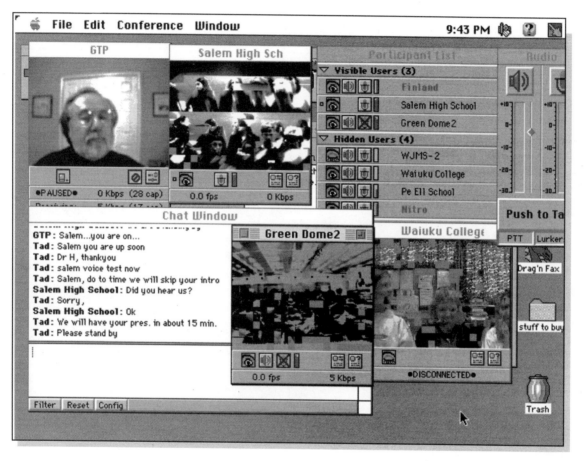

students, visit the eGroups.com site at www.egroups.com and start a group.

Video Conferences

Using inexpensive digital cameras (such as Connectix's black-and-white or color cameras) and desktop video conferencing software (such as CU-SeeMe®), you and your students can communicate with students and teachers from different states or countries not only by "talking," but also by seeing each other.

CU-SeeMe® software, which is available free from a Cornell University site (ftp://cu-seeme.cornell.edu/publ/cu-seeme/),[2] enables you to connect with others on the Internet for group or point-to-point video conferences. A *group conference* provides a collaborative environment in which you can connect with several schools at the same time. A *point-to-point conference*, by

[2] Note that this address starts with "ftp," which stands for "file transfer protocol." Simply type this address into your Web browser from the File menu in the Location box. Once you get to this site, you will be able download a copy of the CU-SeeMe® software.

Figure 6.6
Global School Net CU-SeeMe ® home page.
CU-SeeMe ® Schools home page from
http://www.gsp.org/cu/index.html Web site. Reprinted by
permission of Global SchoolNet Foundation.

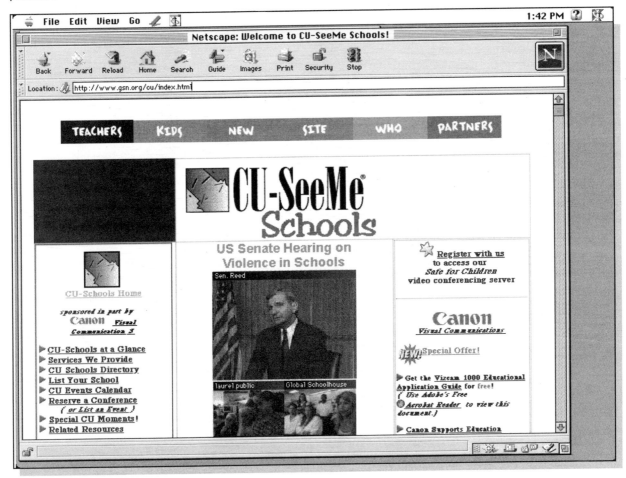

contrast, takes place between your school and
another school. To arrange for "point-to-point"
conferences, you will need the IP (Internet
Protocol) address of the other school. To get this
address, contact the school and ask for its IP
address. This is much like dialing up a friend to
make a phone call. Every computer connected to
the Internet has a unique numerical address
called the IP address. An IP address is a set of
four numbers separated by periods, such as
209.82.68.102. Once you begin collaborating with
other schools using e-mail, arranging for a two-
way conference is a fun, natural next step.

To get started with video conferencing, visit
the Global SchoolNet Foundation CU-SeeMe
page at http://www.gsn.org/cu/index.html/ (Figure
6.6). You will be able to register as a CuSeeMe
participant, and then check to see what conferences are being offered in which you might like
to participate.

Informational Tools

There is an enormous amount of information
residing on computers on the Internet that you
and your students will be able to access. Let's
look at some of the tools that will enable you to
harvest this information, but first, "What is the
Internet?"

Figure 6.7
Gopher Screen
"Gopher Menu" screen from
gopher://gopher-ccs.ucsd.edu:70/1/ Web site. Reprinted
by permission of ADCS and The University of Minnesota.

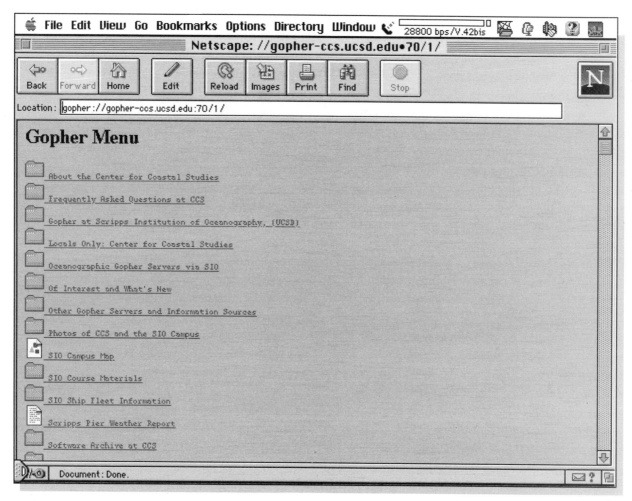

The Internet

The Internet is the network of networks connecting computers and people. It is the world's largest network. You can think of the Internet as the people who use it, and the information that resides on it. It is hard to keep up with the size of the Internet; as of the late 1990s there were millions of people linked through it. This number continues to expand by leaps and bounds. Further, there were at least five million computers on the Internet that were "serving up" information. The information that is available on the Internet includes text, graphics, video, and sound. Most of the information on the Internet is text. However, some pages of information residing on computers can be organized using "hypermedia" documents. These are documents that contain links to other text, images, sound, video, and so on. Computer programs (such as Netscape Communicator, Gopher, FTP, and so forth) have been devised that enable you to retrieve a variety of information from computers on the Internet. Other programs (search engines) have been created to help you search for information on the Internet. Let's take a look at these tools.

Information Please

The information stored in files on computers residing on the Internet can be accessed using different software programs. Three ways of retrieving information on the Internet will be discussed here, including Gopher, FTP, and the World Wide Web.

Gopher. Gopher, which was developed at the University of Minnesota, is a system that enables you to find information on the Internet that uses menus. When the Gopher program is started, you are shown a menu from which you can select an item that shows you another menu (see Figure 6.7). Many of the menu items are files that you can read, print, or copy to your hard drive. All of them are text documents. Web browsers, which will be discussed below, can be used to search for information stored in Gopher files.

Here are some interesting Gopher sites that you might want to visit and use with your students:

- Hurricane Tracking:
  gopher://wx.atmos.uiuc.edu:70/11/
- Flood Disaster Information:
  gopher://ilces.ag.uiuc.edu:70/11/Flood-information/
- Environmental Education Gopher:
  gopher://nceet.snre.umich.edu:70/1/
- Scripps Institution of Oceanography:
  gopher://gopher-ccs.ucsd.edu:70/1/

FTP. FTP stands for "file transfer protocol" and is the name of a program that enables you to move files from one computer to another on the Internet. If you decide that you want to "publish" information on the Internet, you will want to learn more about FTP. FTP means that you are "transferring files" from one computer to another, such as from one of NASA's computers to your computer. If you use a PC, you can use an FTP program called WS_FTP. If you use a Macintosh, you can use an FTP program called Fetch. Each program enables you to easily transfer (either upload a file from your computer to another, or download a file from another computer to yours).

WWW Browsers. In the early 1990s, a system known as the World Wide Web was developed by researchers at CERN in Geneva. This system consisted of connections among computers that developed pages of information using HTML. HTML stands for Hypertext Markup Language, a programming language used to design Web pages. HTML pages, or Web pages, contain text and links to allow you to move about the Web. The original World Wide Web consisted of text-only pages containing links which would move you from one page to another. In 1993 a program named Mosaic was developed by a researcher named Mark Andreesen of the University of Illinois. Mosaic was the first graphical Web browser, and it laid the groundwork for the development of Netscape Navigator™ (Figure 6.8) and Microsoft Explorer.™ Navigator and Explorer will be two of the most important informational tools you and your students use. With these programs, you will be able to "surf the Net," not to mention participate in interactive activities in virtually thousands of Web sites.

Searching for Information

Although the Internet was not developed to be a library, there are tools that can be of help to find information, people, businesses and discussion groups. Three aspects of searching for information will be discussed here: search engines, types of searches, and the use of Boolean Operators.

Search Engines. A number of tools have been developed to help find information on the Internet. There are engines such as HotBot and Exite that will help you find specific information. Tools such as Yahoo! can be used to find categories of information on a topic. Figure 6.9 organizes the engines into categories and then provides you with the Web sites of recommended tools.

Types of Searches. You can use the engines described above to find information by applying one of three types of search strategies: the locating strategy, the sampling strategy, and the collecting strategy. Figure 6.10 outlines these strategies in the context of the kind of information that you want.

Figure 6.8

The Netscape browser shown here enables you to search the World Wide Web for information that is stored on computers all over the world. Today's new browsers also enable you to send and retrieve your e-mail, and create your own Web pages.

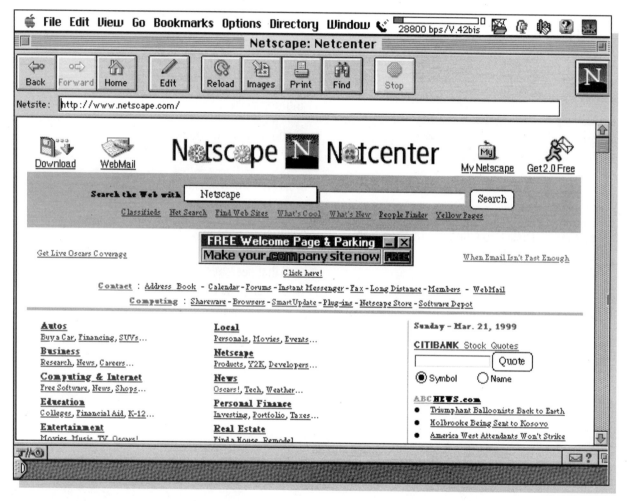

The Netscape browser frame and home page from Netscape website. Copyright © 1998 by Netscape Communications Corporation. All Rights Reserved. Reprinted by permission of Netscape Communications Corporation.

Figure 6.9 Using Search Engines

Engine Category	Web Sites
No search engine is perfect, but here are some of the best.	Yahoo: http://www.yahoo.com/ HotBot: http://www.hotbot.com/ Infoseek: http://www.infoseek.com/ Lycos: http://www.lycos.com/
People Finders: To find people on the Net, use any of these Web sites.	Four11: http://www.four11.com/ (for finding people on the Net) Bigfoot: www.bigfoot.com
Business Finders: This search tool allows you to find businesses on the Net.	Bigbook: www.bigbook.com
Usenet Search: A way to keep track of usenet groups on any topic.	Deja News: www.dejanews.com
Metasearch: These tools find information from multiple search engines.	Profusion: http://www.designlab. ukans.edu/profusion/ (a metasearch tool that searches through several search engines at once!)

Figure 6.10
Search Strategies

What Do You Want?	Search Strategy	Web Site
• "I want specific information on a topic such as the NASA Space Shuttle."	• The locating strategy: In this case, you use a pinpointed search.	• Hotbot: www.hotbot.com
• "I'd like some really good information on geology and astrophysics."	• The sampling strategy: Browse a subject tree. Go to Yahoo! or Magellan and use the existing categories in their directory to find your information.	• Yahoo: www.yahoo.com • Magellan: mckinley.netcom.com
• "I want everything in astronomy."	• The collecting strategy: Do a deep search using a search engine.	• Most of the search engines listed in Figure 6.9 will work.

Figure 6.11
Boolean searches

To	Use	Examples
Narrow your search	AND	Rocks AND minerals means that only documents on the Net that contain both words will be reported in your search.
Broaden your search	OR	Astrophysics OR astronomy means that you get pages that mention either or both astrophysics and astronomy.
Exclude concepts in your search	NOT	Rockets NOT Houston means you will get pages that mention rockets, but exclude those that mention Houston Rockets.

Here are examples of each type of strategy, how you would use it, and some results from actual searches.

Boolean Operators. You will want to teach your students the key Boolean Operators or connecting words—AND, OR, and NOT— to help them as they search for information on the Internet. The table in Figure 6.11 outlines their uses.

Here is an example of how to use a Boolean Operator:

Using AND. You use AND when you want to narrow your search. If your search question is to find documents that discuss rocks, as well as minerals, then the solution is to use the Boolean Operative AND. The procedure would be:

1. Go to Hot Bot: www.hotbot.com/
2. In the "Search" area, type in minerals AND rocks.
3. In the "look for" area, select "Boolean phrase."
4. Select "Search."
5. Examine the results (see Figure 6.12).

Now, go to the Internet and try these examples for using OR and NOT.

Using OR. You use OR when you want to broaden your search and find lots of information. If your search question is information on astronomy and astrophysics, then the solution is to use the Boolean Operative OR. The procedure would be:

1. Go to HotBot: www.hotbot.com/
2. Type in *astrophysics* OR *astronomy.*
3. In the "look for" area select "Boolean phrase."
4. Select "Search."
5. Examine the results.

Using NOT. If you want to narrow your search as well as exclude concepts in your search, then you should use the NOT operative. Suppose you are searching for information about NASA's rockets, not the NBA's Houston Rockets. Follow this procedure:

1. Go to HotBot: www.hotbot.com/
2. In the "Search" area, type in *NASA AND rockets NOT Houston NOT NBA*

Figure 6.12
Hotbot Search

Search results screen for "minerals and rocks" from www.hotbot.com Web site. Copyright © 1994–1999 by Wired Digital, Inc. All Rights Reserved. Reprinted by permission of Wired Digital, Inc.

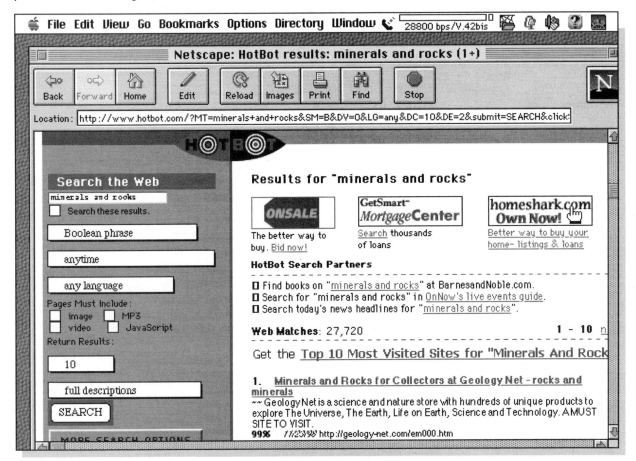

3. In the "look for" area, select "Boolean phrase."
4. Select "Search."
5. Examine the results.

KEY WEB RESOURCES FOR SCIENCE TEACHERS

As a resource, there is nothing comparable to the World Wide Web. It contains hundreds of sites devoted to science, technology, and teaching. Here are some sites that should prove valuable as you begin to use the Internet. Following a brief description of the Web site, you will find the URL (Universal Resource Locator), or the Web address for the site.

Access Excellence

If you're looking for projects of all kinds in the life sciences, then you must visit this site. It contains hundreds of lesson plans that you can download and use in your classroom.
URL: http://www.gene.com/

Classroom FeederWatch

At this site, students build a birdfeeder that is used to carry out a bird-watching monitoring project. Students gather data, and then send the data over the Internet using specially designed Internet forms.
URL: http://teaparty.terc.edu/comweb/ bird/ bird.html/

Discovery Channel Online

This is a must-see site. Always up to date, it includes daily articles, bulletin boards, fact sheets, and activities you can use in your classroom.
URL: www.discovery.com/

Earth Pages

Come here to search NASA's Earth Pages for information about planet Earth.

URL: http://epserver.gsfc.nasa.gov/earth/earth.html/

Eisenhower Web Site

This site compiles information about mathematics, science, and environmental science. Lesson plans, projects, resources, and much more is available here.
URL: http://www.enc.org/

Figure 6.13
If you visit the EnviroNet Web site, one of the pages you will find is BirdWatch. BirdWatch is one of several monitoring projects in which you and your students can participate. BirdWatch screen from www.earth.simmons.edu/birdwatch/birdwatch.html EnviroNet Web page. Copyright © 1998 by Simmons College. Reprinted by permission of Simmons College.

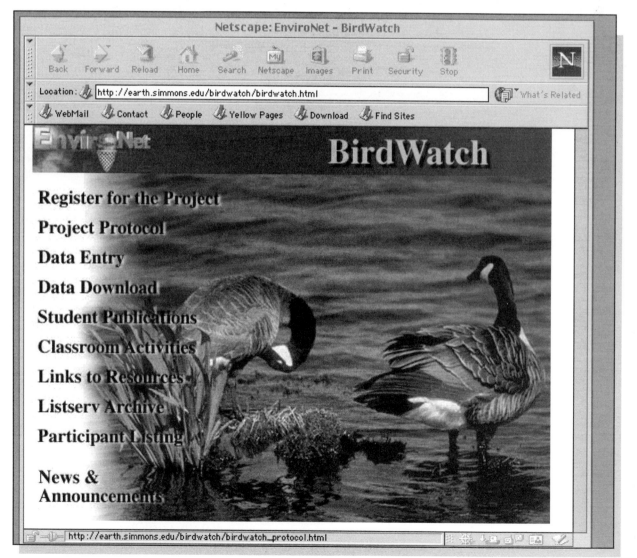

Figure 6.14
ePALS home page

ePALS Classroom Exchange home page from
http://www.epals.com/kpi.html Web site. Copyright ©
1996–1999 by ePALS Classroom Exchange. Reprinted
by permission of ePALS Classroom Exchange.

EnviroNet

This science teaching site, located at Simmons
College in Boston, offers some of the best
Internet projects that you and your students can
join. Topics for collaborative monitoring
include: acid rain, bird watching, plants,
lichens, ozone, road salt, and roadkill. (See
Figure 6.13.) URL: http://earth.simmons.edu/

Franklin Institute Science Museum

If you're looking for a site for a virtual field trip as
well as one containing interactive projects, then
this is a good site for you. Once here, you will find
links to other science museums around the world.
URL: http://sln.fi.edu/

Global Thinking Project (GTP)

This project promotes environmental science on
the Net. The GTP is a hands-across-the-globe
project in which students participate in local
environmental monitoring, global data sharing,
and e-mail collaboration on projects exploring
indoor air pollution, outdoor air pollution, ozone,
water quality, and soil erosion.
URL: http://www.gtp.org/

Figure 6.15
The Global Thinking Project is one of many online projects that utilize the Global Classroom structure. Students work together on one of several global projects by sending and retrieving e-mail, participating in online discussions, sharing data, and reporting on the results of their research.
"Welcome to the Global Thinking Project" screen from www.gtp.org Web site. Reprinted by permission of The Global Thinking Project.

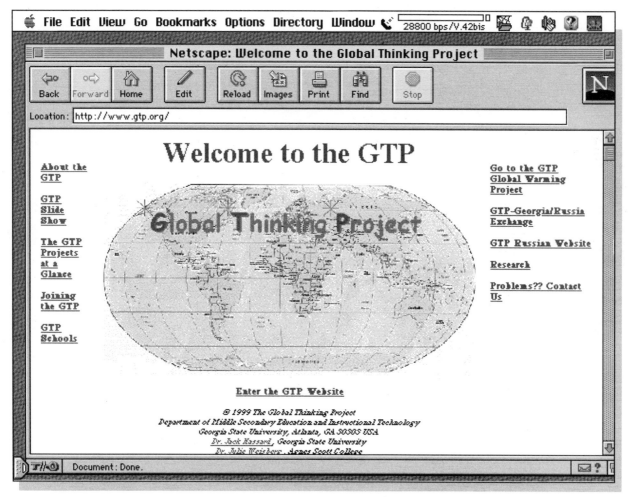

Globe

The Globe Program is an international environmental science and education partnership in which teachers and students monitor environmental factors locally, then pool their data with research scientists across the world.
URL: http://www.globe.gov/

Minds On Science

I developed this Web site to be used in conjunction with this book. You will find a wealth of information and resources organized by content area in science, as well as resources and activities for this book.
URL: http://www.gsu.edu/~mstjrh/mindson-science.html/

Figure 6.16

At the Ask-A-Geologist site, students can send questions about volcanoes, earthquakes, mountains, and other Earth science phenomena to geologists.

National Earthquake Information Center

The National Earthquake Information Center is a data center and archive for all seismic information. If your students want to access current information, this is the site to visit.
URL: http://gldss7.cr.usgs.gov/

Paleontology Without Walls

This site, located at the University of California Museum in Berkeley, contains online exhibits, information about fossils, and other resources guaranteed to enthrall students.
URL: http://www.ucmp.berkeley.edu/exhibit/exhibits.html/

Rockhounds Information Page

Set up by rockhounds, this page has information on images and pictures of rocks, rock shops and galleries, books and magazines, and general Earth science topics.
URL: http://www.rahul.net/infodyn/rockhounds/rockhounds.html/

Zooary

This online zoo is aimed at helping students with zoology. Information is available on Amphibians, Arthropods, Birds and Mammals, Reptiles, and Miscellaneous.
URL: http://www.poly.edu/~duane/zoo/mission.html/

Figure 6.17
Ask Shamu Home Page

"Ask Shamu" and "Shamu Questions" pages from *The Seaworld/BuschGardens Animal Information Database* from Sea World/Busch Gardens Web site. Copyright © 1998 by Busch Entertainment Corporation. All Rights Reserved. Reprinted by permission of SeaWorld/BuschGardens.

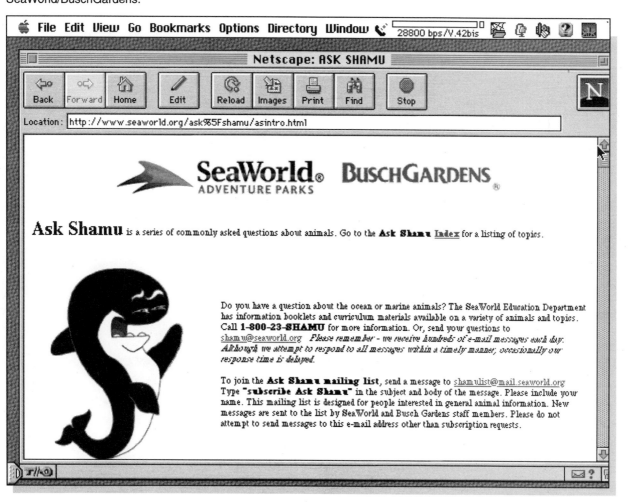

INTERNET ACTIVITIES: WHAT I CAN DO ONCE I'M ONLINE?

The activities that follow are organized into three major categories:[3]

- Interpersonal Exchange Activities
- Information Collection and Analysis Activities
- Problem-Solving Projects

Within each category, you will find several different kinds of activities, or activity structures. Each structure is clearly described so that the goal of the structure is obvious. You will also find important Internet links for each structure, as well as a practical classroom activity based on the structure.

Figure 6.18
Sample Shamu Questions

"Ask Shamu" and "Shamu Questions" pages from *The Seaworld/BuschGardens Animal Information Database* from Sea World/Busch Gardens Web site. Copyright © 1998 by Busch Entertainment Corporation. All Rights Reserved. Reprinted by permission of SeaWorld/BuschGardens.

Interpersonal Exchange Activities

Interpersonal Exchange Activities are interactive experiences on the Internet in which students send e-mail to chat with, talk to, and/or see one another or interact with experts. A range of science activities are possible using Interpersonal Exchanges. These include key pals, global classrooms, question-and-answer services, and impersonations.

Key Pals

The electronic equivalent of pen pals, key pals enables you to design activities in which individual students send e-mail to each other over the Internet. This activity structure is highly motivating for students, but can present managerial problems for the teacher. However, if you organize your classroom into cooperative groups, each one could function as a "key pal group" and could be the unit you use for e-mailing. Finding key pals for your students and/or student groups is relatively easy. One site to

Figure 6.19
Developed by Amy Dominick while an Intern in the
TEEMS Science Education program at Georgia State
University. Used with permission.

INTERNET SCAVENGER HUNT

Using one of the Internet Search Engines, such as Yahoo!, answer the following questions. Please write down the Internet address for each question that you answer.

1. What is the field of science that studies the human fossil record?

   answer:
   _____

   address:
   _____

2. Hominids are included in the super family of all apes, the _____ family.

   answer:
   _____

   address:
   _____

3. Is Ramapithecus still considered a hominid?

   answer:
   _____

   address:
   _____

4. What is the oldest known hominid species?

   answer:
   _____

   address:
   _____

5. How far back does the oldest known hominid species date?

   answer:
   _____

   address:
   _____

6. The species Australopithecus Arafensis had a pelvis and leg bones closely resembling those of modern man. True_____False_____

   answer:
   _____

   address:
   _____

7. Who is Lucy?

   answer:
   _____

   address:
   _____

8. Neanderthal man existed _____ years ago.

   answer:
   _____

   address:
   _____

9. What are some characteristics of Homo Erectus?

   answer:
   _____

   address:
   _____

10. What species is known from one major specimen, the Black Skull?

   answer:
   _____

   address:
   _____

11. What is the Triassic period named for?

   answer:
   _____

   address:
   _____

12. What is the name of the most current epoch?

   answer:
   _____

   address:
   _____

13. Describe and show a diagram of carbon 14 dating.

   answer:
   _____

   address:
   _____

   Illustration:

visit is the Epals Web page at http://www.epals.com/kpi.html (Figure 6.14).

You will be able to access e-mail addresses and secondary school home pages from Africa, Asia, Australia, Europe, Israel, island nations, Japan, New Zealand, North America, and South America. NOTE: You can use Epals in conjunction with problem-solving projects, discussed later in the chapter. For example, students in biology or earth science classes could interview students from other continents to find out about local ecology, biomes, weather, geology, and geography.

Global Classrooms

The Global Classroom activity structure is similar to that of key pals, except that the unit of Internet collaboration is a class of students. Global Classroom activities join together two or more classrooms that participate in a topical activity, which can last from one day to several months to a school year. For an example of a Global Classroom activity, see Project Ozone, described in Chapter 7. In this project, your students join with other classrooms to monitor ground-level ozone locally, and then share the data globally.

The Global Classroom activity structure is a powerful way to involve your class in online discussions of science issues. For other examples of Global Classroom activities, you might visit the following Web sites, each of which fosters Global Classroom collaboration (see Figure 6.15):

- Global Thinking Project: http//www.gtp.org/
- Global Lab: http://www.hub.terc.edu/terc/gl/global-lab.html/
- Globe: http://www.globe.gov/
- EnviroNet: http://earth.simmons.edu/
- Classroom FeederWatch: http://teaparty.terc.edu/comweb/bird/bird.html/

Question-and-Answer Services

Q & A services enable your students to send questions to experts in various fields of science. They can visit Pitsco's "Ask an Expert" site at http://www.askanexpert.askanexpert/. At this site you will find links to e-mail addresses and Web sites of hundreds of experts in science and technology.

Another example of an ask-an-expert service is "Ask a Geologist." (See Figure 6.16.) When students visit this geology home page, they will be greeted with this introduction: Do you have questions about volcanoes, earthquakes, mountains, rocks, maps, groundwater, lakes, or rivers? They will then be invited to e-mail their Earth science questions.

Impersonations

This activity structure is one in which students interact with a "character," such as Dr. Science or Dr. Neutrino. For example, Sea World supports a project called "Ask Shamu." At the Sea World/Busch Gardens Animal Information Database site, students can explore marine science by sending in questions, reading an archive of frequently asked questions, and more. Visit Shamu at http://crusher.bev.net/education/SeaWorld/ask_shamu/asintro.html/.

The set of commonly asked questions at "Ask Shamu" covers babies, birds, dolphins, the environment, fish, invertebrates, rays and eels, reptiles, seals and sea lions, sharks, turtles, walrus, and whales. However, the site is full of links to additional information. As students explore one question, or a related set of questions, they can use the browser to link to further information, as shown in Figures 6.17 and 18.

Information Collection and Analysis Activities

Information collection and analysis activities engage students in activities in which information is gathered, shared, and analyzed. The activities can involve collaboration with other students, teachers, and experts, or they can focus on information available on the World

Wide Web, accessed by means of a browser, such as Netscape. The following three information collection structures are presented: information exchanges, tele-field trips, and pooled data analysis.

Information Exchanges

In the information exchange activity structure, students share information with students in other classrooms on topics typically organized by the teacher that relate to the ongoing science lesson. Students might exchange information on such topics as acid rain, bird watching, local plants, lichens, types of rocks found near the school, weather conditions, or watershed levels. In a typical activity, your students would "collect data" (locally) on some phenomenon, such as the characteristics of the local biome. Other students participating in the information exchange would research their own biome. Then the students would share their data with each other.

Tele-field Trips

Tele-field trips let you and your students share with other classrooms anticipated outcomes and actual results of local field trips; they also offer you online field trips by visiting virtual science museums or participating in project-sponsored tele-field trips. Museums are powerful sources of virtual field trips. For example, you can visit the Franklin Museum of Science in Philadelphia 24 hours a day by visiting their Web site at http://sln.fi.edu/. Once you get there, you can participate in many online exhibits, such as The Heart, Nature Hike, Web Garden, and Animal Migration. An example of a project-sponsored tele-field trip would be Live from Antarctica, organized by NASA as part of its Quest Project, which sponsors Internet interactive learning projects. To participate in the Antarctic project, visit NASA's site at http://quest.arc.nasa.gov/antarctica/index.html/. This rich site will enable you and your students to experience what life is like in the coldest place on the planet. To find other project-sponsored tele-field trips, such as Live from Mars,

Shuttle/Mir Online Research, and Women of NASA, visit the Quest Home Page at http://quest.arc.nasa.gov/.

Pooled Data Analysis

In this activity structure, students and teachers in several schools coordinate the collection of data on some scientific phenomenon, then share the data among themselves. There are many opportunities to create your own projects or participate in those that others have created. Project Ozone, described in Chapter 7, is an example of a pooled data analysis activity.

Problem-Solving Projects

Problem-solving projects involve students in a variety of investigations that require interpersonal exchange as well as information collection. In some cases, students use one or more Internet search engines to find information on a science question or topic. In other cases, students conduct an experiment in their own classroom and then team up with students from other schools to compare and contrast their results. In still other projects, students engage in on-line discussions and problem-solving debates, either in real time or in asynchronous time. And, in some situations, students participate in larger-scale social action projects in which they not only investigate a scientific phenomenon, but also take action on it as well.

Information Searches

Information Searches can be an excellent way for students to become familiar with the Internet and its potential, learn how to navigate from site to site, and begin to utilize the Internet as a resource for research. In this activity structure, the teacher challenges students with "clues," which students use to solve problems, relying on the Internet as their reference system. To help motivate students, try putting together the clues in the form of an Internet scavenger hunt.

Figure 6.19 shows a scavenger hunt activity for an Earth science class. Students work in groups and are assigned two or three of the thir-

Figure 6.20
iEARN is an international project that links teachers and students together from around the world. It is one of the most interesting and well-organized projects on the Web. Not only will you find projects in the area of science, but you'll also find those that deal with human rights, art, music, geography, history, and many other topics.

I*EARN home page from *www.iearn.org* Web site. Reprinted by permission of I*EARN-US.

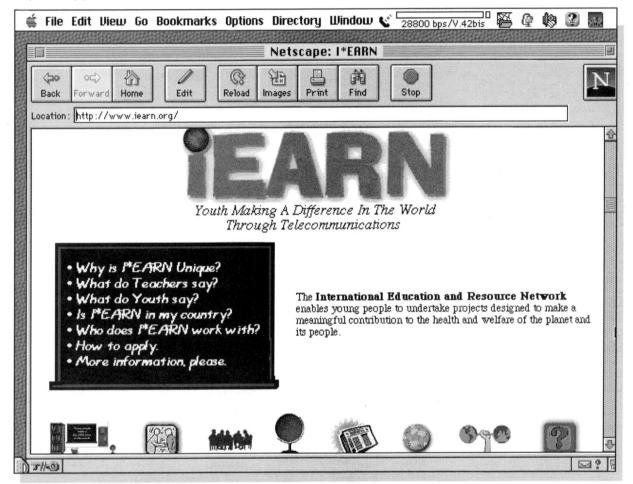

teen questions. They must find answers for each question and document the answer by citing at least two sites per question. To dig up the necessary information, students rely on one of the search engines discussed on page 123.

Visit the *Minds On Science* Web site for more examples of scavenger hunts.

Social Action Projects

Students can become involved in community-based social action projects that focus on humanistic and action-oriented goals. For example, Narcis Vives, a teacher in Barcelona, Spain, organized a project to help children and adults in a refugee camp in Bosnia. He invited schools around the world to raise funds for a school in the camp, arranged for e-mail to be sent to the camp, set up a day of solidarity for the camp in which dozens of nations posted e-mail messages in support of the people in the camp, encouraged class discussions about the refugees and the war in Bosnia, and established an exhibition of art in Barcelona created by children in the camp. Through telecommunications, hundreds of students around the world participated in Vives's social action project.

Helping students become global citizens or citizen scientists is one great potential of the Internet. Social action projects can focus on issues related to endangered species; air, water, or soil pollution; population growth and sustainable development; food, nutrition, poverty, and hunger; and many other topics.

Two Web sites that will be very useful in developing social action projects are epals Classroom Exchange (Figure 6.14), and iEARN (Figure 6.20).

- epals Classroom Exchange: This Web site helps schools find other schools on the Internet (Figure 6.14).
  URL: http://www.epals.com
- iEARN: This international Web site links teachers around the world who wish to participate in collaborative projects (Figure 6.20).
  URL: http://www.iearn.org/iearn/

SUMMARY

The Internet is a dynamic tool that is constantly changing. As you look back on this chapter, keep in mind that it presented information about using the Internet as a tool to enhance your science teaching. The Internet is much more than a virtual place to surf. You can use the Internet to teach your students research skills or to engage your students in a range of interpersonal activities, such as key pals, global classrooms, and question-and-answer service activities. The Internet allows your students to become involved in information exchange activities, as well as a host of problem-solving activities.

CHAPTER 7   **PROJECT OZONE: A WEB-ASSISTED SCIENCE UNIT**

Figure 7.1
The air that surrounds Earth is becoming increasingly polluted. In this chapter you and your students will research ground-level ozone, the principal component of smog, and try to do something about the problem.

Project Ozone is a Web-assisted science unit that uses the Internet to engage students in a science inquiry investigation. It consists of five interrelated activities. It was originally developed for the Global Thinking Project (http://www.gtp.org/) and is presented here, as a stand-alone Internet project, because it provides a good example of many of the activity structures covered in Chapter 6. The following structures will be an integral part of Project Ozone:

- **Key Pals:** Students will be able to correspond with other students who are working on Project Ozone.
- **Global Classroom:** Your school will be part of a group of schools that are using the Global Classroom structure to study ozone.
- **Question-and-Answer Services:** Students will be prompted to go to "Ask-a-Scientist" sites so that, if they have questions, they can seek out the expertise of professional scientists.
- **Information Exchange:** Your students will be collecting data on ozone locally and

exchanging the information with other schools around the world.
- **Tele-field Trips:** Students will be prompted to visit one or more sites on the World Wide Web that function as "virtual field trips."
- **Pooled Data Analysis:** Your students will be using Web forms to pool data with other students; the data then can be analyzed and conclusions drawn.
- **Information Searches:** Using one or more search engines on the Web, your students will find answers to questions presented in the form of a scavenger hunt and report back to their classmates.
- **Social Action Projects:** Your students will be encouraged to take action on the basis of the results of their research, connecting the work they are doing in school to social action in their local, state, and national communities.

INTRODUCTION TO PROJECT OZONE

Several summers ago, more than 200 scientists gathered in Atlanta to study how smog forms. As a newspaper article at the time pointed out, most people try to avoid dirty air, but for the researchers conducting studies of urban smog, the best environment is dirty air!

In another newspaper's editorial column, a letter urged that "the world must move faster to stop making chemicals that destroy the Earth's protective *ozone shield.*"

Ozone (O_3) is a gas that is found concentrated in a small layer in the upper atmosphere, and near the ground in urban areas, especially on hot days. It is a highly reactive gas with a pungent (sharp and biting) smell. It can cause serious damage to plants, and can adversely affect the human respiratory system. High concentrations of ozone

SIDEBAR 7.1

Smog

A dense, discolored fog containing large quantities of soot, ash, and gaseous pollutants.

Ozone Shield

An ozone layer in the upper atmosphere that protects life on Earth by filtering out harmful ultraviolet radiation from the sun

Ozone

A highly reactive gas comprising three oxygen atoms. Ozone is produced by the recombination of oxygen in the presence of ultraviolet radiation from the sun.

Ultraviolet Light

Short wavelengths of light

Ozone Hole

Gap in the ozone layer created by deterioration of ozone in the upper atmosphere, primarily by chlorofluorocarbons

Ground-level Ozone

Concentrations of ozone gas near the ground

pose a serious health threat not only to people with respiratory disorders, but to children and adults, especially if engaged in vigorous activity.

On the positive side, ozone absorbs *ultraviolet light.* The concentration of ozone in the upper atmosphere acts as a planetary shield, preventing most of the sun's ultraviolet radiation from reaching the Earth's surface. In humans, most skin cancers are associated with exposure to ultraviolet radiation. There is evidence that the protective ozone layer above the Earth is deteriorating, and that in some regions, an *ozone hole* has been detected.

level ozone in their cities and towns, and then use these results to collaborate with other schools.

3. Students will use a variety of methods to monitor ground-level ozone.

4. Students will discuss the implications of the deterioration of the protective ozone shield and what should be done to resolve the problem.

5. Students will network with other schools by accessing the Project Ozone Web site.

THE PROJECT OZONE WEB SITE

To help you track your progress and stay in touch with others working on Project Ozone, access the Project Ozone Web site at http://www.gsu.edu/ ~mstjrh/projectozone.html. You can use the site to direct the work of your students in a variety of ways. For example, when students are ready to "post" their data (see project schedule, Figure 7.2) so that other students around the globe can benefit from their work, they can do so from the Project Ozone Web site. One of the links on the Project Ozone Web site (Figure 7.3) is "data sharing." Clicking on this link will take you to an ozone data form that your students can use to post data. You will also find links to retrieve others' data and a link to a bulletin board where you can leave and read messages, as well as links to important environmental science sites related to Project Ozone.

SPECIAL MATERIALS FOR PROJECT OZONE

There are several items that you will need to have available for Project Ozone. Not all the materials that you will need are listed on Figure 7.4, only the ones you are most likely not to have on hand and thus may need to order.

Additionally, on page 158 and following, you will find suggestions for a Project Ozone Mini Learning Log, a Project Ozone Portfolio, and a certificate you can photocopy and present to students when they complete Project Ozone.

GOALS OF PROJECT OZONE

1. Students will explore air pollution by investigating the nature of ozone and how it is formed in the troposphere and the stratosphere.

2. Students will design studies to explore ground-

Figure 7.2 Project Ozone Schedule

Activity	Class Periods	Milestones
1. Ozone: The good and the bad	1	
2. The changing ozone layer	1	
3. Ozone in your community	1–2	Send ozone data
4. Ozone: A global project	1–2	
5. Ozone: What you can do about it	1–3	Send description and then results of action project

Figure 7.3
Project Ozone Web Page

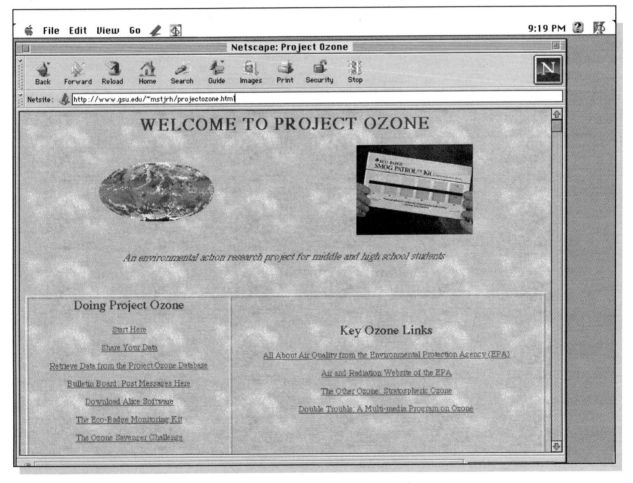

Figure 7.4 Project Ozone Special Materials List

Item	Supplier
Eco-Badge Kit. Chemical strips to monitor ozone. One kit contains 30 eco-badges and a color card. Approximate cost: $45 per kit.	Vistanomics, Inc., 230 North Maryland Avenue, Suite 310, Glendale, CA 91206 (818) 409-6695
Hand-Held Wind Measurer. Sturdy device to measure wind. Approximate cost: $15 per measurer.	Forestry Suppliers, Inc., P.O. Box 8397, Jackson, MS 39284 (800) 647-5368
Psychometers. Wet and dry bulb thermometers to measure humidity. Sold as a kit containing five psychometers. Approximate cost: $20 per kit.	Forestry Suppliers, Inc., P.O. Box 8397, Jackson, MS 39284 (800) 647-5368
Alice Network Software. A science project software tool that your students will use to make data tables, graphs, charts, and maps.	Available free from TERC at this Web site: http://teaparty.terc.edu/tech/tech.html/

ACTIVITY 7.1 OZONE: THE GOOD AND THE BAD

In this introductory activity, students explore what they know about ozone. Then they learn to differentiate between ground-level ozone (the bad ozone) and ozone in the upper atmosphere (the good ozone).

Objectives:
- To discuss prior knowledge of ozone
- To generate questions about ozone
- To explain the difference between ground-level ozone and ozone in the upper atmosphere

Materials: Newspaper and science magazine articles about ozone, sections from science texts about ozone, chart of the atmosphere, large sheets of paper, colored pens or crayons

Web Site Information: The Project Ozone home page has information about ozone, as well as links to important ozone sites on the Internet.

Advance Preparation: Well in advance of doing this project with your class, start collecting newspaper and magazine articles on ozone. Look for articles that focus on any of these topics: ozone, ozone hole, smog. Also, visit the Project Ozone home page, where you will find relevant information.

Procedure:

1. Divide your students into teams of four students each, and give each team a large sheet of paper and colored pens or crayons. Have students draw a picture showing the Earth and the first two layers of the atmosphere (the troposphere and the stratosphere), as well as a satellite in space and the sun in the background (Figure 7.5).

2. Once students have drawn their pictures, give them the following instructions:

In the next 10 minutes, I want you to work as a team to discuss what you know about ozone.

Figure 7.5
Two Layers of Earth's Atmosphere

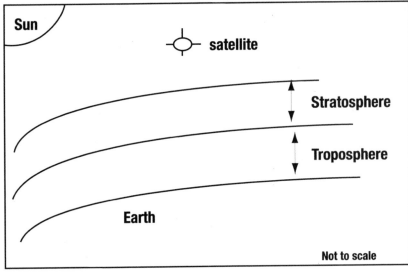

Use the picture to draw and explain what your team knows. In your drawings and explanations, please try to use the following ideas, as well as others that you may know: ozone, smog, car emissions, ultraviolet light, people, plants.

3. Walk around the room and assist the students as needed. At the end of the 10 minutes, tell the students that you are going to randomly call on one person from each group to show the group's drawing to the class and briefly explain it. Give the students another 2 minutes to put their heads together to make sure everyone in the group can explain the picture if called on to do so.

4. Randomly call a number (draw a card from a set numbered 1 through 4) and ask the person from each team who has that number to stand and explain his or her team's drawing. Remember, this activity is intended to give you insight into what the students already know about ozone. Students will exhibit a range of knowledge.

5. When you have finished hearing the reports, ask a member from each team to mount the pictures on the wall in the classroom. Keep these pictures visible throughout the project, and refer to them when appropriate.

6. To help students distinguish between and identify different problems associated with "bad" ozone (ground-level ozone) and "good" ozone (ozone in the upper atmosphere), provide each team of four with two "think pieces." The "think pieces" should be no more than two pages long and, as the name implies, should be used to get the students thinking about the topic under consideration: ozone. Use the "think pieces" that are included in Figures 7.6a and 7.6b or draw on the articles that you have collected from the newspaper or science magazines or have downloaded from the Internet. Whatever you choose, be sure the "think pieces" discuss stratospheric and tropospheric ozone.

7. Further divide the groups of four into pairs so that the pairs have one "think piece" between them. Then have them follow these steps:

a. One student in each pair reads the "think piece" to his or her partner.
b. Following the reading, each pair works by itself to analyze the article. Pairs might make a drawing or write a brief summary of what they discussed.
c. Each pair presents its drawing or summary to the other pair.

Figure 7.6a
Think Piece 1

THINK PIECE 1

Stop Making Chemicals That Destroy the Ozone Shield

According to some scientists, global air pollutants are threatening to destroy the Earth's protective shield against the harsh ultraviolet rays of the sun. This shield, located in the thin upper reaches of the atmosphere (known as the *stratosphere*), consists of ozone.

The chief culprit threatening the ozone layer is a family of industrial compounds known as chlorofluorocarbons (CFCs).

These chemicals include coolants used in air conditioners and refrigerators, as well as chemicals used in hair sprays and dry-cleaning fluids. The CFCs released into the atmosphere eventually reach the stratosphere, where they react with ultraviolet photons. The UV *photons* break the CFCs down, releasing a free chlorine atom that then attacks ozone molecules. According to some scientists, this reaction is devastating to the ozone layer.

The sudden discovery of the ozone "hole" over Antarctica in 1965, showed that the concern was real. Studies indicated that the con-

centration of "ozone" in a column over the South Pole had decreased by 40 percent, and that similar "holes" had been detected since then.

In 1967 more than 40 nations met in Montreal, Canada, to adopt an agreement limiting the release of CFCs into the atmosphere. The Montreal Accord called for a 50 percent cut in CFCs by the year 2000. Soon after the Accord was reached, evidence showed that the ozone shield was being destroyed even faster than predicted. So, in 1990, a revision to the Montreal Accord was written, calling for the complete banning of CFCs by the year

---

d. The groups of four then make a T-chart summarizing the differences between "good" and "bad" ozone.

e. When the teams have finished, post the T-charts in a prominent place in the classroom. Then summarize the work the students did on the "think pieces" by discussing the following concepts:

- Tropospheric (lower atmospheric) ozone is produced when the gases given off from burning fossil fuels combine with sunlight. The result is ozone, or smog.
- More data is needed on the sources, patterns, and effects of tropospheric ozone.
- Lower atmospheric ozone is found in high concentrations in many of the urban centers of the Earth.
- Stratospheric (upper atmospheric) ozone is formed when ultraviolet radiation brings about the breakup of O_2. The free

oxygen combines with another molecule of oxygen to form O_3 (ozone).

- Over a long period of time, the concentration of ozone in the stratosphere has increased enough so that a protective shield has formed. This screens out almost all of the ultraviolet radiation reaching the Earth.
- Presently, there is a concern that certain chemicals called *chlorofluorocarbons* (CFCs) released into the atmosphere in recent years are reacting in the stratosphere by breaking down in the presence of ultraviolet radiation. The free chlorine atoms that are released in this process attack ozone molecules, breaking them into oxygen and chlorine oxide. This process is responsible for the depletion of the *ozone layer,* and has resulted in the presence of a hole in the ozone layer over the Antarctic during spring.

Figure 7.6b
Think Piece 2

THINK PIECE 2

Researchers Study City Smog

In the summer of 1992, more than two hundred researchers descended upon the city of Atlanta to study how smog forms. As one of the chief researchers said, "To study smog, you've got to have ozone." And ozone they had. The days that they were in Atlanta were hot and muggy, just the right conditions for the formation of ozone.

According to scientists, ozone forms at ground level when *hydrocarbons* and *nitrogen oxides* from factories, automobiles, and trees react in the presence of sunlight on hot, sunny days when the air is stagnant.

Ozone formed in one location may be blown by the wind miles away to another location and cause serious health problems there. Ozone flowing from cities may do enormous damage to crops and forests in rural areas.

The scientists in the Atlanta study were trying to learn more about how ozone forms and how ozone from Atlanta impacts the surrounding areas.

According to one report, the researchers were bombarding Atlanta's skies with laser beams, high-altitude balloons, and helicopters. Air samples were being collected at 14 locations in the city on a 24-hour basis for the eight-week study.

Ozone is a growing problem, not only for urban areas, but for rural areas too, where winds carry the polluted urban smog (the chief constituent of which is ozone). In the Atlanta study, monitoring sites have been placed "upwind," to see what the air is like before it reaches Atlanta, and "downwind," to measure the air that flows out of the city. Scientists want to know what the effect is of the city's dirty air on surrounding areas. Another monitoring site is set up in the Fernbank Forest, a preserved area in the middle of the city. Measurements are being made of the hydrocarbons being released from trees.

More information is needed on ground-level ozone, and you, like these researchers, can begin to study the ozone patterns in your community and share your results with others.

• Depletion of the ozone layer could result in an increase of ultraviolet radiation reaching the Earth's surface, which would cause damage to nearly every form of life.

Optional Extensions

1. Have your students keep a scientific log or journal of their work on Project Ozone. Students can collect articles and relevant newspaper clippings about ozone, as well as keep track of their work on the project. (For more about student logs, see the information at the end of this chapter.)

2. Students might like to produce a newsletter on ozone. Newsletters typically are short—perhaps two pages—and summarize interesting ideas about a topic. A Project Ozone Newsletter could be shared with other students in school, and over the Web.

3. You and your students might want to work together to create an "air pollution" or "SmogWatch" Web site. Be sure to make it known to other schools by posting a note on the ozone bulletin board.

4. Provide students with a set of questions similar to the ones shown in Figure 7.7 (and accessible from the Project Ozone Web site) and send them on a virtual scavenger hunt. Have students use one of the following search engines to find answers to the these questions.
• Yahoo: http://www.yahoo.com
• HotBot: http://www.hotbot.com/

Figure 7.7

PROJECT OZONE SCAVENGER HUNT QUESTION SHEET

Using the Internet as your source of information, find answers to the following five questions. Make sure that you provide not only an answer, but also the site from which you obtained the information.

1. What are the six "criteria pollutants" that the EPA uses as indicators of air quality?

    Answer:

    _____

    _____

    Source:

    _____

2. What is a nonattainment area, as defined by the EPA's Clean Air Act of 1990?

    Answer:

    _____

    _____

    Source:

    _____

3. What are at least two human health problems associated with high levels of ground-level ozone?

    Answer:

    _____

    _____

    Source:

    _____

4. How is ozone produced in the Earth's lower atmosphere?

    Answer:

    _____

    _____

    Source:

    _____

5. Scientists refer to two types of ozone: good ozone and bad ozone. What does this mean?

    Answer:

    _____

    _____

    Source:

    _____

ACTIVITY 7.2 THE CHANGING OZONE LAYER

In this activity students explore the nature of the all-important ozone layer, which, as they have learned, protects the surface of the Earth from the ultraviolet radiation of the sun. They discover how ozone is produced in the upper atmosphere and what appears to be causing the deterioration of the Earth's protective layer. In addition, students discuss ways of curbing this trend and, in the optional extensions, explore a means for detecting total-column ozone levels.

Objectives:
- To explain how ozone is destroyed by CFCs in the stratosphere
- To identify ways of curbing the deterioration of ozone
- To discuss ways of detecting and measuring ozone (total column)

Materials: Aerosol spray can, set of polystyrene foam spheres or a variety of colors of clay to make molecular models

Web Site Information: From the Project Ozone Web site, students might take a tele-field trip to investigate upper atmospheric ozone and its depletion by visiting the EPA Web site (Figure 7.8) at http://www.epa.gov/ozone/index.html/

Procedure:
1. Divide your students into several small teams. Begin the lesson by showing an aerosol spray can product, and spraying a small amount into the air. Then say: "Some of the chemicals in spray cans can affect the ozone layer. How can this be?" Give students a few minutes to discuss in their groups what they know about this statement and what might be creating the problem.

2. Explain to students that, over millennia, a layer of ozone (O_3) (see Figure 7.9) has built up in the atmosphere as a result of the interaction of photons of ultraviolet light and oxygen (O_2), as shown in the chemical reaction given in Figure 7.10. This reaction is one you might refer to as the ozone formation cycle. Point out that the ozone in the stratosphere absorbs ultraviolet radiation and accomplishes two things: it shields the Earth from dangerous ultraviolet photons and it participates in the ozone formation cycle, in which more ozone is produced when an ozone molecule is broken down as it absorbs photons.

3. Explain to students that the concentration of ozone in the stratosphere is very small. If it could be compacted and brought to the surface of the Earth, it would be a layer about 3 mm thick. Explain to students that chemicals produced by human activity now endanger the ozone layer. Of greatest concern are the molecules known as CFCs (chlorofluorocarbons). CFCs are chemicals typically used in hair

Figure 7.8
Ozone Depletion Web Page

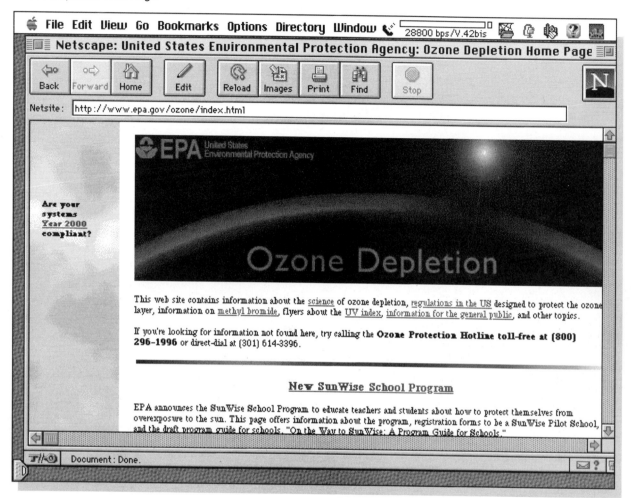

Figure 7.9
Buildup of the Ozone Layer

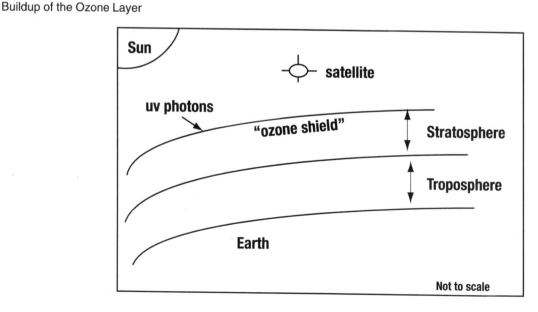

Figure 7.10
How Ozone Is Created in the Upper Atmosphere

$$O_2 + \text{Ultraviolet photon} \rightarrow O + O$$

$$O_2 + O + M \rightarrow O_3 + M^*$$

$$O_3 + \text{Ultraviolet photon} \rightarrow O_2 + O$$

M* = A molecule that is needed to take away the excess energy in a reaction.

Text copyright © Jack Hassard. Illustration copyright © Good Year Books

SIDEBAR 7.4

Photochemical Reactions

Reactions in the atmosphere that take place between air pollutants in the presence of sunlight

sprays, refrigerants, and cleaning fluids. Structurally, they are very stable; consequently, they do not have to be replaced very often. While this makes them practical to use, it also means that if they are released into the environment, they will remain there for a long time.

In the mid-1960s, using ground-based and satellite measuring devices, scientists determined that the total-column ozone over the Antarctic had decreased by 40 percent in a single year. Total-column ozone is a measure of the amount of ozone in a column of air from the ground to the upper atmosphere. This led to the concept of an "ozone hole," a concept that has reappeared several times since that time. Then, in the late 1970s, scientists reported that CFCs that drift into the stratosphere react with ultraviolet photons, releasing chlorine atoms that attack ozone molecules (Figure 7.11). They predicted a further depletion of the amount of ozone if large amounts of CFCs drifted into the stratosphere.

In the stratosphere, the reaction that continues to concern scientists appears in Figure 7.12. It shows what happens to a CFC molecule—normally made up of 1 carbon (C), 2 chlorine (Cl), and 2 fluorine (F) atoms—in the presence of UV light. Specifically, a photon of ultraviolet light

(UV) breaks the bond holding one of the chlorine atoms to the CFC molecule and a chlorine atom is released. It reacts with ozone, destroying the ozone and creating another molecule that can, in turn, react with oxygen to produce free chlorine, which can attack another ozone molecule. Thus an individual CFC molecule can end up destroying many ozone molecules.

4. To help students understand these processes, give them a number of polystyrene foam spheres (or clay) and have them make the following:

- O (one sphere)
- O_2 (two spheres of same size)
- O_3 (three spheres of same size)
- CFC (three different spheres: 1 carbon, 2 chorine, 2 fluorine)
- UV photons (very tiny spheres)

Then have the students use the spheres to replicate the following reactions:

- The way ozone is produced in the atmosphere
- The way ozone is destroyed in the atmosphere

Once finished, have the teams display their models and explain their creations.

5. Ask students to talk about the implications of these *photochemical reactions*. How do they impact students' lives?

Figure 7.11
Chemical Reaction in Which Chlorine Reacts with Ozone

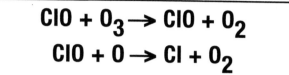

$$ClO + O_3 \rightarrow ClO + O_2$$
$$ClO + O \rightarrow Cl + O_2$$

Figure 7.12
Photochemical Reaction in Which UV Breaks Down a
CFC Molecule

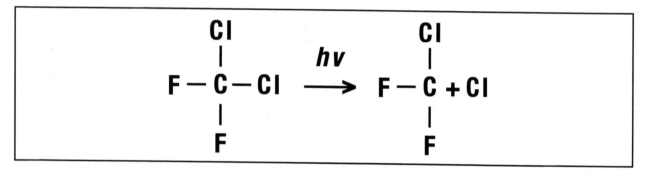

Optional Extensions

1. Have students visit the Project Ozone home page and the links there to other resources devoted to the study of the problem of ozone in the stratosphere (ozone hole, ozone depletion). Then have them do a search of the literature in the school media center and find several articles on the topic in science-oriented journals or magazines. How do the reports compare?

2. Students living in the northern hemisphere might want to collaborate with their counterparts in the southern hemisphere—especially those living in Australia and New Zealand—where ozone depletion is a very real problem. Students could share information and agree to collaborate in the sharing of total-column ozone data.

3. Students might find it interesting to explore ways at the personal, local, regional, and global levels for dealing with the problem of ozone depletion. What actions might and should be taken, and why would they be effective?

ACTIVITY 7.3 OZONE IN YOUR COMMUNITY

In this activity, students explore ozone in their community by using the Eco-Badge, an ozone test-strip monitoring system. Students set up monitoring sites in order to make inferences about ozone levels in the greater area. They use the Internet to contact other students living nearby in order to increase their knowledge of ozone in the region.

Objectives:
- To conduct experiments to determine levels and patterns of ozone in the local community
- To analyze the data and present it in graphical and map form

Materials: Eco-Badges (Figure 7.13), ozone colormetric chart, hand-held wind measurers, thermometers, psychrometers, plastic tape, acetate sheets, clock, map of the city and surrounding towns, markers, small plastic bags, Alice Network Software[1]

[1] You can download this software from the following Web site:
http://teaparty.terc.edu/tech/tech.html

Web Site Information: Consider letting students draw on the expertise of scientists who can help them answer questions they might have on ozone and techniques used to monitor ozone. One site that should be of assistance here is Pitsco's "Ask an Expert" site: http://www.askanexpert. askanexpert/

Procedure:

1. Show your students a topographic or road map of your region, and explain to them that they are going to study ozone in the local community. To do this, they are going to set up some monitoring sites (students' homes make suitable sites), and then collect data on ozone levels for a short period of time. The purpose of the study is to measure ozone concentration levels and correlate these with local weather conditions—especially temperature, wind direction, and sunlight. Explain to students that their work will contribute to a better understanding of ozone in the local community and, at the same time, help them understand how ozone forms and its patterns of concentration.

2. Divide students into four-member research teams. Make each team responsible for at least one ozone monitoring site. Suggest that since the students live varying distances from school, using their homes as sites will expand the region that the class can monitor. In addition, one of the sites should be the school. Once each team has agreed on a site, the site should be identified on a map of the community. A good highway map of the area will do; however, if you can, try to get a topographic map of your community. Place the map on a wall and use markers to identify the location of the sites.

3. Describe for students how the ozone test strips are used. Basically, begin by taping the ozone test strip onto a small index card (see Figure 7.13). Since the chemical on the test strip is activated when it is exposed to the air, students must work quickly. If the teams are going to do a 1-hour test, you can cut the strips in half and give students only the top part of the strip (the 1-hour test

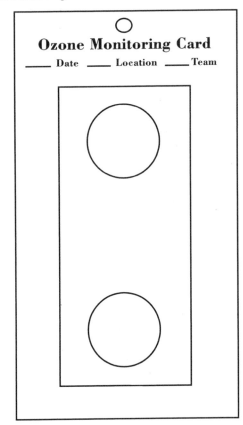

Figure 7.13
Ozone Monitoring Card

circle). (In this case, just half the strip would be taped to the card.) Copy this template onto card stock. Students can tape the Eco-Badge to the card, and use it as a device to monitor ozone.

Alternatively, you can cover the test strip with a piece of clear acetate. Cut small holes the size of the two test sections and tape the acetate directly over the ozone test strip. Cover the 1-hour test section with one of the circles of acetate. This way, students can run the 8-hour test (bottom part of the strip), and wait to do the 1-hour test later.

Students then place the cards in the monitoring locations that have been selected. When they do so, they should observe the temperature, humidity, wind, cloud cover, cloud type, visibility, and weather. Let them know that data tables (see Figure 7.15) will be provided for recording data.

4. Students can perform several tests at each site.

- Test 1: Measure ozone levels over four or five 1-hour intervals throughout the day. To do this, students will need four or five 1-hour test strips.
- Test 2: Measure the ozone level over an 8-hour period using an 8-hour test strip.
- Test 3: Measure ozone levels over several days using several 8-hour test strips.

5. Each team should be responsible for conducting experiments for a one-week period. This will enable students to monitor ozone over an extended period of time, as well as take daily ozone readings.

6. Work with your class to set up the experiments it will conduct. In each case, have students formulate hypotheses that they will test through the experiments they conduct. For example, if the students do an experiment in which they measure ozone throughout the day, an hypothesis for this experiment might be the following:

Hypothesis: There will be no differences in the ozone levels measured in the shade at 1-hour intervals throughout the day.

In addition to ozone levels, students should monitor other weather data, including air temperature, humidity, wind direction, and wind speed. Additional hypotheses can be formulated with respect to these data.

7. Following hypothesis formulation, students should write out brief proposals describing the studies they wish to conduct. The proposals should include a statement of the problem, one or more hypotheses, and a description of the methods students will use in their study.

8. Now students are ready to begin monitoring ozone and other weather variables. Distribute copies of the Project Ozone Observation Form so students can record their data (Figure 7.14).

9. After students have completed their data collection, they can use the Global Lab program (which you can download for free) to create a data table. Have the students set up a data table, similar to the one shown in Figure 7.15. (Be sure they include latitude and longitude so that they can utilize the Global Lab program's data mapping capability.) Once students have entered the data into the program, they can create graphs (see Figures 7.16, 7.17, and 7.18).

Include a column for each variable such as time, date, ozone, temperature, wind, latitude and longitude. NOTE: Latitude and longitude are required if you want to make use of the Global Lab program's mapping feature.

Students can also display their data on maps. The map shown here, drawn using the Global Lab program's software, depicts ozone readings collected by students in different countries. Note the ozone levels in the legend.

Figure 7.17, for example, shows one way the ozone readings should be analyzed, which is in terms of the number of days that exceeded the optimal level of ozone (120 parts per billion). This value will change to 60 ppb as the EPA's new recommendations are put into practice. Note that in this case, the optimal ozone level was exceeded on three days.

10. Have students propose explanations of the data they have collected and analyzed. Ideally, they should look at the data gathered from all of the sites monitored by the class and try to make sense of the data. Have students compare their data to that in the Air Quality Chart shown in Figure 7.19. What is the pattern of ozone in their community? What is the level of ozone over the period they studied? What is the cause of the ozone? What can be done to reduce the level of ozone in their community?

11. Once each team has studied the data and formulated a set of explanations, conduct a class session in which each team has an opportunity to present its data to the others. To encourage inter-

Figure 7.14

PROJECT OZONE OBSERVATION FORM

Team Name: _____   Team Members: _____

Measurement Location: _____ Inside: _____   Outside: _____

Date: _____   Latitude: _____

Start Time: _____   Longitude: _____

Quantitative Measurements

Ozone (Eco-Badge readings):

Location	Start Time	End Time	Reading 1 (parts per billion)	Reading 2 (parts per billion)	Reading 3 (parts per billion)	Average (parts per billion)

Temperature: _____ °C

Relative Humidity: _____ %

Wind Speed: _____ km/hr

Wind Direction: _____ degrees

Precipitation: _____ cm

Qualitative Observations

Circle one of the words to describe your observations.

Ozone	Good	Moderate	Unhealthful	1st Stage Alert
Temperature	Hot	Warm	Cool	Cold
Humidity	High	Average	Low	None
Clouds	Cumulus	Cirrus	Stratus	None
Sunlight	Sunny	Mainly sunny	Mainly cloudy	Cloudy
Wind Speed	Strong	Medium	Light	Zero
Wind Direction	North	East	West	South
Precipitation	Rain	Drizzle	Snow/sleet	None

Figure 7.15 Sample Data Table

Row	Time	Date	Ozone in ppb	Temp. °C	Humidity	Wind Speed	Latitude	Longitude
1								
2								
3								
4								

Figure 7.16
Graph of Data Collected at Ozone Monitoring Sight

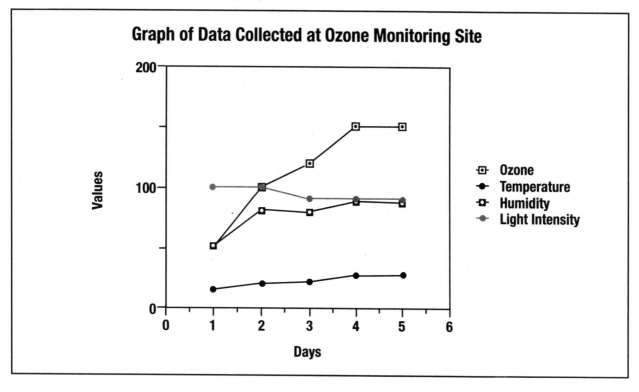

Graph of Data Collected at Ozone Monitoring Site

Figure 7.17
Bar Graph Comparing Daily Ozone Levels

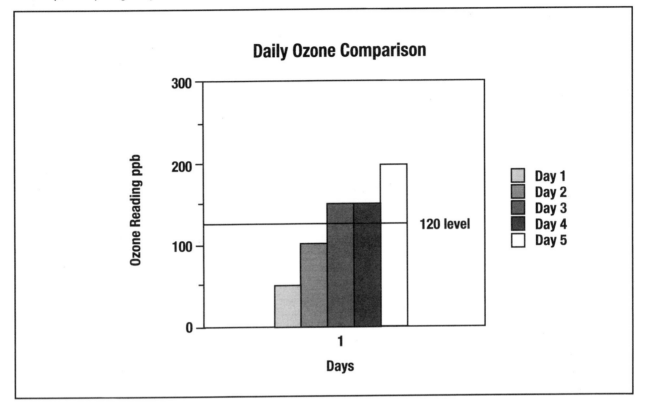

ACTIVITY 7.4 OZONE: A GLOBAL PROJECT

Students use the Project Ozone Web site to collaborate with other schools on the problem of ozone and share data in order to gain knowledge about ozone at the global level. Students also discuss what can be done to halt the trend toward increasing urban smog levels.

Objectives:
- To use the Project Ozone Web site to send and retrieve data collected on ground-level ozone
- To use the data submitted by other schools to compare and contrast ozone levels in different regions, cities, and countries

Materials: Data and conclusions from Activity 7.2; large map of the world; string, pins, labels, or

dependence within each group and the class as a whole, tell students that you will randomly call on a student from each group to present the data, and that the whole class will be responsible for making a general statement about ozone in the community based on the reports.

12. As a final step, have students compare their findings to real-time ozone data collected by the EPA. Students can visit a clickable map of the United States and find out how their readings compare with those collected by professional scientists. To find the map, have students check this Web site: http://www.ecobadge.com/
 At this site, your students can click on any state and receive real-time data from the Environmental Protection Agency (Figure 7.20).

Figure 7.18

This map, drawn with the Global Lab program, shows the locations and values of ozone monitored by students in different countries.

Ozone Map from the Global Lab program. © TERC. Reprinted by permission of TERC.

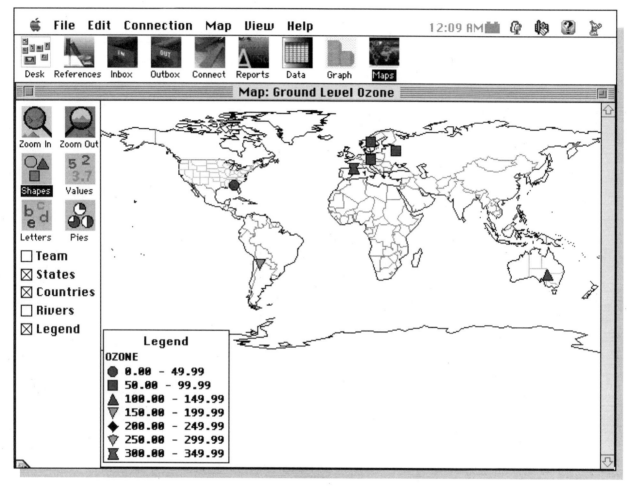

Figure 7.19 Air Quality Chart for Interpreting Ozone Data

Air Quality	Good	Moderate	Unhealthful	1st-Stage Alert	2nd-Stage Alert
Ozone, ppb on Eco™ Filter	10–50	50–200	200–300	300–350	>350
Part per billion	<50	50–120	120–190	190–340	>340
Ozone index reported to public (ozone level/ 120 x 100)	50	50–100	100–156	156–260	>260

Figure 7.20
EPA Web site. At this site, your students can click on any
state and receive real-time data from the EPA.

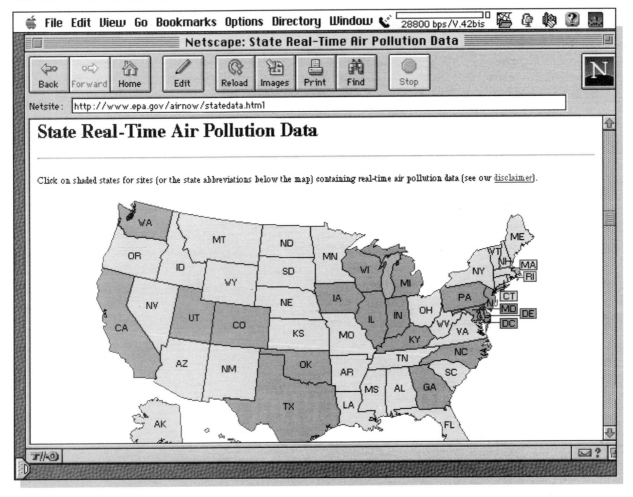

cards (to post information on the map); access to
the Internet (to submit and retrieve data and to
participate in a Web discussion)

Web Site Information: The Project Ozone
home page lets students send and retrieve data
and participate in Web discussions about ozone.

Procedure:
1. Discuss with students the value of cooperating
globally with other people to share data, draw
conclusions, and make decisions about important
problems, such as ground-level ozone. Explain to
students that they are going to collaborate with
other students to find out about the problem of
ozone in other regions or countries, and, at the

same time, to share the results of their local ozone
research.

2. Work with your students to help them understand how to use the Project Ozone Web site to
submit the data they collected on ozone and other
weather-related elements in Activity 7.2.

3. Data Transmission. Once the data have been
compiled, student teams submit their data to the
Project Ozone Database. From the Project Ozone
home page, students select "Data Sharing."
Students will be able to enter their data directly
into a Web form (Figure 7.21a), and send it elec-
tronically to the Project Ozone Database.
This is the submission form for Project Ozone.

Figure 7.21(a)
Ozone Submission Form

"Cybermarch Ozone" page from Cybermarch Web site. Reprinted by permission of Vistanomics, Inc.

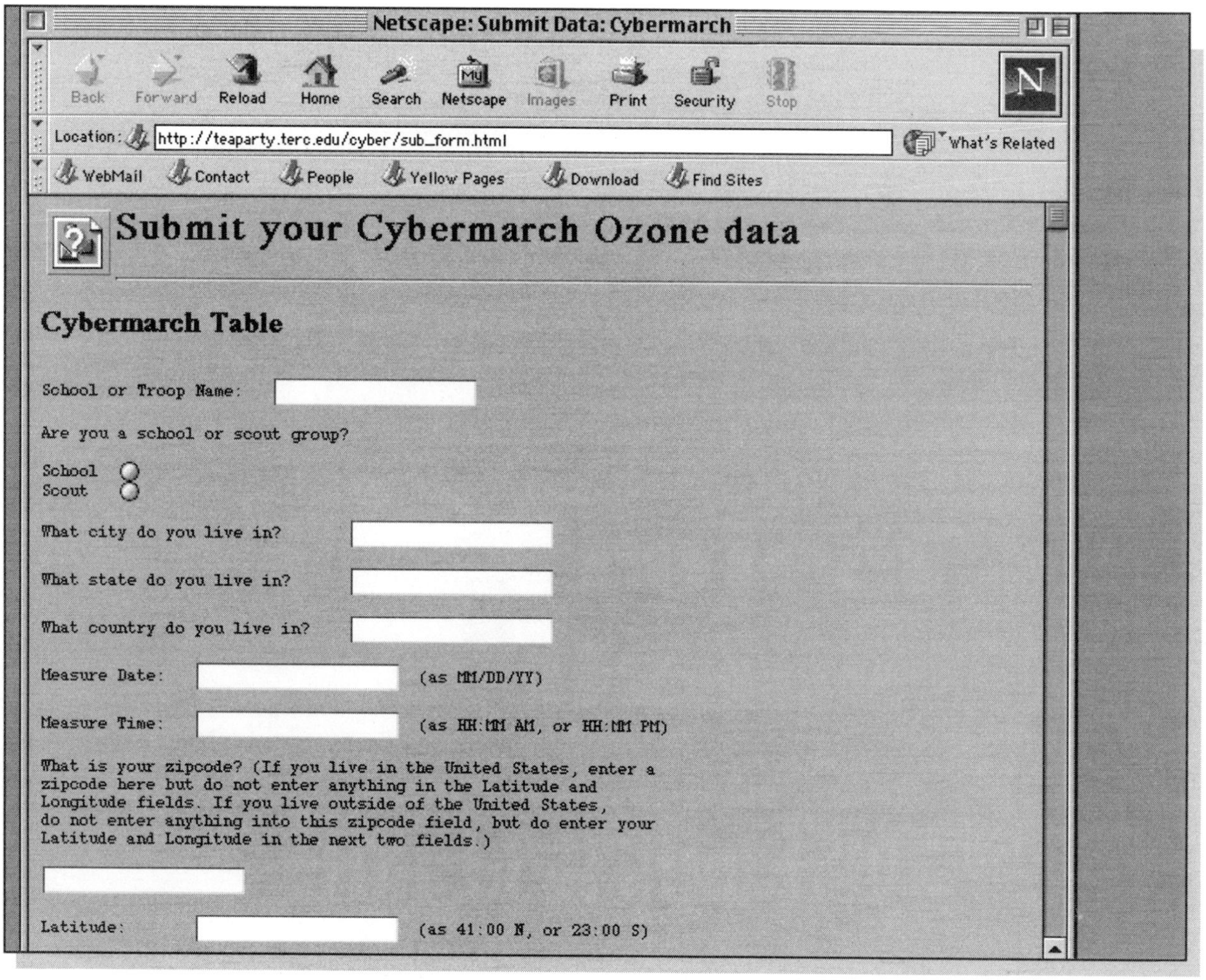
Netscape: Submit Data: Cybermarch

Back Forward Reload Home Search Netscape Images Print Security Stop

Location: http://teaparty.terc.edu/cyber/sub_form.html What's Related

WebMail Contact People Yellow Pages Download Find Sites

Submit your Cybermarch Ozone data

Cybermarch Table

School or Troop Name:

Are you a school or scout group?

School
Scout

What city do you live in?

What state do you live in?

What country do you live in?

Measure Date: (as MM/DD/YY)

Measure Time: (as HH:MM AM, or HH:MM PM)

What is your zipcode? (If you live in the United States, enter a zipcode here but do not enter anything in the Latitude and Longitude fields. If you live outside of the United States, do not enter anything into this zipcode field, but do enter your Latitude and Longitude in the next two fields.)

Latitude: (as 41:00 N, or 23:00 S)

You can reach this page from the Project Ozone Web site. Simply click on "Submit" and then have your students enter the data they collected and submit it to the Project Ozone Database.

Following is a list of the data that will be submitted:

- School name
- City
- State
- Country
- Latitude
- Longitude
- Number of students in the class
- Date
- Time of observation
- Ozone in parts per billion
- Ozone description
- Outside air temperature
- Temperature description
- Humidity
- Wind speed
- Wind direction
- Precipitation
- Weather conditions

4. From the Project Ozone home page, students select "Data Retrieval" (Figure 7.21b) and down-

Figure 7.21(b)
Results table

"CyberMarch Table" page from CyberMarch Web site.
Reprinted by permission of Vistanomics, Inc.

Netscape: CyberMarch Retrieval

Location: http://teaparty.terc.edu/cgi-sh1/dbml.exe?Action=Query&cType=HTML&Template=/cyber/cybrtrv.dbm

CyberMarch Table

(Only the last 50 entries will be displayed to your browser)

SchoolName	MeasureDate	MeasureTime	Latitude	Longitude	Temperature	Ecobadge	Location	LanduseLocal	WindDir	WindSt
none	3/16/99	4:17			45.0	40	Rural	Residential	Southwest	15
East Clinton Middle School	11/20/98	2:40PM			16.0	40	Other	Residential	Southwest	10
East Clinton Middle School	11/19/98	2:45PM			15.0	32	Rural	Residential	Southwest	10
East Clinton Middle School	11/18/98	9:30AM			10.0	99	Rural	Residential	East	2
East Clinton Middle School	11/17/98	2:41PM			16.0	50	Rural	Residential	Northwest	5
East Clinton Middle School	11/16/98	9:30AM			11.0	95	Rural	Agriculture	Southeast	7
Earhart Middle School	11/17/98	01:00 PM			17.0	204	Rural	Residential		5
Earhart Middle School	11/17/98	12:00 PM			18.0	174	Rural	Residential	North	5
Earhart Middle School	11/17/98	11:00 AM			15.0	194	Rural	Residential	Southeast	6
Earhart Middle School	11/17/98	10:00 AM			13.0	156	Rural	Residential	South	2
Earhart Middle School	11/17/98	09:00 AM			11.0	146	Rural	Residential	South	2

load the data that appears in the Ozone data table. Have students generate questions, then use the Global Lab program graph and map tools to find answers to their questions. Have the students stick pins on the world map for each location represented in the data. Discuss the results as a class. Have students draw comparisons among the reporting cities to explain differences in levels of ozone.

5. Have students write brief analyses of the data, using their graphs and maps to support their ideas. Have students share the results in class and send e-mail reports over the Internet. From the Project Ozone home page, students select

"Discussion" and then submit brief reports. Students should also respond to student discussions at other schools.

Optional Extensions

1. Encourage your class to make contact with one or more schools that would like to carry out a collaborative study. Have your students look at the data from the Ozone Database and pick out a school whose ozone data differ significantly from those they collected. Have students formulate some questions aimed at finding out about the town or city in which the comparison school is located, in order to understand its ozone problem (or lack thereof). Using e-mail, students can con-

tact the school and explore these differences and possible explanations for them.

2. Assign students to look into the laws that regulate the emission of gases that contribute to the formation of smog. For example, in the United States, the EPA has established compliance laws regarding the ozone standards for U.S. cities. Students also may want to check out the standards that regulate emissions in other countries.

3. Similarly, ask students to inquire into legislation regulating pollution. For example, American schools should examine the EPA's Clean Air Act of 1990 and the revision of the Clean Air Act in 1997, and then share essential parts of it with schools in other countries.

4. Students might find it interesting to explore ways—at the personal, local, regional, and global levels—for dealing with the problem of ozone depletion. What actions should be taken, and why would they be effective?

ACTIVITY 7.5 OZONE: WHAT YOU CAN DO ABOUT IT

Understanding the nature of an air pollutant, such as ozone, through data collection and analysis, and collaboration with other schools is an important part of protecting the atmosphere. However, students can go even further than this by becoming informed about the local and global dimensions of ozone.

Objectives:
- To investigate the laws that protect the quality of the atmosphere
- To become aware of public and private groups concerned with air quality and air pollution control
- To identify actions that students, as citizen-scientists of their community, can take to protect and improve the atmosphere

Materials: Access to the Internet, phone books, newspapers, books on environmental organizations, poster paper, pens, art materials

Web Site Information: Project Ozone home page: http://www.gsu.edu/~mstjrh/projectozone.html/

Procedure:
1. Discuss with students some ideas for short projects they might carry out in small groups to help them take action and learn to make responsible decisions concerning the atmosphere. The focus could be this: How can we inform others about what we have learned about ozone and air pollution? See the suggestions that follow for ozone action projects that students might do.

- **Ozone Web Site:** Students might want to develop their own ozone or Smog Watch Web site, modeling it after the Project Ozone Web site. They could then put it on the Internet and inform others of its existence.
- **Newsletter:** Students might like to draw on their research, and the research of others with whom they've collaborated, to put together a newsletter on ozone. The newsletter could be distributed to others (students, parents, teachers, citizens) in the local community. Some students might decide they want to publish an electronic equivalent of the newsletter.
- **Video Program:** A team of students might get together to produce a consumer-oriented videotape that informs the public about ozone and explores ways to resolve the problems associated with tropospheric and stratospheric ozone. The video program could be presented to other classes in the school or to citizens' groups in the community. If students wish, they might investigate putting their video up on their own Web page.
- **Poster Reports:** Students might opt to create poster reports of the work they did in Project Ozone; the posters might also display work done by their classmates and other students with whom they've collaborated. The

poster reports could be displayed in the school and/or in the community.

- **Research Paper:** Some student groups might be interested in writing fairly brief research papers (three to five pages) that describe the investigations they conducted in Project Ozone. Students could try to get one or more other schools to collaborate. Thus, the final product might be a collection of student papers bound together as a comprehensive report. These could and should be published on the Internet.

2. Give cooperative groups time to meet to decide what kind of project they wish to work on. Decision making might involve making contacts with government agencies or environmental groups. This is a good opportunity for students to search the Internet for information that might be related to their project. Have them begin by consulting the Project Ozone home page.

3. Once students finalize their projects, they should present reports to the class. Cooperative teams should write brief summaries of their projects. From the Project Ozone home page, students select "Discussion" and send their reports on to others working on Project Ozone. Be sure that if your class develops its own Web page, you inform others of its existence.

STUDENT MATERIALS

Project Ozone Mini Learning Log

You may want students to organize their work on Project Ozone using the Project Ozone Mini Learning Log (Figure 7.22). Photocopy the pages and then fold them to produce an eight-page log for each student.

Project Ozone Portfolio

In addition to or as an alternative to the Mini Learning Log, consider having students keep a portfolio of their work on Project Ozone. (For some background on portfolios, see the discussion in Chapter 8.)

Materials: Three-ring binder for each student (1" binder), index tabs to separate binder sections, marking pens, folder for each student in which he or she keeps all completed project work.

Portfolio Elements: Have students set up their portfolios so that they contain the following elements:

- Title Page: Name, course, dates
- Personal Log: Excerpts from the student's log or journal
- Growth Through Writing: Students respond in writing to an open-ended question at the beginning of the project and then again at the end of the project. Sample Question: Using the following ideas and concepts, discuss the differences between ground-level ozone and upper atmospheric ozone. (Terms: sunlight, CFCs, automobiles, refrigerants, smog, ozone shield, urban areas, southern hemisphere)
- Ozone Research: A report of research conducted by the student during Project Ozone
- Social Issue: Either a written report or a collection of newspaper articles and editorials about the implications of ozone on humans and other living things
- Ozone in the News: A collection of newspaper and magazine articles on ozone.
- E-mail messages: A collection of all e-mail messages sent to and received by the student during the project
- Overall Reflection: An at-the-end reflection on and assessment of the portfolio written by

Figure 7.22
Project Ozone Mini Learning Log

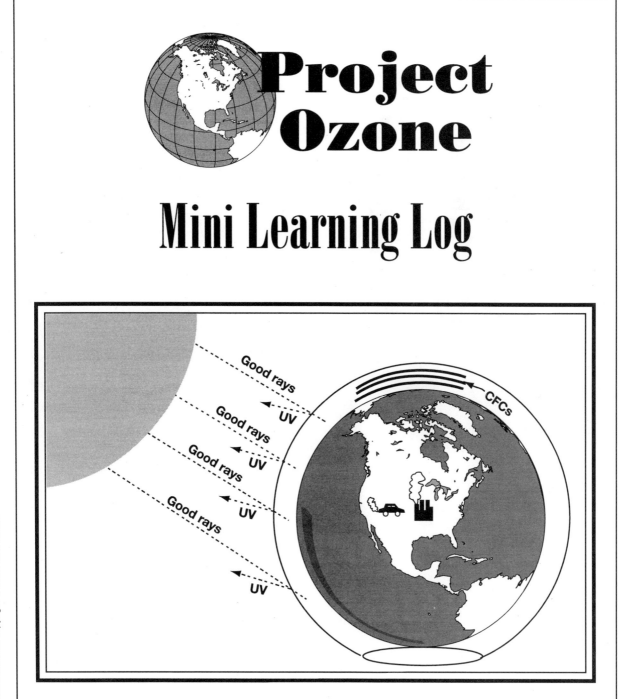

Directions: Photocopy the next four pages (front to back). Fold them to make an eight-page *Mini Learning Log.*

Figure 7.22
Project Ozone Mini Learning Log

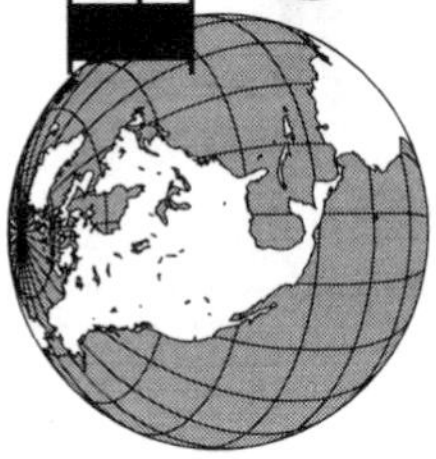

Project Ozone
Mini Learning Log

Name

Date

1

Ozone Resources

8

Figure 7.22
Project Ozone Mini Learning Log

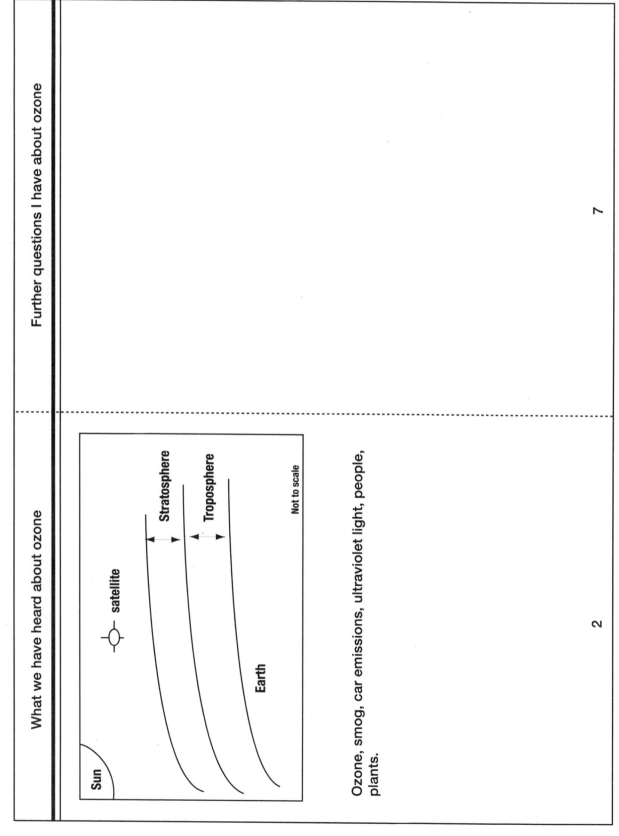

Figure 7.22
Project Ozone Mini Learning Log

Group Your Ideas: Put two or three ideas together to form categories.

3

What I have learned about ozone

6

Figure 7.22
Project Ozone Mini Learning Log

Predict what you think you'll learn about ozone.

5

List some things you want to learn about ozone.

4

Figure 7.23
Project Ozone Certificate

This is to Certify that

_____

has successfully completed

Project Ozone

the student. The student should answer these questions: Which element of the portfolio represents your best piece of work? What does this portfolio show about your abilities? How would you change your portfolio if you were to do another one?

Project Ozone Certificate

If you wish, use the certificate in Figure 7.23, which is designed to be presented to students when they complete Project Ozone.

This chapter presented a complete web-assisted teaching unit on a problem that has global consequences. The quality of the air that

humans breathe is a critical health issue around the world. In this project your students can become part of an effort among students and teachers to learn more about their own environment and then use the Internet to share their findings, and learn about other city's environments as well. Your students will learn to use the Internet using many of its tools, including key pals, global classrooms, information exchanges, and data sharing. And your students will be participating in a social-action project in which they make use of their findings to help improve the quality of the environment in their community.

CHAPTER 8 ASSESSING PERFORMANCE IN SCIENCE

Figure 8.1
Science learning is an active process of engagement, cooperative exchange, and problem solving. This type of learning requires a different way of assessing student progress.

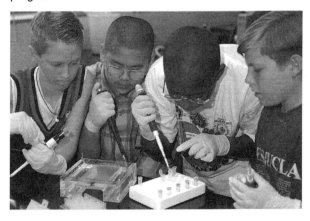

This chapter presents a variety of ways to assess student performance in science. Science teaching that is full of active learning strategies requires assessment methods that are active as well. In recent years, the emphasis on assessment has shifted away from paper-and-pencil tests and toward an array of performance-based and alternative assessment practices. The assessment strategies that are presented here will provide you with the tools you need to implement a performance-based assessment approach in your classroom.

ASSESSING PERFORMANCE: WHAT'S IT ALL ABOUT?

Performance assessment is rich with ways to evaluate the progress of students in a science class. Following are some strategies and the types of science outcomes they reveal.

- **Portfolios.** Portfolios consist of materials that students and teachers select to represent a student's best work. Portfolios can reveal many things—for instance, gains in a particular subject area over a short or long period of time, progress on long-term projects, or performance in group work.

- **Journals or Logs.** Journals or logs consist of writings, drawings, and illustrations created by students to document their thinking in science. They can be used by students to record their feelings and attitudes about science, as well as their responses to group and cooperative work.

- **Computers.** Computers help track the process of learning and thinking. Because they are interactive, they provide a sort of record of how well students learn with feedback, as well as their ability to deal with realistic situations.

- **Videotapes.** Videotapes record ongoing activities and student explanations in rich detail. This makes it possible to determine such things as how students present their ideas and answer challenging questions, and how students carry out tasks and perform experiments. For example, you might videotape a group presentation and then use the tape to review the group's communication skills; also, send the tape home for parents to observe.

- **Hands-On or Performance Tasks.** Hands-on tasks ask students to show what they know by working with or manipulating concrete materials. Science students might be instructed to design and conduct an experiment to test a hypothesis, using scientific equipment or procedures to do so. For example, they might use a hand-held lens to analyze and interpret the crystals in a rock.

- **Group Activities.** Group tasks can be quite helpful in assessing certain science skills. For example, group tasks show how well team members work cooperatively, communicate, and integrate each member's contributions into a final product.

- **Paper-and-Pencil Assessments.** Continue to use pencil-and-paper assessments as appropriate, to measure students' knowledge of facts, concepts, and procedures; their ability to read and understand text; and their ability to solve problems.

- **Multiple-Choice Tests.** Expect multiple-choice tests to continue to play a role in the science classroom—both because their format is efficient and scores on some multiple-choice standardized tests correlate moderately well with subsequent academic performance as measured by grades. However, as this chapter demonstrates, we as teachers can make improvements in multiple-choice tests to bring them in line with new science curricular goals.

ASSESSMENT: THE BIG PICTURE

The trend in science education reform is toward assessments that

- are embedded within instructional materials
- use a variety of methods to assess student progress
- emphasize teacher observation and judgment
- provide methods for getting at the reasons behind student answers

This perspective follows naturally from the active learning strategies presented earlier in the book. In this context, assessment is an integral aspect of each of the following phases of instruction: pre-instruction, during instruction, and post-instruction. The active assessment strategies that follow can be used in one or more of these phases of instruction, as summarized in Figure 8.2.

INFORMAL ASSESSMENT STRATEGIES

Observing

Observing students doing science in the classroom is a valid way to assess student learning. Often it is during these informal assessments that we see evidence of learning and achievement that is not necessarily apparent using other, more formal methods.

Observing Social Behavior

Observation of social behavior is an effective way to determine the level of involvement of students working in groups. Paying attention to students' behavior—verbal as well as nonverbal—is also a good way to gain insight into their learning. One useful idea is to create an observation form. This enables you, the teacher, to observe student behavior during cooperative learning activities and to record instances of the social/interpersonal skills that are being encouraged. The interpersonal skills "active listening," "staying on task," "asking questions," and "contributing ideas," for example, lend themselves to an observation chart (Figure 8.3). The teacher records the names of the students in each group, spends a few minutes watching each group individually, and then records instances of the interpersonal skill. Later, the teacher returns to the group and provides specific feedback to the group about its interpersonal skill development.

Observing Hands-on/Minds-on Behavior

Observing students as they experiment, collect data, draw conclusions, and communicate helps you assess their problem-solving ability. A checklist, such as the one in Figure 8.4, can be useful in such situations. The form has been set up for observing students engaged in cooperative learning activities.

Asking Questions

Asking questions is another means for informally assessing student learning. One of the most powerful uses of classroom questions as an assessment tool is during cooperative learning activities and/or laboratory activities. The role of the teacher at such times is one of classroom monitor. He or she visits individual groups to explore the content of and the methods that students are using in their investigations and small-group work. The following techniques should be useful in assessing student understanding.

Figure 8.2
Model of Assessment for Science Teaching

Pre-Instruction	During Instruction	Post-Instruction
Goal: Assess students' prior knowledge, ideas, beliefs, and attitudes	**Goal:** Embed assessment within instruction to gain insight into students' knowledge, ideas, beliefs, and attitudes (a seamless process linking instruction and assessment)	**Goal:** Evaluate students' progress and reflect on the effectiveness and quality of instruction
Strategies:	**Strategies:**	**Strategies:**
• T-charts	• Portfolio—collections of student work	• Survey of student opinions and attitudes (learner satisfaction form)
• Journal writings	• Journals and logs—document student thinking and reflection	• Student interviews
• Drawings	• Activities as assessment—hands-on activities that assess performance	• Written assessments (standardized or open-ended—see Plant in a Jar)
• Interviews/conversations	• Observations	• Performance assessments (problem-solving tasks)
• Questionnaires	• Interviews	• Assessment of portfolios (rubrics)
• Concept maps	• Products	
	—journal or log	
	—drawings	
	—list of readings	
	—collections	
	—written assessment	
	—videotapes	
	—audiotapes	
	• Paper-and-pencil tests	
	• Written tests	
	• Alternative multiple choice	

Figure 8.3 Observation Chart

Interpersonal Skills	Team 1	Team 2	Team 3	Team 4	Team 5
• Active Listening					
• Staying on Task					
• Asking Questions					
• Contributing Ideas					

Figure 8.4 Scientific Observations Checklist

Scientific Skills	Student 1	Student 2	Student 3	Student 4
Problem Solving • Solved problem with little guidance • Stayed on task				
Experimenting • Recognized a number of problems • Created sound hypotheses • Used sound experimental design • Used materials creatively				
Collecting Data • Made unique observations • Used measuring devices correctly • Data collected was complete				
Drawing Conclusions • Provided in-depth analysis of data • Developed well-supported conclusions				
Communicating • Student did not need prompting • Student communicated orally				

Ask a Variety of Questions

Try to strike a balance between low-order (recall) and high-order (application, synthesis, evaluation) questions. The use of higher-order questions has been shown to be motivational, whereas the use of lower-order questioning is an effective probing strategy.

Allow Wait Time

Science teachers who practice waiting at least three seconds after asking a question establish a classroom atmosphere that is beneficial to a student's cognitive, as well as affective, learning. Rowe found that the length of student response increases, the number of failures to respond decreases, confidence increases, speculative responses increase, student questions increases, and variety of student responses increases.[1]

Probe

If, after asking a question and waiting at least three seconds, a student gives an incorrect answer, then the teacher should probe the student answer with other questions. Probing provides a second opportunity for the student to express his or her understanding. Berliner explains that probing for the purpose of helping students clarify and improve on their answers is a more effective way of increasing student achievement than probing for the purpose of getting an answer.[2]

Redirect

If you are working with a cooperative group, redirecting a question to another group member can be a useful technique. Suppose you ask one student in the group a question and this student is unable to answer or gives an incorrect answer, you might then redirect by asking another student in the group the same question.

Student Talk

Student talk can serve as a good guide to (science) understanding. Use either small-group or whole-class talk to document student learning and knowledge. Discussions are especially helpful ways to discover the range of prior knowledge among a group of students. Here are suggestions for generating student/teacher discussions:[3]

- Discussions should begin with open-ended questions, such as these:
  What have you noticed lately about the caterpillars?
  What are some things you know about shadows? What is shade?
  What sorts of questions do you have about the sun? Is there anything in particular that you have wondered about?
- Refrain from correcting or unduly modifying the students' comments.
- Let discussions proceed in a manner encouraging the involvement of most of the students.
- Try to record the students' statements.

Here are some specific teaching strategies designed to encourage student talk as an assessment strategy.

T-chart Conversations

Provide a sheet of newsprint and marking pens for each group of students in your class. Suggest a topic, have students make a T-chart (Figure 8.5), and then provide two thinking prompts: What have you heard about the topic? What questions do you have about the topic? (In this strategy, the T-chart serves to involve all members of the group in the topic and to help structure student conversations.) Students brainstorm for 5 minutes, then discuss the data they have recorded. At this point, you may need to ask questions related to the charts in order to encourage students to talk aloud about their ideas.

---

[1] Rowe, M. B. *"Science Silence, and Sanctions,"* in Science and Children *(October 1969)*, pp. 22–25.

[2] Berliner, D. C., *"But Do They Understand?"* in Educating Handbook: A Research Perspective, *Virginia Richardson-Koehler, ed. New York: Longman, 1987, p. 270.*

[3] *After Chittenden, Edward, and Wallace, Vivian. "Reforming School Assessment Practices: The Case of Central Park East" in* Planning and Changing 22 (1993), *pp. 141–46.*

Figure 8.5
Use T-charts to encourage students to talk about their writing and to consider the ideas and questions they have about the topic of the chart.

Rocks and Minerals

What have we heard about rocks and minerals?	What questions do we have about rocks and minerals?
They can be classified into three main groups-- igneaous, metamorphic and sedimentary. Rocks are comprised of one or more minerals. There are hundred of different kinds of rocks and minerals. Fossils are sometimes found in sedimentary rocks. Sedimentary rocks are formed when sediments are deposited in an ocean.	How are rocks formed? Do rocks last forever, or do they disintegrate? What is the oldest rock on the Earth? What causes rocks to have different colors? Why are some rocks heavier than others?

Word Webs

Word webs are another excellent tool for stimulating student talk about a topic or concept. Give pairs or small groups of students a sheet of newsprint and ask them to write down a concept in the center of the sheet. From the central concept, suggest that students brainstorm what they know about the concept by writing down other words that connect to the central idea (Figure 8.6). When the webs are completed (about 10 minutes), ask students to share their webs with students in another group, or ask team representatives to discuss their team's ideas with the whole class.

STUDENT WRITING AS AN ASSESSMENT STRATEGY

Writing is a powerful way to help students learn science; it is also a powerful way to find out what students are thinking and thus it is a valid assessment strategy. The purpose of writing in science bears highlighting. Here are four goals suggested by Lesley Bulman:[4]

- To help the growth of understanding of science concepts

- To provide a record of concepts and activities that can be used for revision later
- To provide feedback to the teacher on the growth of the students
- To develop students' ability to communicate

More than 70 percent of the writing in science classes is of the following two types: (1) copying dictated notes, or "teacher talk," and (2) answering questions on worksheets, exercises, tests, or exams. Clearly, there is room for change in the ways that we ask students to write. Over-reliance on multiple-choice and true–false formats, in particular limits our opportunities to document student knowledge and understanding through writing.

There are many alternative assessment strategies that include writing as a means of documenting student thinking. Here, you will find just a few of those strategies. Later in the chapter, you'll see how writing is integrated into hands-on performance tasks, as well. Let's start with a science lesson that focuses on writing.

Rocky Writing: An Alternative Writing Assignment

Objectives:
- Assess students' observational skills
- Record notes about a natural object—a rock
- Reconstruct notes in poetry form

[4] Bulman, L. (1985). *Teaching Languages and Study Skills in Secondary Science.* London: Heinemann.

Figure 8.6
After students have completed a team web, they are ready to discuss their ideas with other teams of students. Have a student representative from each team in the class rotate to another team and present his or her team's web. Help students field the questions and comments that emerge.

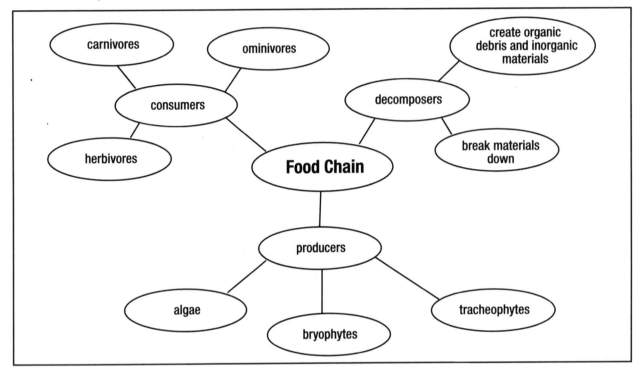

Overview: As part of a science unit on local geology, students select a rock, which they observe carefully, using all five senses. They then write down words and phrases based on their observations. After reading and thinking about what they've jotted down, students write an ode to their rock. This assignment is an example of an embedded assessment activity in which students' abilities to make observations and write (poetically) about them are assessed.

Procedures:
Have students gather rocks, perhaps as part of a field trip, or bring in enough rocks yourself so that each student will have one to observe.

1. Stimulus
Once all students have a rock on their desks, discuss what the students can observe about a rock based on each of the five senses. Have a student recorder write down key words on the board or on chart paper, such as these:

Sight—size, shape, color
Hearing—rattle, scraping
Taste—mineral content, dirt
Touch—contour, roughness, smoothness, unevenness, bumpiness
Smell—sweet fragrance, earthiness

Have students fold a sheet of composition paper five times, labeling one section for each of the senses, and the sixth section "Other Ideas." Ask students to observe their rocks and to jot down notes about what they observe.

2. Writing
After students have had time to observe and take notes, ask them to use their observations to

write an ode to their rocks. Tell them that an ode is a lyric poem that frequently begins "Oh (subject) . . ." and praises a person. Thus students would begin their poem with "Oh rock . . ." and speak to their rock as though it were a person, using personification.

3. Follow-up
After students have written for a while, have them read their poems to a partner. Partners can assist each other in adding ideas or revising the poem, as needed. Students' poems might go something like this:

> Oh, wonderful little gray rock,
> Bumpety, lumpety, and tough.
> You have tumbled down from the high
>   mountain,
> You have survived the trampling of many
>   rough feet,
> The crush of an automobile's wheels.
> I will give you an easier life now
> Perched on my bedroom windowsill.

4. Assessment
Circulate through the room to observe student activity as students observe, write, and share. After students have shared their work, have them determine criteria (scientific and poetic) for an especially good poem, answering the question: *What made some poems stand out as especially effective?* Students can revise their poems based on the established criteria. Have students display their rock writing along with their rocks on a table or shelf. Note: An alternative way to assess the students' work is to use a scoring rubric that examines their "notes" and their final poem.

Scoring Rubric for Ode
0 = Student did not include observations in the poem, included observations in the poem that were very inaccurate, or did not write a poem.

1 = Student included some observations in the poem, but the poem did not reflect accurate observations of the rock.

2 = Student included more than one sensory observation in the poem, and the poem accurately described the rock.

3 = Student included more than two sensory observations in the poem, and the poem reflected outstanding observations of the rock.

ALTERNATIVE MULTIPLE CHOICE
This strategy asks students not only to select an answer to a multiple-choice question, but also to provide one or more reasons for their choice. Begin by looking over the multiple-choice questions you are currently using and selecting those that lend themselves to this new strategy. Change the questions as needed. Following is a multiple-choice question that fits the alternative format:

1. Which of the birds pictured below probably lives around ponds and eats snails and small fish?

   What are your reasons for the choice you made?

Figure 8.7
Drawings of Birds
Educational Testing Service

OPEN-ENDED QUESTIONS

The use of the open-ended question is another powerful way to assess student's scientific understanding of the natural world. It is a strategy consistent with the new National Science Education Standards as set out in the Introduction to this book:[5]

- An understanding of scientific facts, concepts, principles, laws, and theories
- The capacity to reason scientifically
- The ability to inquire
- The capacity to use scientific principles to make personal decisions and to take positions on societal issues
- The ability to communicate effectively about science

Open-ended questions provide a means for students to inquire, to apply scientific ideas to solve a problem, and to communicate effectively. In so doing, they enable us, as teachers, to assess students along the lines outlined in the Standards. Some of the characteristics of open-ended questions that make their use compatible with current reform trends include the following:

- There are many ways to answer the question.
- There is a range of appropriate responses.
- The questions are typically problem-oriented, thereby requiring the application of science knowledge.
- Students can use many means to respond: a short paragraph, a picture or diagram, or perhaps a data table or graph.
- Assessment can be flexible, thereby allowing for a range of responses.

Designing Open-ended Questions

Process

As summarized in Figure 8.8, the first step in designing an open-ended question is to identify a big idea in science. Scientific inquiry, forces and motion, origin of the Earth system, personal and community health, and the structure of the atom are examples of big ideas in science.

Once a big idea has been selected, you can develop subconcepts to help you refine the focus of the open-ended question that will emerge. Create a writing format by thinking about the format of the question. For example you might want to write a scenario that outlines a real problem in the community, for example, how students might solve a pollution problem reported in the media. Next you should write the question, and then design an assessment rubric.

Following are some tips for designing open-ended questions:

1. "Big ideas" in science refers to the fundamental ideas in science. The National Science Education Standards, basing its work on the AAAS Project 2061 and NSTA's Scope, Sequence, and Coordination, has attempted to identify some of these "big ideas" in science. Here are two possible examples:

- All organisms must be able to obtain and use resources, grow, reproduce, and maintain a relatively stable internal environment while living in a constantly changing external environment. (Life Science Standard)

Figure 8.8
Developing Open-ended Questions

- Identify the "big idea" → •Develop subconcepts → •Create a writing format → •Write the question → •Design an assessment rubric

[5] *National Research Council. (1995). National Science Education Standards. Washington, DC: National Academy of Science.*

Figure 8.9 Scoring Rubric

SCORING RUBRIC FOR OPEN-ENDED QUESTIONS

Outstanding: 4 points

The student's response clearly demonstrates superior understanding of the concepts and processes. Rationale is clear and logical, and, where appropriate, diagrams and illustrations are provided.

Competent: 3 points

The student's response effectively presents knowledge of the concepts and processes. No serious flaws are evident, but one or more elements in the response is missing. Rationale is logical for the most part.

Satisfactory: 2 points

The student's response shows a limited understanding of the concepts and processes; the response is incomplete and the rationale appears to be unclear.

Unsatisfactory: 1 point

The student's response shows serious flaws in terms of understanding the concepts and processes, and shows little or no understanding of the words, drawings, and diagrams that may have been included.

No Response: 1 point

The student provides no relevant response.

- Scientific explanations use evidence and logically consistent arguments, and propose, modify, or elaborate principles, models, and theories in science. (Inquiry Standard)

2. Using a demonstration, diagrams, pictures, graphs, data tables, and, sometimes, hands-on materials enhances the quality of open-ended questions.

3. Open-ended questions are appropriate for individual or small-group use. When working in small groups, students are free to talk and discuss the question among themselves, but each student should respond individually.

4. Try using a scoring rubric to assess open-ended questions. You can design your own rubrics inductively. Begin by reading a sample of responses to the open-ended question; then identify the qualities of "good" or "complete" responses as opposed to those that are "poor" or "incomplete." Examining already-developed rubrics, like the one shown in Figure 8.9, should help you develop your own rubrics more easily.

---

[6] *Based on an example in* National Science Education Standards. *1996. Washington, DC: National Academy of Science.*

Examples of Open-ended Questions

Two examples of open-ended questions that you might try in your own classroom are "Plant in a Jar" and "Heating the Air." Plant in a Jar is an assessment task that emphasizes the importance of the explanation of scientific phenomena as a way to assess student understanding of big ideas in science.[6] Each assessment task possesses attributes that make them good assessment exercises:

- The situation can be described with words, diagrams, or real materials.
- The situation can be understood by students of various ages.
- The explanation for the prediction can be developed at several levels of complexity.

Plant in a Jar

For the Plant in a Jar assessment (Figure 8.10), you'll also find information on what we might expect from typical elementary, middle, and high school students (Figure 8.11), along with sample student responses accompanied by typical ratings (based on the rubric in Figure 8.9; see Figure 8.12) that teachers have given the responses.

Heating the Air

"Heating the Air" (Figure 8.13) is an example of a physical science open-ended question. Note that in this case, the question is designed to be answered by a small group of questions. In this case, students explain how the air is heated, but they must also illustrate their ideas by using terms given.

PERFORMANCE TASKS

Performance tasks typically involve students, either individually or in small teams, in the act of solving a problem or thinking critically about a problem, data, or an observation. Performance tasks also engage students in activities that draw on their ability to use science thinking skills, such as sorting and classifying, observing and formulating hypotheses, interpreting data, and designing and conducting an experiment.

Characteristics of Performance Tasks

Performance tasks are creative approaches to student evaluation that you can employ in an overall assessment plan. They are creative because the emphasis is on the methods that students use as well as the ideas that students generate. Performance tasks place the student in situations that are in accordance with what science instruction should look like. Studies indicate that there is a high correlation between performance tasks and a hands-on, conceptual approach to science teaching. Following are some of the characteristics of performance tasks:[7]

- They typically involve students in real-world contexts.
- They involve students in sustained work, sometimes over several days.
- The focus is on the "big ideas" and major concepts in science, rather than isolated facts and definitions.
- They are broad in scope, usually involving several principles of science.
- They involve students in the use of scientific methods and the manipulation of science tools.
- They present students with open-ended problems.
- They encourage students to collaborate and brainstorm.
- They stimulate students to make connections among important concepts and ideas.
- Scoring criteria are based on content, process, group skills, and communication skills.

---

[7] *Excerpted from Joan Boykoff Baron, "Performance Assessment: Blurring the Edges Among Assessment, Curriculum, and Instruction." In* Assessment in the Service of Instruction, *Washington, D.C.: American Association for the Advancement of Science, 1987.*

Figure 8.10
Plant in the Jar

Adapted from *National Science Education Standards,*
pp. 92, & 95–96. Copyright © 1996 by the National
Academy of Sciences. Reprinted by permission of the
National Academy Press, Washington, D.C.

Plant in a Jar

Task: Explaining a Prediction
Some moist soil is placed inside a clear glass jar. A healthy plant is
planted in the soil. The cover is screwed on tightly. The jar is located
in a window where it receives sunlight. Its temperature is maintained
between 60°F and 80°F. How long do you predict the plant will live?
Write an explanation supporting your prediction.

Directions: Use relevant ideas from the life, physical, and earth
sciences to make a prediction. If you are unsure of a prediction, your
explanation should state that and should tell what information you
would need to make a better prediction. You should know that there
is not a single right prediction.

Figure 8.11 What Should We Expect of Students in the Plant in the Jar Task?

- Elementary school students: Elementary school students would likely base their predictions on their work with plants; they would probably use very few scientific terms.

- Middle school students: Middle school students should use more scientific language and mention concepts such as light, heat, carbon dioxide, water, energy, and photosynthesis.

- High school students: High school students might see the plant in the jar as a model of the Earth's ecosystem, noting the complementary processes of photosynthesis and respiration.

Figure 8.12
Student Responses to the Plant in the Jar Task.

Adapted from *National Science Education Standards*, pp. 92, & 95–96. Copyright © 1996 by the National Academy of Sciences. Reprinted by permission of the National Academy Press, Washington, D.C.

STUDENT 1 (AGE 10)

- The plant could live. It has water and sunlight. It could die if it got frozen or a bug eats it. We planted seeds in third grade. Some kids forgot to water them and they died. Eddie got scared that his seeds would not grow. He hid them in his desk. They did. The leaves were yellow. After Eddie put it in the sun it got green. The plants in our terrarium lived all year long. (Typically rated a 3.)

STUDENT 2 (AGE 12)

- I predict the plant will not live for more than 3 days. Why? Because the lid on the jar is screwed on tightly and it has no holes in it, therefore it can't get any air or oxygen. The plant can't live with water so the plant will die very soon. Living things can't live without air or water so therefore it won't live more than three days. (Typically rated a 1 or 2.)

STUDENT 3 (AGE 14)

- If there are no insects in the jar or microorganisms that might cause some plant disease, the plant might grow a bit and live for quite a while. I know that when I was in elementary school we did this experiment. My plant died—it got covered with black mold. But some of the plants other kids had got bigger and lived for more than a year. The plant can live because it gets energy from sunlight. When light shines on the leaves, photosynthesis takes place. Carbon dioxide and water form carbohydrates and oxygen. This reaction transforms energy from the sun into chemical energy. Plants can do this because they have chlorophyll. The plant needs carbohydrates for life processes like growing and moving. It uses the carbohydrates and oxygen to produce energy for life processes. After some time the plant probably will stop growing. I think that happens when all the minerals in the soil are used up. For the plant to grow it needs minerals from the soil. When parts of the plant die, the plant material rots and minerals go back into the soil. So that's why I think that how much the plant will grow will depend on the minerals in the soil. The gases, oxygen, carbon dioxide, and water vapor just keep getting used over and over. What I'm not sure about is if the gases get used up. Can the plant live if there is no carbon dioxide left for photosynthesis? I'm pretty sure a plant can live for a long time sealed up in a jar, but I'm not sure how long or exactly what would make it die. (Typically rated a 3 or 4.)

Figure 8.13
Heating the Air: An Open-ended Question

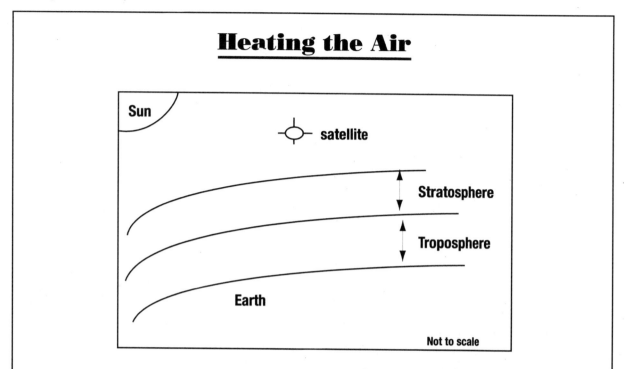

Heating the Air

Directions: Working with your teammates, use all of the following terms (you may add other terms if you wish) in a diagram to explain how you think Earth's atmosphere is heated. After you have made your diagram, write an explanation of it.

Terms: atmosphere, warming, carbon dioxide, soil, sun, energy, heat, molecules

Examples of Performance Tasks

Here are five performance tasks ready for use with your students.

Milk-Carton Cars

Your group is given two identical "milk carton" cars. One has full-width wheels. The second has had its wheel width reduced by one-half. Design an experiment to test the variable of wheel width and its effect on distance traveled. After you have designed the experiment, test each car at least three times. Record and then analyze the data. Write a report describing your project and presenting the results.

Plant Study

Your group wants to study the effect of different amounts of exposure to sunlight each day on the growth of identical plants. Design an experiment that varies the sunlight from 0 hours per day to 24 hours per day. Use at least four identical plants and collect data for at least one month. Graph and then analyze the data. Write a report describing your project and presenting the results.

Can Crusher

Your group is given design paper, cardboard, clay, pencils, half-gallon milk cartons, and cardboard tubes from rolls of paper towels. It is also given some "model" aluminum cans made from aluminum foil. The model cans are approximately one-third the size of actual beverage cans. Using the principles behind simple machines, construct a prototype can crusher that can effectively crush the model cans. After testing the prototype, present a demonstration and an oral report to the class. Make a scale drawing of the can crusher device, and write out step-by-step instructions for its construction.

Recycling

Your group is presented with large quantities of the following: plastic containers from consumer products, beverage cans, vegetable and fruit cans, newspaper, cardboard, magazines, and

Figure 8.14
Water Filter System

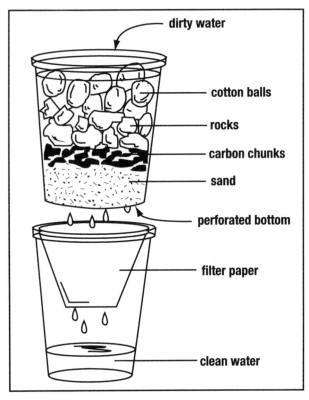

- dirty water
- cotton balls
- rocks
- carbon chunks
- sand
- perforated bottom
- filter paper
- clean water

glass bottles and jars. It is also given plastic bags, twist ties, labels, a can opener, a magnet, an aluminum can-crushing device, and a plastics-recycling key. Design a system that can be used to separate, package, and store the recyclable materials for delivery to a recycling center. Based on the experience gained from this activity, apply your system to the school's recycling program. Write a report describing the program's strengths and weaknesses. Present the report to the class and to the school administration.

Dirty Water

Prior to presenting this task to students, obtain the necessary materials (see below) and use the recipe to make dirty water.

Materials:

Small plastic cups, some with holes in the bottom; cotton pieces; activated charcoal; clean sand

Figure 8.15

The student log can contain a variety of examples of student work, including answers to questions, lab reports, articles from newspapers, student reflections, and more.

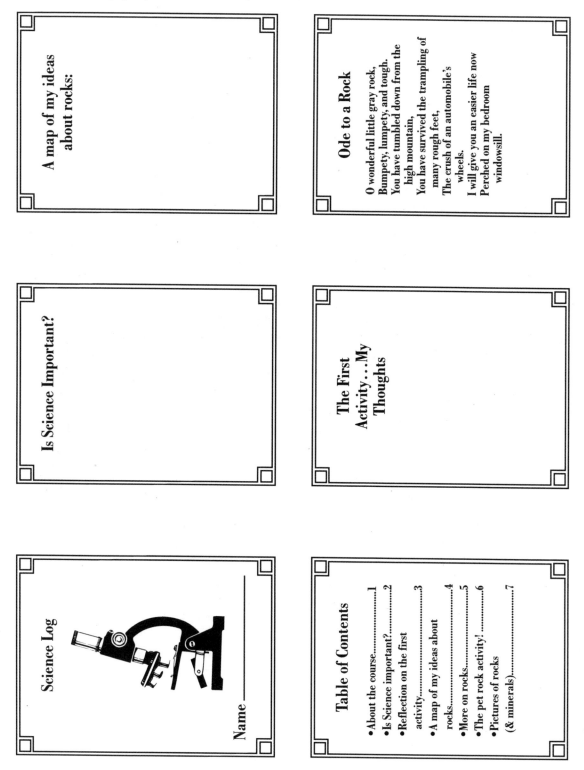

A map of my ideas about rocks:

Ode to a Rock

O wonderful little gray rock,
Bumpety, lumpety, and tough.
You have tumbled down from the high mountain,
You have survived the trampling of many rough feet,
The crush of an automobile's wheels.
I will give you an easier life now
Perched on my bedroom windowsill.

Is Science Important?

The First Activity...My Thoughts

Science Log

Name —————

Table of Contents

- About the course..............1
- Is Science important?........2
- Reflection on the first activity.......................3
- A map of my ideas about rocks........................4
- More on rocks...............5
- The pet rock activity! 6
- Pictures of rocks (& minerals).................7

Dirty Water Recipe:
To 1 liter of water, add a few drops of blue food coloring, 50 cc of vinegar, and a handful of dirt.

Your team has been asked to find a method to clean up water that will be used subsequently in a fish tank. The water is located in the large jar at the materials table. One possible method of cleaning the water is to make a simple filter. Figure 8.14 shows one such filter system. Find the best method you can to clean up the water using the materials that are provided. As you begin your experiments, be sure to write down the question you are investigating. You might begin the question this way: "What would happen if . . . ?" Make drawings of your models and write a report summarizing your findings. Be prepared to give a short presentation to the class.

THE STUDENT LOG

Of all the approaches to performance assessment, the student log is, without a doubt, my favorite choice for enhancing thinking and providing students with a place to "do science." Students can use many different forms of expression as they work in their logs, encouraging both right- and left-brain thinking (Figure 8.15). Here's a look at just some of what students can do:

- Write in narrative form.
- Ask questions.
- Make designs for prototypes.
- Record quotes they've found about science.
- Write an (essay about a science issue).
- Jot down ideas.
- Draw or paste in a cartoon.
- Make diagrams illustrating a concept or theory.
- Record the teacher's pearls of wisdom.
- Create concept maps or webs.
- Draw a picture with pen and ink.
- Draw a picture with crayons, paints, or color marking pens.

- Paste in lab reports, data, and activities, then comment on them.
- State an opinion about an issue, theory, or science concept.
- Write letters.
- Doodle (scientifically, of course!).
- Paste pictures from magazines and comment about them.

These logs themselves can take many forms, including:

- Spiralbound notebooks
- Loose-leaf notebooks or binders
- Folders
- Files in a computer

Spiralbound journals are more permanent, and if students "add" papers to the log (such as data sheets, graphs, drawings, or pictures clipped from a magazine), they can be glued or taped to it. Similarly, they can be open-ended or highly structured (perhaps teacher-generated and based on a single lesson plan or unit of teaching).

HOW SHOULD LOGS BE ORGANIZED?

Take some time to work with your students to get their logs organized. Plan a day when the students bring the materials for their log to class (spiralbound notebook, binder and paper, etc.). Provide colored marking pens for students' use in illustrating their logs. Here are some specific tips:

1. Have students organize their log according to your overall plan for using the logs. If you want the logs to be chronological, without regard to categories of items, then students can write and include items in the log in the order in which activities take place. If, however, you want a topical organization, then have the students use dividers or labels to separate the log into parts—for example,

reflections on class sessions, notes from class, project work, and so on.

2. Students should reserve the first five pages of the log for a table of contents. Some teachers like to have students reserve the last five pages for a student-generated glossary.

3. Students should number each page of the log from beginning to end.

4. Students should date each entry in their log.

When Should Logs Be Used?

If you consistently make time for logs, students will value "logging" as meaningful work. Following are two suggestions for incorporating the log into a busy class schedule:

1. **At the end of class.** Ask the students to reflect on the lesson by giving them a prompt that encourages writing, drawing, and illustrating. Some teachers find that five minutes at the end of the class period works well for this type of activity. Here are some ideas for prompts:

- How did your group do today?
- What did you enjoy most about class today? (Least?)
- What connections can you make between the content of today's lesson and a real-world situation?
- How would you visualize today's class? Can you find a picture or draw one that helps you?
- How would you chart or diagram what you learned today?

Here are some other visual stimulators:

- A map of my ideas would look like this. . . .
- This illustration or cartoon expresses. . . .
- The movie (movie title) reminds me of. . . .

Here are some verbal stimulators:

- I was disappointed that. . . .
- I discovered that. . . .
- I didn't realize that. . . .
- I learned. . . .
- My group thought that. . . .
- My group contributed. . . .

2. **During class.** You can build logs into ongoing lesson plans by having the students work for approximately five minutes on a specific logging activity (drawing a map, making an illustration, expressing the meaning of a concept, etc.). Students can then share their work with others in their group or with the whole class.

How Should Logs Be Used?

Logs can be an integral part of students' work. Thus they should be available during class time for students' use in taking notes, making diagrams and illustrations, and doing narrative writing. They can be an integral part of hands-on activities, as well as a place for minds-on work that encourages students to reflect on the activity. Some teachers occasionally use logs as part of homework assignments. Here are a few other suggestions:

1. **Eliciting student ideas.** Logs are perfect tools for encouraging students to think and write about their knowledge of ideas in science. Use them as a place for students to brainstorm what they know about a topic, as well as a place for students to jot down questions they have about a topic. Logs can help students see how their thinking has changed over time.

2. **Reflecting on past work.** After students have worked in their logs for several weeks, have them look back over their entries. They should read what they've written, study the pictures and drawings, and look over the other entries. This way, students think about their thinking, as well as try to identify patterns in their work.

3. **Sharing with others.** This is a very powerful use of student logs. However, it can be

Figure 8.16
Typical Portfolio

intimidating. What the student shares with others should be his or her choice, and students should not be coerced into sharing if they are uncomfortable with it. Sharing is generally less threatening in small groups. You can structure a sharing session simply by asking students to share a favorite drawing, picture, poem, or statement in their log. You can also ask students to share a common assignment—perhaps a concept map or a reflection on a class session.

THE PORTFOLIOS

Typically, when science teachers are asked whether they are using portfolios in their science classes, very few of them say that they are. This may be due to the fact that there are many misconceptions floating around about portfolios. The materials that follow will, hopefully, dispel some of these misconceptions and encourage you to use

portfolios in your class. You'll find two models for portfolios presented here. The first is a generic approach—one you could use in most any science class. The second is based on a model developed for a biology or life sciences class. After looking it over, however, you may well be able to modify it for an Earth science, environmental science, marine science, or physical science course.

Model 1: Basic Portfolio for Any Science Class

What Is a Portfolio?

A portfolio is a folder or binder in which students can place their work to show what they have done in science class over a defined period of time. A three-ring binder that is not more than 1" wide seems to work best. Students should use dividers to separate one section from another (see Figures 8.16 and 8.17). Portfolios should NOT be designed for a full year's worth of work—that is too long a time period for students to be responsible for a project. You might consider a grading period as defining the maximum length of time that a portfolio should be kept. Some teachers assign portfolios for specific projects. See, for example, the portfolio suggested for Project Ozone in Chapter 7.

Why Should Students Put Work into Portfolios?

There are a number of answers to this question. Here are a few you might wish to share with your students.

- To show what you have learned
- To show you are a self-directed learner
- To gather evidence of the quality of your work
- To show your progress in science
- To go through the process of choosing work you think says something important about you
- To communicate to others what you know and understand

Figure 8.17
Sample Portfolio Pages

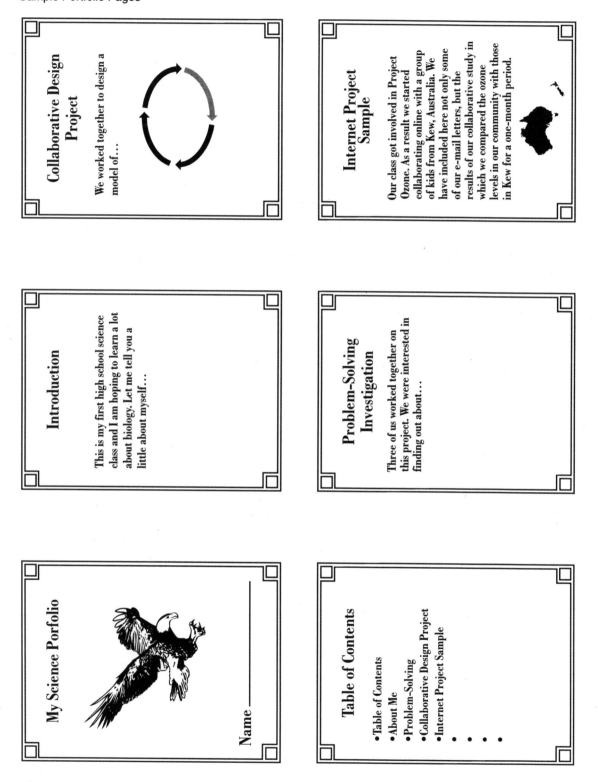

What Samples of Work Should Students Include in a Portfolio?

The following list of items can be used to form the content of a portfolio. Depending on your science class, you should select items from the following list.

- **Cover.** Include the student's name, course title, and a science illustration.
- **Table of Contents.** Include a list of the entries as well as page numbers.
- **Goals.** Students should make a list of the goals that are being accomplished.
- **Biography:** Students tell about themselves, including history and interests and how science has affected their lives.
- **Log Excerpts:** If your students keep a log of their work in your course, have them include samples from their log to reflect growth and interest in science.
- **Writing Samples**
  - Open-ended Questions. Students include samples of pre- and post-question writing to illustrate their growth through writing.
  - Book Reviews. Include brief summaries of books related to the topic.
  - Fuzzy Situations (see Chapter 4). Include the results of writing on one fuzzy situation related to the topic of the portfolio.
- **Problem-Solving Examples**
  - Laboratory Reports. Include any of the laboratory activities that included data collection, analysis, and summarization.
  - Group Investigations. Include any laboratory activity or research project that was completed as part of a research team.
  - Internet Projects. Include a sample of an Internet activity accomplished alone or with a research team.
- **Creative Projects**
  - Web page. Print out a copy of the Web page that was developed as part of a project or activity.
  - Models. Include a diagram or photograph of any scientific model constructed.

- Poetry/Plays/Creative Writing. Include a sample of any work in these categories.
- **Self-Reflection:** Include a self-evaluation of each item included in the portfolio.
- **Overall Self-Reflection.** Have students write a short statement in which they look back over the unit of instruction and discuss what they learned about science. They should also indicate the goals met and what they need to work on in the future.

Model 2: Biology/Life Science Portfolio[8]

Background for Students

Many people continue to learn about biology after they have completed a high school biology course. They learn because they are seeking information on a topic of special interest to them. As part of this course, you have learned not only biology content, but also how to learn. For your portfolio, you are asked to demonstrate that you have developed skills that will enable you to be an independent learner who can seek information and apply that information to new situations.

Directions for Students. As part of your final examination, you will be asked to submit a portfolio. It will be worth ten points toward your final examination. To prepare your portfolio, you will be expected to select five samples of your independent work in biology from the list of possible portfolio elements described on the following pages. You are encouraged to think carefully about this list and to choose portfolio elements that reflect your interests and/or talents.

You should add samples of your work to your portfolio throughout the year so that you have a diversity of potential portfolio elements to select from as the due date approaches. For each portfolio element that you select, you must complete a self-reflection card. The self-reflection should be written on a 3" × 5" index card and should include answers to these questions:

---

[8] *This is a shortened version of a portfolio plan developed by Susan Holt, Williamsville East School, NY. Used with permission.*

Figure 8.18
Self-Reflection Form

Self-Reflection Form
(Rationale for including this item in my portfolio)

Name: _____ Date: _____

Title of the Assignment:_____

Please describe this entry:_____

_____

How long did you work on this entry?_____

Who else worked with you? _____

Why did you choose this piece for your portfolio? _____

_____

Why do you think it is a good piece of work?_____

_____

What does this work show about your abilities?_____

_____

---

1. Why did you choose this portfolio element?
2. What did you learn about biology/life science by doing this element?

NOTE: In lieu of the index card, you might instead want to use the self-reflection form shown in Figure 8.18.

Your selection of portfolio elements must be done so that your portfolio includes evidence of your abilities in the following areas:

- Using decision-making skills to seek a solution to a personal or societal issue
- Using the inquiry process to plan and carry out an extended laboratory investigation
- Learn independently by acquiring and processing information
- Communicating in written, oral, and graphic form

- Improving your work through peer and self-evaluation
- Working collaboratively

Figure 8.19 lists a variety of possible portfolio elements and offers supporting examples. Portfolio elements that are asterisked are ones that may be accomplished by doing regular classroom assignments during the school year. You do not need to complete a portfolio contract for these. The portfolio elements that are not asterisked are ones that you may choose to do as independent projects. You will need to submit a contract for any independent project. This contract will ensure that independent projects will be appropriate for the portfolio. Your contract should include a description of the element and the method you will use to accomplish your task.

Figure 8.19 Portfolio Elements and Examples

Possible Portfolio Elements	Examples
LAB EXPERIMENT AND REPORT* Complete an individual lab experiment in which you select a question, then design, conduct, and report on an experiment that answers this question.	• Rapid Radish or Fast Plant Experiments
ORGANISM LOG* Complete a log/diary with information on a plant or an animal that is raised in the classroom for a period of at least 10 weeks. Your log should include information that you have gathered from both observation and library research.	• Diary of a Plant • Diary of an Animal
WRITTEN REPORT-BIOLOGY* Complete a two-page written report during class time. To prepare for writing your report, you will be expected to research a topic related to biology, organize the information, and prepare a concept map or an organized set of note cards.	• Human Genetic Disease Report
ORAL REPORT—BIOLOGY* Produce a videotaped ten-minute oral report on a topic related to biology. To prepare for videotaping your report, you will be expected to research the topic, organize the information, and prepare a concept map or an organized set of note cards.	• Human System Malfunction Report
DECISION MAKING—ECOLOGY* Participate in a cooperative learning project in which three students work together to investigate an issue related to ecology. Members of the group cooperate to produce a written report, an oral report, and a poster on the causes of, effects of, and possible solutions for problems resulting from human technology. All members of the group then take an individual essay examination on the topic.	• Impact of Humans on the Environment Project
DECISION MAKING—BIOETHICS* Participate in a cooperative learning project in which three students work together to investigate an issue related to bioethics. Members of the group cooperate to learn about the personal, scientific, social, and ethical dimensions of the issue and prepare to participate in a debate on the issue.	• Do People Have the Right to _____ Project
CAREER RESEARCH AND SHADOWING* Prepare an oral report, a written report, a scrapbook, or a videotape on a biology or biology-related career that you have selected. Collect information on this career and interview several individuals working in this field.	• Select a biology career. • Select a career such as law or history or journalism that may be related to biology.

*Can be accomplished during school year.

Text copyright © Jack Hassard. Illustration copyright © Good Year Books

Figure 8.19 Portfolio Elements and Examples (continued)

Possible Portfolio Elements	Examples
COMPUTER TECHNOLOGY/TELECOMMUNICATIONS PROJECT* Use a variety of computer network facilities to collect information for one of the reports or projects that you do this year. Keep a journal on the types of computer technology that you have used, how this technology was used, and the kinds of information available through that technology.	• Keep a record of how you used the computer facilities to gather information on a biology topic such as cloning, ecosystems, and human diseases.
MULTIMEDIA PRESENTATION Produce a multimedia presentation that uses slides, videotape, laser disk images, and a written or taped script to present information on a biology-related topic.	• Produce a multimedia presentation for the school's "Unity and Diversity Day" or for a future biology class.
SCHOOL/COMMUNITY SERVICE PROJECT Complete twenty hours of biology-related community or school service. You will be expected to keep a journal that details what kinds of things you did and explains how your experiences related to biology concepts.	• Volunteer to work at a hospital, research lab, nursing home, zoo, park, or museum. • Volunteer to be a tutor or lab assistant for biology classes.
FIELD TRIP REPORT Plan a field trip to a museum, nature sanctuary, park, research lab, or other biology-related location. Collect information on the site, visit the site, and prepare an oral report, a written report, a scrapbook, or a videotape about the field trip.	• Select a local site and plan a trip for your classmates. • Select a distant site and plan a trip for your family.
TEACHING EXPERIENCE Present a hands-on biology lesson for preschool or elementary schoolchildren that you prepare and actually teach. Submit your lesson plans before you teach the lesson. Following the teaching, write a report on the teaching experience.	• Show preschool children how plants grow from seeds. • Help elementary school children set up a school garden or a classroom aquarium.

*Can be accomplished during school year.

Figure 8.19 Portfolio Elements and Examples (continued)

Possible Portfolio Elements	Examples
GRAPHIC REPRESENTATION Create an original graphic such as a bulletin board, model, mobile, computer graphic, or series of photographs to represent related biological concepts. Your graphic should be accompanied by a written explanation or an explanatory key.	• Make a three-dimensional model illustrating a biology concept. • Make a mobile on a biology concept.
CONCEPT EXPLANATION Become a "specialist" on a unit that you find particularly interesting by reading beyond the required course level. Make a concept map for this unit that includes your independent study. Your teacher will interview you and ask you to explain your concept map.	• Concept-map the chapters in a unit using three Advanced Placement biology texts.
INTERDISCIPLINARY PROJECT Select a biology topic and demonstrate/explain how it relates to four other subject areas, such as English, social studies, math, art, music, physical education, or business.	• Explain how "Unity and Diversity" or "Constancy and Change" is a theme that is common to many subject areas.
SCRAPBOOK OF BIOLOGY IN THE NEWS Prepare a scrapbook of newspaper and magazine articles that relate to biology. Collect at least ten articles per week for ten weeks. Organize the scrapbook into sections that correspond to the units of study in your biology class. Write a brief explanation of how the information in each article relates to your life.	• Collect biology articles from your family's newspapers and magazines. • Select a topic of interest to you, then photocopy and collect recent articles on this topic.
CREATIVE PROJECT Use your ingenuity, your talent, and/or your sense of humor to demonstrate independent learning about a biology topic that interests you. Consult the card file of suggestions in the classroom to give you an idea of the diversity of projects that you can do, but remember that you are not limited to these.	• For ideas, see the "How to Show What You Know" poster or the "Idea" card file in the classroom.

EVALUATING PERFORMANCE USING ACTIVE ASSESSMENT TOOLS: A THEORETICAL PERSPECTIVE

An effective assessment strategy should be based on the philosophy or rationale of the course or unit that students are studying, as well as the intended learning outcomes of the experience. Advocating a curriculum based on science thinking skills and hands-on learning, but assessing outcomes using true-false and fill-in-the-blank tests is incongruent.

A valid assessment system must take into account three major learning outcome areas: psychomotor skills, cognitions and cognitive skills, and attitudes. One plan that meets this requirement is the Florida Assessment Plan, which was developed at Florida State University and Georgia State University. Based on separate research and development projects at these universities, the system incorporates learning outcomes with assessment items based on psychomotor learning, cognitive thinking, and affective learning.

In this system, eight categories of intellectual skills or types of learning were identified and used to create a matrix of outcomes and assessments in Earth science, life science, and physical science. Let's take a look at the system, and then use it to develop test items for our science courses.

The eight categories of intellectual skills or types of learning were these:

1. Motor skills
2. Verbal skills
3. Discrimination
4. Concept learning
5. Rule learning
6. Problem solving
7. Cognitive strategy
8. Attitudes

As you can see, the first category describes psychomotor skills; categories two through seven cover cognitions and cognitive skills; and the final category identifies attitudes. Using this system enables you to take a systematic approach to developing effective assessment items for quizzes and tests. Take a moment to look at the table in Figure 8.20, which shows how the eight intellectual skills correlate to learning outcomes, human performance, and assessment items.

Let's look at some examples of assessment items given several learning outcomes. You can refer to these examples as model assessment items and make use of them as you design your own.

(Psycho)motor Skills

In an inquiry-oriented, hands-on science course, students will be involved in the manipulation of laboratory apparatus, scientific instruments, and the tools necessary to carry out investigations and activities. Although the assessment of motor skills, or chains, may seem to involve motor skills only, it's worth noting that cognitive skills are usually involved in any activity of this type. In any case, providing students feedback through psychomotor assessments is a powerful way to reinforce the importance of motor skills and learning in the science classroom.

Example: Motor Skills
Learning Outcome

Given a graduated cylinder, colored water, and an empty container and asked to put 40 mL of liquid into the empty container, the student manipulates the beaker and the graduated cylinder by measuring the 40 mL of the liquid and pouring this measured amount into the empty container.

Assessment Item

Here is a graduated cylinder, some colored water in a beaker, and an empty container. Pour 40 mL of the colored liquid into the empty container.

Cognitions and Cognitive Skills

As previously noted, there are six categories of assessment items that, when combined, provide measures of cognitions and cognitive skills. There is a hierarchy implied in the categories. In this section we will use the Florida approach

Figure 8.20 Active Learning Assessment System

Learning Skill	Learning Outcome (Action Word)	Human Performance	Assessment Example
1. Motor Skills	Manipulates	Executes a skilled motor performance	Weighs substance on a balance
2. Verbal Skills	Recalls	States a fact, makes a generalization, or gives a description	Lists minerals in Mohs' scale of hardness
3. Discrimination	Discriminates	Distinguishes objects or object features as the same or different	Tells whether photographs of galaxies are the same or different
4. Concept learning	Identifies or classifies	Classifies an object or a situation in accordance with a definition	Classifies granite as an igneous rock
5. Rule learning	Demonstrates	Applies a rule, law, or concept to a specific example	Determines the density of a mineral
6. Problem solving	Generates	Generates a solution to a novel problem	Determines the effect of velocity on erosion along a stream
7. Cognitive strategy	Originates	Originates a novel problem and solution	Gets an answer to "I wonder what would happen if . . ."
8. Attitudes	Chooses	Chooses a course of action and/or expresses a feeling toward a person, an object, or an event	Writes a letter to a Congressional Representative supporting air-quality standards

---

Figure 8.21 Rock Chart

Characteristic	Color	Crystal Size	Hardness	Texture
Rock 1				
Rock 2				
Rock 3				

---

because it is more closely aligned with the recent emphasis on cognitive thinking and cognitive science. Following, then, are the six categories of cognitive thinking, along with examples of each.

1. Verbal Skills

This form of thinking finds students involved in recalling information, either verbally or in writing. Correct answers indicate that the student knows the proper sequence of words in response to a request for verbal information. This category represents the lowest level of cognitive thinking—the recall of information.

Example: Verbal Skills
Learning Outcome

Given a volume of a liquid (melted paraffin) that is changing from a liquid to a solid, the student identifies the change by stating that the liquid is "freezing."

Assessment Item

When the liquid paraffin forms solid paraffin, what process has taken place?
(Answer: The process is called freezing.)

2. Discrimination

When students discriminate, they decide whether or not things are identical. Discrimination does not imply, however, that students can identify the specific properties of the things that are the same or different.

Example: Discrimination
Learning Outcome

Given granite and a set of igneous rocks, the student discriminates between granite and other plutonic rocks.

Assessment Item

For each characteristic listed, indicate with a *d* or an *s* whether the rocks in the new set are the same as or different from granite (Figure 8.21).

3. Concept Learning

In concept learning, students do one of two things. (1) They recognize a class of objects, object characteristics, or events. In this case, students have learned the concept of class to the extent that they can classify examples by instant recognition. Recognition can involve any one or all of the senses—sight, touch, smell, taste, or sound (see Example 1). (2) Concept learning also involves classification per se. In this case, students use a definition to put something into a class (or to put some things into classes). Correct responses indicate that students know the parameters of the class or classes, and they can either verbalize them or use them when asked to do so (see Example 2).

Example 1: Concept Learning
Learning Outcome

Given the names of parts of a typical plant cell, the student draws a cell and names the given parts.

Figure 8.22
Moon Map

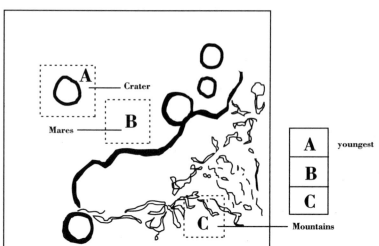

Assessment Item
Draw a plant cell with these parts shown and labeled.

a. Cell wall
b. Nucleus
c. Chloroplasts

Example 2: Concept Learning
Learning Outcome
Given a map of the moon with features labeled, the student classifies the labeled features according to age.)

Assessment Item
The map (see Figure 8.22) shows a region of the moon with three areas marked. In boxes to the right of the map, place the letters of the features in order of age, listing the youngest first.

4. Rule Learning
Rule learning engages students in applying specific concepts, rules, or procedures to a specific task. The key notion here is the process of applying rules. Indeed application is an important part of the learning cycle that has been developed throughout this book. Students need

Figure 8.23 Moon Problem

_____50-foot nylon rope

_____star map

_____5 gallons of water

_____box of matches

_____two 100-pound tanks of oxygen

_____food concentrate

_____life raft

_____first-aid kit

_____solar-powered heater

_____magnetic compass

_____signal flares

_____case of powdered milk

_____solar-powered FM walkie-talkie

_____parachute silk

opportunities to apply what they are learning, and they need assessment feedback on their progress.

Example: Rule Learning
Learning Outcome

Given a hypothetical situation in which the student crash lands on the moon's surface and given a list of items that survive the crash, the student ranks those items in terms of their importance to reaching the safety of a moon base.

Assessment Item

Imagine that you are a member of a moon landing crew whose spaceship has just crashed on the lighted side of the moon's surface. Your survival depends on reaching a moon base some 5 miles away. Figure 8.23 shows 14 items left intact after the crash landing. Rank them in order of importance to reaching the moon base. Place a number 1 by the most important, number 2 by the second most important, and so on.

5. Problem Solving

When students use two or more rules, definitions, or concepts to solve a problem, they are generating ideas, solutions, and procedures. Like rule learning, problem solving involves the application of scientific concepts; however, it occurs at a higher level of cognitive functioning. Students benefit from many opportunities to solve problems and, by extension, from assessment strategies that test their problem-solving abilities.

Example: Problem Solving
Learning Outcome

Given a hypothetical situation describing an individual's energy requirements and given materials that model these needs, the student generates a system to fulfill the energy requirements.

Assessment Item

Imagine this situation. Your neighbors are planning to add a garage to their house. Their energy needs include lighting, heating, and power to run a motor for the garage door. The energy they have selected is electricity. You have been given a dry-cell battery, a light bulb, a piece of nichrome wire, and a small motor. Using any or all of these materials, make a system that shows how your neighbors can meet their energy needs.

6. Cognitive Strategy

Cognitive strategy ultimately refers to student creativity. The key notion here is originating a plan or an idea. Cognitive strategy means combining ideas to propose and solve problems. Students know the material sufficiently well to identify a problem area and organize the proper concepts and procedures to solve it. Many of the performance tasks that were introduced earlier in this chapter involve cognitive strategy.

Example: Cognitive Strategy
Learning Outcome

Given an organic and inorganic fertilizer, soil, containers, and seeds, the student designs and conducts an experiment to find out which fertilizer is more effective.

Assessment Item

(For individuals) You will find before you the materials you may use to carry out an experiment. You are to design the experiment yourself. Its purpose is to determine which fertilizer is better for making the plants healthier and able to produce more peppers.

(For groups) You will find before your team the materials you may use to carry out an experiment. You are to work together with your team members to design the experiment. Its purpose is to determine which fertilizer is better for making the plants healthier and able to produce more peppers.

Attitudes

Affective outcomes, like psychomotor and cognitive outcomes, can and should be assessed. In the model being presented here, "affects" are classified as "attitudes."

Attitudes involve, among other behaviors, choosing. If students make a choice, they are deciding to behave in a certain way. A student might choose to say that smoking is harmful, but after school be seen smoking a cigarette. Similarly, a student might say that recycling is an important part of a family's responsibility to the environment, but not make use of trash stream separators at restaurants or in the school cafeteria.

Example 1: Attitudes
Learning Outcome
Given a list of endangered animal species and a statement that the animals are being killed in such numbers as to risk their extinction, the student chooses to speak in favor of protecting the animals.

Assessment Item
The bald eagle, blue whale, California condor, Everglades kite, red wolf, key deer, cougar, alligator, and whooping crane are all examples of animals in the United States that are endangered species. These animals may all become extinct, never again to be part of the Earth's ecosystem. What should be done about this problem?

There are other techniques that you can use to assess attitudes. One technique involves the semantic differential. To use the technique, you select a concept or an idea, then develop a set of relevant bipolar adjectives or adjective phrases. For example, suppose you wanted to assess your students' attitudes toward science. You could use the following semantic differential scale.

The students simply check a line along the continuum, indicating what their attitude is with respect to each bipolar pair. NOTE: You'll probably find it useful to summarize the class's responses first, then calculate a mean for each bipolar adjective pair. Of course, many other "concepts" can be assessed using this technique. You might, for example, assess student attitudes about the following:

- Chemistry
- Rocks
- Science course
- This unit
- Alcohol/drugs
- Space exploration

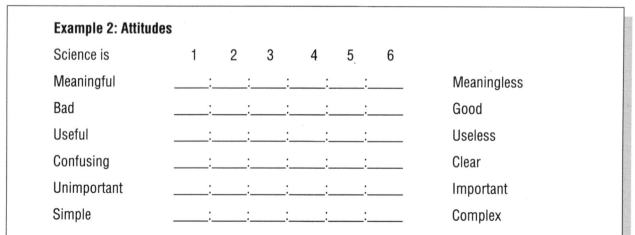

Example 2: Attitudes

Science is	1	2	3	4	5	6	
Meaningful	___:___:___:___:___:___						Meaningless
Bad	___:___:___:___:___:___						Good
Useful	___:___:___:___:___:___						Useless
Confusing	___:___:___:___:___:___						Clear
Unimportant	___:___:___:___:___:___						Important
Simple	___:___:___:___:___:___						Complex

SUMMARY

Teaching science as inquiry behooves us to reconsider the way that student learning is assessed. The key concept in assessing student learning is the connection between the goals of science teaching and the expression of student learning. Not all student learning can be expressed in terms of answers on a multiple-choice test. In this chapter you were introduced to informal (observations, asking questions, listening to student talk) and formal assessment tools (student writing, performance tasks). As you look back and decide which tools to employ, keep in mind the importance of science as inquiry and how you will "measure" student inquiry.

PART III CONSTRUCTIVISM IN THE BAG:
ACTIVE SCIENCE LESSONS

This book has focused on the importance of establishing classroom environments in which students are active learners. Research has shown that regardless of the strategy being used by the teacher—questioning, cooperative learning, discrepant events (EEEPs), and so on, the most important element in fostering achievement and learning is an active student.

Chapters 9 and 10 contain thirty-one active science lessons organized into the following subject areas: Earth Science, Environmental Science (both in Chapter 9), Life Science, and Physical Science (in Chapter 10). Every lesson includes Internet resources that complement the subject matter. Additionally, many of these lessons incorporate the use of the Internet into their design.

DEVELOPING THE LESSONS

The lessons you'll find here are based on sketches and outlines developed at teaching seminars conducted over the past several years.

In preparation for the seminars, a four-stage plan based on the Constructivist Learning Model (CLM) was developed. The four stages used are: Invitation, Exploration, Explanation, and Taking

Figure III.1
Bags of science equipment as shown here were used by teachers to develop active learning and Web-based lessons in the activity "Constructivism in the Bag" in the author's seminars.

Action. Figure III.2 outlines the key elements of the constructivist learning cycle.

In a session entitled "Constructivism in the Bag," teacher participants selected from a bag of science materials grouped into Earth, environmental, life, and physical sciences. An Earth science bag, for example, might contain a collection of rocks, a hand-held lens, and a metric rule. Physical science bags might contain lenses, batteries, motors, wire, light bulbs, Slinkys™, prisms, and/or mirrors; life science bags might contain animal replicas, shells, soil, and/or seeds (Figure III.1).

The teacher teams then worked together on lesson sequences using the "Constructivism in the Bag" form (Figure III.3) to guide their work. This form outlines the four key elements of the constructivism lesson (Invitation, Exploration, Explanation, and Taking Action). The task for the teams was to develop a lesson sequence as well as to design posters summarizing their work. Some of the posters are shown in Figure III.4. As a final step, the teachers exchanged materials and shared ideas.

INVITATION
Purpose: The CLM begins by engaging the student with an invitation to learn. The invitation stage helps spark interest and expose initial ideas students have about the topic.

Figure III.2
Constructivist Learning Cycle

Constructivist Learning Model (CLM)

Invitation

Purpose: The CLM begins by engaging the student with an invitation to learn. The invitation stage helps spark interest and expose initial ideas students have about the topic.

• Teacher establishes a context for learning and invites student to learn about a topic by:
 —asking provocative questions
 —conducting a demonstration of a discrepant event or an EEEP and asking students to ponder, think about, and predict
 —asking students what they know and questions they have about a topic

Exploration

Purpose: To provide an opportunity for students to explore phenomena or concepts through focused activities.

• Teacher plans specific activities that enable students to test their predictions or initial ideas as well as engage in observation, data collection, and data interpretation experience.

• Students work in cooperative groups to brainstorm, test ideas, discuss, and debate ideas.

Explanation

Purpose: To enable students to propose explanations based on their own activity and to help them construct new views of the concepts.

• Teacher plans activities that will enable students to communicate their ideas to each other as well as construct new explanations for concepts and phenomena.

• Students work in small groups, but share ideas with the whole class through public displays of their work, poster reports, and class discussion.

Take Action

Purpose: To take action on what they learned.

• Teacher works with students to help them take personal and social action on issues related to the content of the concepts and phenomena.

• Students apply knowledge and skills, share information about the topic, ask new questions, make decisions, develop products, and write letters.

Figure III.3

CONSTRUCTIVISM IN THE BAG

THE DESIGN TEAM ACTIVITY

CREATING CONSTRUCTIVIST SCIENCE LESSON SEQUENCES

Inquiry. This is an open-ended inquiry activity. You will work with your science curriculum design team and create a sequence of activities using a four-stage learning cycle. Obtain a "constructivist science baggie" and use it to frame your team's thinking and planning as you design a sequence of activities. Be prepared to mini-teach and/or share your product with others.

Topic of the Teaching Sequence

_____

Key Preliminary Decisions

    Grade Level and Subject

_____

    Big Idea

_____

_____

_____

    Fundamental Concept(s) That Your Team Wishes to Teach

_____

_____

_____

    Key Objectives/Goal

_____

_____

_____

Grouping of Students

_____

Materials

_____

Key Elements of the Learning Cycle Sequence

1. Invitation. (Invite student ideas.) Describe how you will find out about students' prior knowledge, ideas, and beliefs about the concepts in your sequence.

- Provocative Questions
- EEEPs
- Discrepant Events
- T-charts

- Interview Questions
- Interesting Challenges
- Demonstrations
- Concept Maps

Describe your activity or procedure:

_____

_____

_____

2. Exploration. (Students explore phenomena through focused activity.) Describe at least one activity that you will use to assist your students in exploring the fundamental concept(s).

- Inquiry
- Writing to Learn
- Hands-on
- Observation
- Data Collection

- Data Interpretation
- Asking Questions
- Constructing Explanations
- Communicating Ideas
- Cooperative Groups

Describe your activity:

_____

_____

_____

What are some questions you will be asking students to help them focus on fundamental concept(s)?

_____

_____

3. Explanation. (Help students propose and compare ideas.) Describe how the students will have the opportunity to hear differing views to talk aloud about their ideas to test ideas against the "the scientist's" ideas.

- Small-Group Discussion
- Debating Alternative Ideas
- Large-Group Discussion
- Displays of Concepts
- Constructing Models

- Journal/Log Writing
- Active Reading
- Collaborative Group Questioning
- Explaining Ideas
- Defending Models

Describe how you will assist students to form explanations of the fundamental concepts:

_____

_____

_____

4. Taking Action. (Students apply their knowledge.) Describe at least one activity that will assist students in taking personal and/or social action on issues related to the content of the concepts, or to assist them in applying the concepts to new situations.

- Designing a long term research project
- Writing letters
- Making posters about the topic
- Hands-on activities

- Sharing knowledge
- Journal/log writing
- Concept maps
- Seeking answers to their own questions

Describe the plan to assist student in taking action:

_____

_____

_____

- Teacher establishes a context for learning and invites student to learn about a topic by:
- Asking provocative questions
- Conducting a demonstration of a discrepant even or an EEEP and asking students to ponder, think about, predict about the topic
- Asking students what they know and questions they have about a topic

EXPLORATION

Purpose: To provide an opportunity for students to explore phenomena or concepts through focused activities.

- Teacher plans specific activities that enable students to test their predictions or initial ideas as well as engage in observation, data collection, and data interpretation experience.
- Students work in cooperative groups to brainstorm, test, discuss, and debate ideas.

EXPLANATION

Purpose: To enable students to propose explanations based on their own activity and to help them construct new views of the concepts.

- Teacher plans activities that will enable students to communicate their ideas to each other as well as construct new explanations for concepts and phenomena.
- Students work in small groups, but share ideas with the whole class through displays of their work, poster reports, and class discussion.

TAKE ACTION

Purpose: To take action on what they learned.

- Teacher works with students to help them take personal and social action on issues related to the content of the concepts and phenomena.
- Students apply knowledge and skills, share information about the topic, ask new questions, make decisions, develop products, and write letters.

USING THE LESSONS

The lessons that follow can be used in any sequence. They integrate many of the strategies that are developed earlier in the book. Each lesson plan includes eight elements:

- Goal—Lesson objective(s)
- Overview—Description of student responsibilities
- Materials—listing of simple and easily obtainable supplies needed for the lesson
- Invitation—Stage 1 of Constructivist Learning Model, in which students' prior knowledge and ideas are identified
- Exploration—Stage 2, in which students explore the key phenomena in the lesson
- Explanation—Stage 3, in which students propose and compare ideas
- Taking Action—Stage 4, in which students take personal and/or social action on issues

Figure III.4
To turn posters into lessons, the author collaborated with Daniel Whitehair, a science educator in New York and graduate student in science education at Georgia State University, to develop the 31 complete lessons that form the basis of Chapters 9 and 10.

CAN T-REX LIVE IN NEW YORK?

Invitation
Students create a T-Rex T-chart and share results with class

Exploration
Students go on a "scavenger hunt" on the Internet answering key questions about dinosaurs' living environments

Explanation
Students construct model of T-Rex's niche and habitat

Take Action
Students view "The Lost World."

related to the content of the lesson
- Internet Resources—Identification of relevant sites on the Internet

Chapters 9 and 10 contain a collection of lesson plans that are based on a constructivist and inquiry approach to science learning. Each lesson is self-contained, and thus you can choose to use the lessons in whatever sequence that you wish. Each lesson also includes Internet sites that you might wish to use in the lessons. NOTE: All of the Web sites listed for the lessons in Chapters 9 and 10 can be found in the *Minds On Science* Web site: http://www.gsu.edu/~mstjrh/mindsonscience.html

CHAPTER 9   **EARTH SCIENCE AND ENVIRONMENTAL SCIENCE LESSONS**

EARTH SCIENCE LESSONS

- Making a Cloud

- Igneous Rocks: Granite

- The Center of the Earth

- Rock Types: Igneous, Metamorphic, Sedimentary

- Geysers

- Mohs' Scale of Mineral Hardness

- Geology: Mohs' Scale

- Rock Formations

MAKING A CLOUD

Goal: Students become more aware of cloud formations after completing this activity, which illustrates the principles involved in cloud formation. More specifically, students observe the importance of a nuclei-providing medium on which water vapor can condense, forming a "cloud." Lab skill, observation skills, and ability to deduce will be enhanced.

Overview: Initially, students will complete a T-chart on clouds. Groups of students then formulate a hypothesis on how clouds are formed. Groups make a cloud in a jar using simple equipment; they then formulate a new hypothesis on the formation of clouds. Students finish up by researching local weather and finding out how technology is used to predict weather patterns.

Materials: Bags containing a wide-mouth gallon pickle jar, a heavy-duty clear plastic bag, rubber bands, matches

INVITATION
Students complete a T-chart on clouds. One column should read "Things we know about clouds"; the other should read "Things we would like to know about clouds." Cloud formation should emerge as a topic in either column. Discussion focuses on a study of how clouds form.

EXPLORATION
Students are divided into small cooperative learning groups. Each group should develop a hypothesis about how clouds are formed and record its ideas. Groups are given a bag containing the lab materials. Groups should then follow this procedure: Place 20 ml of water in a jar. Place a lit match into the jar. Quickly place a plastic bag over the mouth of the jar and secure it with (a) rubber band(s). Push the bag into the jar quickly, then pull the bag out. Observe and

Figure 9.1
Making a Cloud

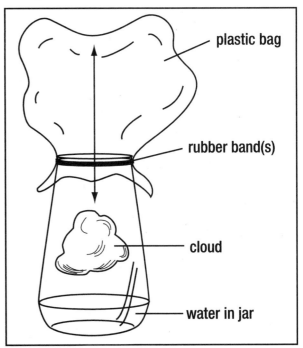

record what happens. Each group should formulate a new hypothesis on the formation of clouds.

EXPLANATION
Groups present their hypotheses and observations to the class. The teacher intervenes to ensure that information is accurate. The water produces high humidity in the jar and the smoke provides nuclei on which the water vapor can condense. As the bag is pushed in, the pressure and temperature in the jar increase, causing the jar to clear. Upon pulling the bag out, pressure and temperature drop, allowing water vapor to condense and produce a "cloud" inside the jar.

TAKE ACTION
Students could track local weather conditions for a few days and make predictions about cloud coverage according to conditions. Students could also contact and/or visit a local meteorologist, or research radar and other technology used in weather detection and forecasting.

Internet Resources

http://www.cis.hut.fi/~jucca/cloud/cloud.html
Cloud Classifier Home Page

http://covis.atmos.uiuc.edu/guide/clouds/high.
clouds/html
UIUC Cloud Catalog

http://www.usatoday.com/weather/wcirrus.htm
Cirrus Clouds

http://msslsp.mssl.ucl.ac.uk/orgs/cp/html/atmos/
secondary/clouds.html
Clouds–Climate Predictions

http://web1.earthwatch.com/
3-D Weather Web Site

http://www.weather.com/weather/maphowto/
doppler.html
Doppler Radar Maps

IGNEOUS ROCKS: GRANITE

Goal: This activity, done in cooperative learning groups, challenges students' abilities to observe, examine, inquire, and conclude. Students become familiar with igneous rocks, their formation, and composition.

Overview: Students brainstorm about rocks and create a concept map based on their brainstorming. In groups, students examine a sample rock and try to deduce facts about its composition. Students share resulting observations/deductions with the class. Groups then reevaluate their initial concept map and modify it, if necessary. This concept map is to be turned in.

Materials: Bags containing a sample of granite, a small magnifying glass, newsprint, markers

INVITATION

As a class, students brainstorm about rocks. Terms are written on the board/large newsprint by the teacher. Groups then create a concept map utilizing the terms on the board.

EXPLORATION

Each group receives a bag containing a sample of granite. Groups examine the sample, make observations about the sample, and attempt to determine facts about its composition. Groups then answer questions such as the following: How many different substances make it up? What are some characteristics of those substances? *What type of rock is it? What is it?* All observations and deductions should be recorded on newsprint.

EXPLANATION

Students share resulting observations/deductions with the class. Teacher intervention, if necessary, consists of informing the class that the sample is granite, an igneous rock composed of feldspar, quartz, and mica. The class discusses the characteristics of igneous rocks. Groups then

Figure 9.2
Granite

reevaluate their initial concept map and modify/change it if necessary. The concept map is turned in, along with observations. See Figure 9.3 for the components of granite.

TAKE ACTION
Students could conduct research on the other two types of rocks (sedimentary and metamorphic) and/or on feldspar, quartz, and mica. Students could also research the type of rocks found in their geographical area, then make conclusions about that area.

Internet Resources
http://www.geosociety.org/index.htm
Geological Society of America

http://geology.usgs.gov/index.shtml
USGS–Geological Survey

http://www.esd.mun.ca/~gac/GEOSITES/geosites.html
University Sites–Geology

http://www.colby.edu/geology/geology.html
What Geologists Do

http://seis.natsci.csulb.edu/GRANITE/GRANITE.html
Granite Photo, Info

THE CENTER OF THE EARTH

Goal: In this activity, students become familiar with the composition of the Earth. They learn to identify the Earth's four main layers, and the effects they may have on us. In cooperative learning groups, students apply knowledge and exercise their creativity.

Overview: Students read and discuss an excerpt from Jules Verne's *Journey to the Center of the Earth.* In groups, they create a small model of the Earth, revealing its composition. Students pre-

sent their models to the class. Models are then displayed. As a final step, students investigate the composition of the moon and other planets for comparison with the Earth's composition.

Materials: Bags containing materials for making a model: small polystyrene foam ball, various colors of modeling clay, cotton, paper, etc.; colored pencils/markers; other basic supplies, as desired; copies of an excerpt from *Journey to the Center of the Earth*

INVITATION
Students receive a copy of an excerpt from *Journey to the Center of the Earth.* They discuss the reading and Verne himself, answering such questions as: Would such a journey be possible? Did people in Verne's time believe that such a journey was possible? If it wouldn't be possible, why not?

EXPLORATION
Students are divided into cooperative learning groups. In these groups, they research the composition of the Earth and design and create a small model. Accompanying this model should be a written summary of the group's work and its findings.

EXPLANATION
Once the models and the reports have been completed, each group presents its final project (model and report) to the class. Final projects are then displayed. Teachers should use an alternative form of assessment to evaluate the model and teamwork.

TAKE ACTION
Students could review the questions they answered in the Invitation section, and con~ their responses to those they would give They could also investigate the comr~ moon and other planets for comp~ Earth's. Additionally, students~ any of Verne's books and/or~

211

Figure 9.3
Igneous Rocks Web page
"Igneous Rocks" home page from http://www.science.ubc.ca/-geo1202/igneous/igneous.html Web site.
Reprinted by permission of the University of British Columbia.

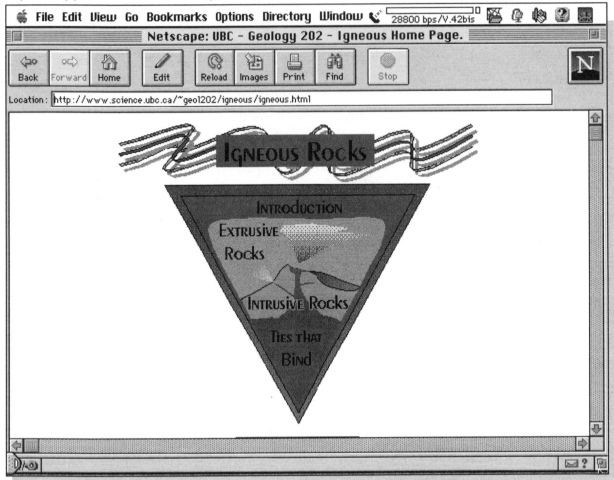

Internet Resources
http://www.primenet.com/~oznet/index.html
Earth Science Home Page

http://avery.med.virginia.edu/~mtp0f/flips/
jules.html
Life and Works of Jules Verne

ROCK TYPES: IGNEOUS, METAMORPHIC, SEDIMENTARY

Goal: In this activity, students gain insight into three different types of rocks and how each is d. Observational, research, and inference-kills are enhanced in this cooperative ity.

Overview: Students brainstorm about rocks. In groups, students make observations and inferences about a rock, utilizing as many of the terms from their brainstorming list as possible. Each group then conducts research to verify its inferences and presents its findings to the class. The class revises its initial brainstorming list. To finish up, students research types of rock from the local area.

Materials: Bags containing a rock and a magnifying glass (use different rock types in the various bags); books; computer(s) with Internet access

INVITATION

Students are asked to brainstorm about rocks. Teacher records all suggestions on the board/ newsprint. Students are then divided into groups and given a bag containing a rock and a magnifying glass. Groups observe their rock and make at least five inferences about it, using as many of the terms as possible from their brainstorming list. Observations and inferences should be recorded.

EXPLORATION

Groups research their rock in order to verify their five inferences. Utilizing the Internet can be a very fruitful and efficient way for student groups to conduct their research. Some informative sites that groups may want to access are listed under the Internet Resources section that follows. Teachers may need to assist the groups in determining what type of rock they have. Once the type has been determined, students' search can be facilitated.

EXPLANATION

Groups present to the class their rock, their five inferences, and their factual findings. After the final presentation, the class revisits its initial list and amends it to make it a more accurate and comprehensive list about rocks.

TAKE ACTION

Students could collect rock samples from their geographical area. The samples could be classified and certain inferences made about the geological history of that area. Visits to any local rock formations could be interesting as well.

Internet Resources

http://dekalb.dc.peachnet.edu/~pgore/geology/ geo101/igneous.htm
Igneous Rocks

http://duke.usask.ca/~reeves/prog/geoe118/ geoe118.013.html
Igneous Rocks Classification

http://dekalb.dc.peachnet.edu/~pgore/geology/ geo101/meta.htm
Metamorphic Rocks

http://www.willowgrove.district96.k12.il.us/ RocksandMinerals/metamorphic.html
Metamorphic Rocks

http://scienceweb.dao.nrc.ca/burgess/geology/ cycle6.html
Sedimentary Rock

http://www.dc.peachnet.edu/~pgore/geology/ geo102/sed102.htm
Sedimentary Rock

http://www.purchon.co.uk/science/sediment.html
Sedimentary Rock

http://geology.usgs.gov/index.shtml
USGS–Geological Survey

GEYSERS

Goal: Students participate in a hands-on cooperative activity giving them insight into how geysers function. In the process, they gain experience in laboratory work and hone their observational skills. At the end of the activity, students will be able to describe how a geyser works.

Overview: Students watch and discuss a video on Old Faithful. In groups, students theorize about the mechanism of a geyser. Groups then conduct an experiment that demonstrates geyser functioning. Groups record the procedure and results. To expand their knowledge, students can research geyser numbers and activity in their area, in the country, or worldwide.

Materials: Bags containing a funnel, a large coffee can or pot as tall as the funnel, a piece of plastic tubing (about 1 m); video on Old Faithful

Figure 9.4
Old Faithful Web page
Old Faithful Geyser of California home page from
www.oldfaithfulgeyser.com/index.html Web site.
Reprinted by permission of Old Faithful Geyser of
California.

INVITATION

Students watch a video about Old Faithful, located in Yellowstone National Park. As part of the discussion, any student who has seen a geyser can share his or her experience with the class. Students are then divided into small cooperative learning groups and theorize about the mechanism of a geyser. A member of each group records the group's theory.

EXPLORATION

Groups are given a bag containing the lab materials. Each group should conduct the following experiment recording each procedure and result:

Fill the pot with water; set the funnel mouth down into the water; place the end of the plastic tubing under the rim of the funnel; blow. Groups then answer the following questions regarding their experiment: Describe what happened and relate this to what you know about the structures of geysers. Some geysers erupt every few minutes, while others erupt every few years—what could be causing this difference?

EXPLANATION

Groups present their results and their answers to the class. As they do so, teachers can make a listing of answers on the board. A teacher-led

Figure 9.5
Geyser

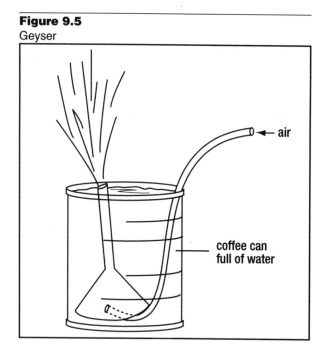

air

coffee can
full of water

discussion helps put the results in perspective and answer any remaining questions.

TAKE ACTION

Students could expand their knowledge by researching geyser numbers and activity in their area, in the country, or worldwide. Research on Yellowstone National Park would make for an excellent longer-term project.

Internet Resources

http://www.yellowstone.net/geysers.htm
Yellowstone Net Geyser Page

http://science.cc.uwf.edu/sh/curr/geothermal/geothermal.htm
Geothermal Energy

http://www.wyoming.com/~yellowstonejournal/YellowstoneGeysers.html
Yellowstone Geysers

http://vose.placo.com/geysers.html
Geysers

http://monhome.sw2.k12.wy.us/west/wyo/yellow.html
Yellowstone Geysers

MOHS' SCALE OF MINERAL HARDNESS

Goal: This lesson introduces students to Mohs' hardness scale and teaches them how it relates to the classification of minerals. Students create their own hardness scale using scientific and imaginative skills.

Overview: In groups, students answer questions related to the hardness of certain substances. Students then create a simple hardness scale using some of the items from Mohs' base scale. Student groups share their scales with the class. Further discussion and research might focus on some of the substances on Mohs' scale.

Materials: Bags containing substances from the scale: talc, gypsum, calcite, fluorite, apatite, feldspar, quartz, topaz, sapphire, diamond; small blackboards or items made of another slatelike substance; a chart with Mohs' scale; newsprint; markers

INVITATION

Teacher begins lesson by asking students thought-provoking questions such as these: "What are some differences between talc and diamonds?" "Why do we use chalk on blackboards?" "What if we used other substances on a blackboard?" "What is the principle behind the process of engraving?" "What is used to cut glass?" Questions should inspire discussion relating to the hardness of substances.

EXPLORATION

Groups of students receive a bag containing the lab materials. Groups test the hardness of the various substances in the bag, and make observations; small blackboards or items made of another slatelike substance are provided for scratching. Groups then design a simple scale of

Figure 9.6	Mohs' Hardness Scale
Hardness	**Material**
1	Talc—easily scratched by the fingernail
2	Gypsum—just scratched by the fingernail
3	Calcite—scratches and is scratched by a copper coin
4	Fluorite—not scratched by a copper coin and does not scratch glass
5	Apatite—just scratches glass and is easily scratched by a knife
6	Orthoclase—easily scratches glass and is just scratched by a file
7	Quartz—not scratched by a file
8	Topaz
9	Corundum
10	Diamond

hardness—one appropriate for ranking not only the substances provided in the bag, but other substances as well. Groups create their scale on newsprint and present it to the class.

EXPLANATION

Teacher introduces Friedrich Mohs and his scale of hardness. Class discussion focuses first on how Mohs' scale compares with the various scales designed by the students. Should there be questions about the ranking of the items, additional class tests can be run on any of the substances. Discussion then turns to why hardness is an important feature, and who might need to use Mohs' scale.

TAKE ACTION

Each group could choose one of the items from the scale and do additional research on that substance. Research might focus on the answers to

these (and other) questions: What is it used for? Why is it relevant? Why is its position in Mohs' scale important to its features and functions? Research might be carried out via the Internet. Each group could create a brief report on the selected substance and present it to the class.

Internet Resources

http://bohler.com/moh.html
Mohs' Scale

http://www.agso.gov.au/education/crystals/crystals.html
Exploring Crystals—A Resource for Teachers

http://www.mcli.dist.maricopa.edu/aaim/linear/L0.html
Testing Mineral Hardness

GEOLOGY: CLASSIFYING ROCKS

Goal: This lesson provides students with insight into classification by feature. Working in cooperative groups, students utilize a streak plate, learn about degrees of hardness in geology, and design classification systems.

Overview: Groups of students create and share a classification system for the six rocks given them. Groups then reclassify their rocks based on one feature (hardness), and present their new classification system to the class. An informative discussion follows. To finish, students research nongeology professions that require knowledge of geology.

Materials: Bags containing 6 rocks and a scratch plate

INVITATION

Students are divided into groups. Each group receives a bag containing the six rocks. Groups are instructed to classify the rocks according to whatever system they design. They then summarize/explain their system in writing and present their final classification system to their classmates.

EXPLORATION

After a discussion of the different types of classification systems that the groups created, teacher introduces/expands on classification based on one feature. He or she asks students the following question: Why would classification by one feature even be useful? Teacher then asks for examples (e.g., horses classified by speed and not height). Class discusses "hardness" as a feature of rocks and how hardness can be significant. Teacher distributes scratch plates and instructs the groups to create a new classification scale utilizing the scratch plate and making "hardness" the principle feature by which to classify the rocks.

Figure 9.7 Mohs' Hardness Scale	
The scale has been extended as follows:	
Hardness	**Material**
1	Liquid
2–6	As indicated on the scale in Figure 9.7
7	Vitreous pure silica
8	Quartz
9	Topaz
10	Garnet
11	Fuzed zirconia
12	Fuzed alumina
13	Silicon carbide
14	Boron carbide
15	Diamond

EXPLANATION

Each group presents its new scale to the class. The teacher introduces Mohs' scale and explains/expands upon geologists' use of hardness as a critical feature of rocks. Teacher initiates class dialogue on this subject and assigns or distributes reading material on Mohs' scale, geology, etc. Alternatively, the teacher might opt to proceed to the Take Action section, in which students research careers in geology.

TAKE ACTION

Students should make a list of five nongeology professions that require knowledge of geology. (Teacher assistance may be required.) They should select one of the five on their list and use Internet resources to write a brief one-page report on that profession. If possible, students should interview an individual currently working in that profession (refer to Pitsco's "Ask an Expert" site) to complement their report.

Internet Resources

http://www.hws.edu/ACA/depts/geo/links.html
Geoscience Career Information

http://www.uwrf.edu/pes/geol/goejobs.html
Geology Careers Page

http://www.tntech.edu/www/acad/earth/CAREER.html
Career Opportunities in Geosciences

http://www.carleton.edu/curricular/GEOL/Career Opps.html
Career Information

http://www.colby.edu/geology/geology.html
What Geologists Do

http://www.geosociety.org/educate/career.htm
GeoSociety Career Center

http://www.brookes.ac.uk/geology/geoljobs.html
Geology Jobs Links Page

http://www.gphs.vuw.ac.nz/boards-of-studies/geol/geol-careers.html
Careers in Geology

http://www.askanexpert.askanexpert/
Pitsco's Ask an Expert

ROCK FORMATIONS

Goal: Students learn about the features of different types of rocks as they become familiar with famous rock structures around the world. Students hone their research, Internet, creative, and cooperative learning skills.

Overview: Students are asked to name famous "Rock Stars," and then are led to name famous "Rock" stars. In groups, students examine an image of a famous rock structure. Each group writes an informative article about that rock structure. All articles are combined into one

Figure 9.8
Mt. Rushmore, South Dakota

bound document. As a final step, students visit local rock structures.

Materials: Bags containing one labeled picture of the following: Ayers Rock, Stone Mountain, Mt. Rushmore, Rock of Gibraltar, Devil's Tower, Plymouth Rock; books; computer(s) with Internet access. NOTE: Pictures of all of these are available on the Internet.

INVITATION

Ask students to name famous "Rock Stars." Record students' ideas on the board. Obviously, students will name musicians. Repeat the question, this time emphasizing the "Rock." If, after a few minutes, students don't name a rock, write the following on the board:

"Rock" Stars, not "Rock Stars"

Give an example. Make a list of famous rocks and rock structures on the board.

EXPLORATION

In groups, students remove the labeled image of a famous rock structure from their bag. Each group then writes an informative article about that rock structure. The article should include geological information as well as any cultural, social, or other impact the structure may have. Groups conduct their research through the Internet and at their local libraries (see Web sites at end of lesson). Articles should be written as though they were being submitted to a magazine for publication. Encourage student creativity.

Figure 9.9
Stone Mountain, Georgia

EXPLANATION

Groups present their final article to the class. Each article is assessed and then bound into one magazine, which can be submitted to the school library and/or other teachers. All students should receive a copy of the magazine as well.

TAKE ACTION

Students could visit local rock structures, if any, that are of geological interest. Alternatively, expansion projects could focus on geothermal energy or geological problems, such as erosion, volcanic activity, plate tectonics, or earthquakes.

Internet Resources

http://www.gorp.com/gorp/resource/us_nm/sd_mount.htm
Mt. Rushmore

http://www.state.sd.us/state/executive/tourism/rushmore/mtrush.htm
Mt. Rushmore

http://www.americanparks.com/parklist/sdrush.htm
Mt . Rushmore

http://www.stonemountainpark.org/index_2.html
Stone Mountain

http://www.gibnet.gi/~dparody/gibmap/home.htm
Gibraltar

http://www.travel-library.com/north_america/usa/arizona/
Grand Canyon

http://www.interlog.com/~bgcarr/ayers.html
Ayers Rock

http://www.mountainzone.com/nationalparks/deto/index.html
Devil's Tower

ENVIRONMENTAL SCIENCE LESSONS

- Acid Rain

- Rain Forest Deforestation

- Air Pollution

- Waste Disposal

- Clean Water

- Hydroelectric Power

ACID RAIN

Goal: This lesson provides students with a general awareness of what acid rain is, what it affects, and what is being done about this worldwide problem. Students will gain experience utilizing computers and the Internet. In the end, the lesson raises school consciousness about the pressing problem of acid rain.

Overview: Students brainstorm about and complete a T-chart on acid rain. In groups, students research via the Internet, one concept/question and write a one-page summary of it, which they present to the class. Summaries are compiled into a final Acid Rain Folder. To finish, students make informational posters about acid rain and post them around the school.

Materials: Posterboard, markers, resources on acid rain (Internet, books, pamphlets, etc.), computer(s) with Internet access

INVITATION
To spark a brief discussion of acid rain, ask students questions such as the following: "How do sulfur emissions from power plants in the United Kingdom affect Scandinavia?" "How do Canadian emissions (from cars) contribute to biodiversity in lakes in northeastern United States?" "Why does the Canadian government complain to the U.S. government about sulfur falling in eastern Canada?" Once class discussion leads to acid rain as the answer, a T-chart should be constructed with the following column headings: "What we know about acid rain" and "What we want to know about acid rain."

EXPLORATION
Teams select one of the questions/concepts from the T-chart for research. Teachers make resources available to the students, and involve themselves in students' research as needed. Each group should utilize at least one Internet resource in its research. That Web site should be properly read,

referenced, and mentioned in the team's report (and Take Action posters). Each team prepares a final written report of its findings, which it hands in. Note: Teachers may want to assign one or two of the following Web sites to each team and have teams either use those sites to research their question/concept, or summarize each site and then share that information with the class.

Internet Resources
http://www.epa.gov/docs/acidrain/ardhome.html .
EPA Acid Rain Program

http://www.ns.ec.gc.ca/aeb/ssd/acid/acidfaq.html
FAQs on Acid Rain

http://www.beakman.com/acid/acid.html
Acid Rain

http://www.soton.ac.uk/~engenvir/environment/
air/acid.home.html
Acid Rain Pollution

http://www.unite2.tisl.ukans.edu
University of Kansas: Acid Rain

http://www.stevensonpress.com/acidrain.html
Saving the Pyramids

http://btdqs.usgs.gov/manilles/qafactpg.html
Acid Rain Monitoring

EXPLANATION
Each team briefly shares its report with the class. It should be clear from the report what question/concept the team selected, and their findings on that issue. Following the presentations, groups turn in their written reports, which are compiled into an Acid Rain Folder, and placed in the school library as a resource.

TAKE ACTION
Each team should make one to three posters about acid rain. By hanging up posters around the school, students help to make other students aware of the acid rain problem. Be sure students

Figure 9.10
Acid Rain

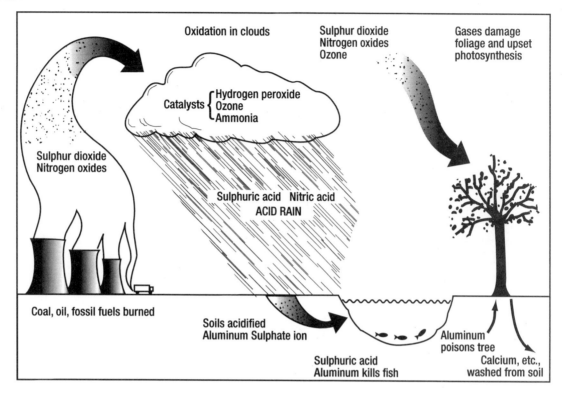

Oxidation in clouds

Sulphur dioxide
Nitrogen oxides
Ozone

Gases damage
foliage and upset
photosynthesis

Catalysts { Hydrogen peroxide
Ozone
Ammonia

Sulphur dioxide
Nitrogen oxides

Sulphuric acid   Nitric acid
ACID RAIN

Coal, oil, fossil fuels burned

Soils acidified
Aluminum Sulphate ion

Aluminum
poisons tree

Sulphuric acid
Aluminum kills fish

Calcium, etc.,
washed from soil

understand that the posters are to be informational and aimed at raising school consciousness. Each individual student could also research and prepare a one-page report on legislation regarding acid rain. This one-page report could be included in the Acid Rain Folder, along with any newspaper articles on the subject. Consider evaluating the folder with a rubric.

Internet Resources
http://www.unfccc.de/index.html
Climate Change Convention

http://www.unep.ch/iucc/bulltn0.html
UN Climate Change Bulletin

http://www.mannlib.cornell.edu/
Cornell Database

http://www.lib.uwaterloo.ca/discipline/SpecColl/acid/
Canadian Coalition–Acid Rain

http://www.agu.org/sci_soc/venusian.html
Acid Rain on Venus

http://www.dep.state.pa.us/dep/deputate/air-waste/ aq/default.htm
Cleaner Air

RAIN FOREST DEFORESTATION

Goal: Students learn how the deforestation of the rain forest relates to the greenhouse effect. Students observe changes, record data, and conduct research utilizing the Internet. In the end, student awareness of deforestation and the greenhouse effect is raised.

Overview: Students are asked to speculate on how the clearing of land in Brazil can affect the temperature in Siberia. Students share their theories with the class; discussion of the greenhouse effect follows. A class experiment/demonstration shows the release of carbon dioxide from forest fires. The relationship between deforestation and global warming is verified and further research is conducted via the Internet.

Materials: 10-gallon fish tank with lid, sand/gravel, wooden matches, limewater (calcium hydroxide), two small glass beakers or jars, water, fireplace matches; computer(s) with Internet access

INVITATION
Ask students, working in cooperative learning groups, to hypothesize about how clearing land in Brazil for crops and livestock can affect the temperature in Siberia. Have each group share its theory with the class. Note theories on the board/newsprint.

EXPLORATION
Tell students you are going to use limewater (calcium hydroxide) as an indicator to demonstrate how the burning of a forest releases carbon dioxide; in the presence of carbon dioxide, limewater will turn cloudy in color and a white

sediment (calcium carbonate) will collect at the bottom of the beaker. Each team is to observe the experiment and record its observations. Cover the bottom of the fish tank with 8 cm of sand/gravel, and place 30 to 40 matches in a tight circle in the center of the tank. Fill the two beakers with limewater and place one inside the tank and the other just outside the tank. Light the matches using one of the fireplace matches and immediately seal the tank. The matches will burn and give off billows of smoke, soot, and ash. Leave the lid on the tank. Have students observe the beakers of lime water and record their observations. Students should continue to make observations for the next 2 to 3 days.

EXPLANATION
At the conclusion of the experiment, each group should revise its theory (as needed) about the relationship between the clearing of land in Brazil and temperature changes in Siberia. As part of this activity, groups should research global warming/deforestation on the Internet, utiliz-

Figure 9.11
Deforestation Experiment/Demonstration

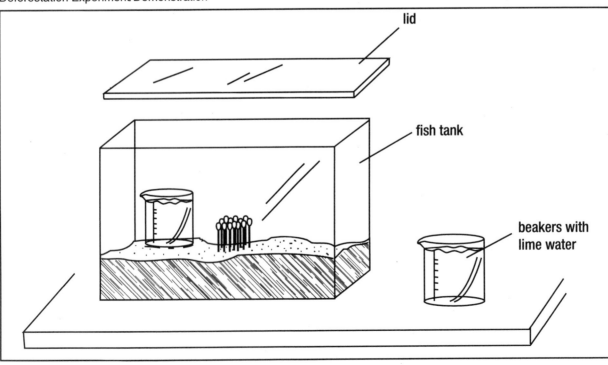

ing the Web sites listed below. This information should be used to refine theories and/or develop new theories. Have students share their theories with the class (if they have changed). Inform students that deforestation by fire emits carbon dioxide, which is a greenhouse gas. Greenhouse gases absorb and redirect heat down to Earth, thus causing global warming.

http://www.beakman.com/warm/warm.html
Global Warming

http://www.ciesin.org/docs/011-464/011-464.html
Ozone and Global Warming

http://www.gsu.edu/~wwwgtp/
Global Thinking Project global warming activity

http://www.ucsusa.org/global/gwwhatis.html
What Is Global Warming?

http://www.ran.org/ran/info_center/whysave.html
Why Save the Rain Forest?

http://www.centralamerica.com/cr/crrobs/outrain.htm
Save the Rain Forests

TAKE ACTION
Students might opt to do one of several things: make a list of steps they can take to help prevent rainforest deforestation; or investigate other gases that pollute the air; or research the long-term effects of global warming. Students might also write letters to their U.S. Senators and Representatives regarding deforestation.

Internet Resources
Deforestation/Rain Forests

http://www.free.cts.com/sd/s/srood/rain.html
Deforestation Links

http://www.cybercom.net/~faculty/rainforest/pictures.html
The Virtual Rainforest

http://www.bagheera.com/clasroom/spotlite/sprain.htm
Tropical Rain Forests

http://www.mat.auckland.ac.nz/~king/Preprints/book/diversity/cathed.html
Deforestation

http://www.ran.org/ran/info_center/whysave.html
Why Save the Rainforest?

http://ceps.nasm.edu:2020/CEPSDOCS/AMAZON/amazon.html
Amazon Deforestation

Acid Rain

http://www.epa.gov/docs/acidrain/ardhome.html
EPA Acid Rain Program

http://www.ns.ec.gc.ca/aeb/ssd/acid/acidfaq.html
FAQ's on Acid Rain

http://www.beakman.com/acid/acid.html
Acid Rain

AIR POLLUTION

Goal: Students become familiar with terminology related to air pollution. They enhance their computer and Internet navigational skills as they raise their awareness of the serious problem of air pollution.

Overview: Students are asked to identify problems they believe are facing our growing population. In groups, they search for key words on the Internet related to air pollution. Each team shares the results of its search with the class. A discus-

Figure 9.12
List of Terms for Air Pollution Word Search

Ash	Automobile
Carbon Dioxide	Car Pool
Exhaust	Government
Industry	Lungs
Population	Smoke
Atmosphere	Breathe
Carbon Monoxide	Disease
Filters	Hydrocarbons
Inversion	Mucus
Smog	Waste

sion on air pollution follows. NOTE: This activity might be used as an introduction to "Project Ozone" in Chapter 7.

Materials: Newsprint, markers, computer(s) with Internet access

INVITATION
Divide students into groups of four to five. Give each group 5 minutes to make a list of five major problems facing the world as population increases. Have each group share the problems it identified by writing them on newsprint or on the board. A brief discussion should follow, focusing on pollution and, specifically, air pollution, as a major problem.

EXPLORATION
Challenge the groups with an Internet word search. Working from a list of terms (Figure 9.14), each group must find a site on the Internet (using either Hotbot.com or Yahoo.com) that relates each term from the list to the subject of air pollution. Each group should record the

site in which each term/concept is located. After 20 minutes, have each group count the total number of terms/concepts it located. It should also select the two Web sites that were the most interesting to group members.

EXPLANATION
Each group shares with the class the number of terms it was able to locate and reference, the two sites that proved most interesting, and a brief explanation as to why. If the students have access to a printer, the two sites should be printed and shared with the class. Once the presentations are complete, a T-chart can be created to see what information the class is still lacking. At this point, you may opt to provide the missing information or assign it as part of the Take Action activity.

TAKE ACTION
Students could research local air pollution legislation, recording methods, organizations, and so on. Research might also focus on cities, such as Los Angeles and Mexico City, that have extremely high levels of air pollution.

Internet Resources (including those for word search)
http://www.tnrcc.state.tx.us/air/aqp/
Air Quality Planning (25 Links)

http://www.awma.org/awards.html
Air & Waste Management

http://www.lungusa.org/learn/environment/
envairpolex.html
Air Pollution–Exercise

http://www.intr.net/napenet/sspr.html
Air Pollution–Impact on Body

http://science.cc.uwf.edu/sh/curr/airpollution/
airpoll.htm
Air Pollution

Figure 9.13
Environmental Protection Agency Web page

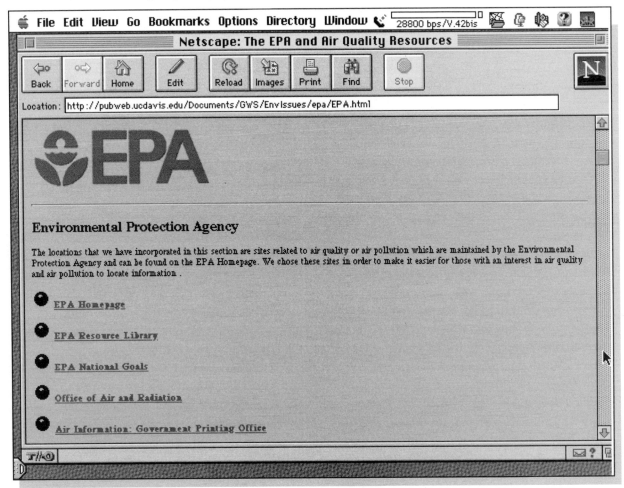

http://pubweb.ucdavis.edu/Documents/GWS/
EnvIssues/epa/EPA.html
EPA (Links)

http://www.sej.org/env_airp.htm
Air Pollution (40+ Links)

http://www-wilson.ucsd.edu/education/
airpollution/airpollution.html
Air Pollution Images

http://www.twoten.press.net/stories/95/10/19/
headlines/HEALTH_Asthma.html
Asthma Sufferers

http://www.alaw.org/pmfact.html
American Lung Association

WASTE DISPOSAL

Goal: Students learn about terms and concepts associated with waste disposal and other pollution problems. Students also conduct research on this topic utilizing the Internet, raising student awareness of waste management in the process.

Overview: Students are asked to brainstorm about waste disposal. In teams, students research, via the Internet, one of the concepts identified during the brainstorming. Teams present their findings to the class.

Materials: Computer(s) with Internet access

INVITATION

Ask students to brainstorm about waste disposal. Encourage them to list as many terms, concepts, procedures, methods, and so on, related to waste management as they can. Encourage the brainstorming by providing background information, such as the following:

Did you know that hogs used to act as garbage disposals in New York City? Long ago there were no garbage trucks or city dumps. In the 1700s, people threw their garbage out of their houses into the streets. Hogs roamed the streets eating garbage. Times have changed. Today, 90 percent of solid waste is currently disposed of in landfills. Several common methods are used to dispose of garbage. They range from burning to burying it in sanitary landfills. The current design of landfills does not promote the breakdown of wastes but does help to reduce their environmental impacts. In New York State, all new landfills have a plastic and clay liner at least 10 feet thick under the garbage, and a 4-foot-thick cover over the top. These layers minimize the immediate environmental impacts of landfills but exclude the water, air, and temperature changes needed to degrade waste. Still, some degradation takes place over time, and leachate must be collected. Each modern landfill in New York State has a leachate collection system to help keep the leachate from polluting groundwater and surface water supplies.

EXPLORATION

Divide students into groups. Each group should select a term, concept, or method from the brainstorming list. Each group then conducts research, via the Internet, on what it has selected (see Web sites at the end of this lesson).

EXPLANATION

Each group presents to the class its findings on the concept it researched. The report should have an oral component, as well as a written/printed component. Reports should draw heavily on the Web sites used to research the concept. If possible, printed versions of the sites should be included in the reports. Time permitting, the class can create a concept map using terms from the initial brainstorming. Should any major concepts have been omitted, the teacher can request additional Internet research.

TAKE ACTION

Students could research local waste disposal systems, including those in their home, school, community, city, and state. This lesson also lends itself to school and community involvement through waste awareness, recycling, disposal, and other activities. Be creative and allow the students to be creative!

Internet/ Resources

http://ecosys.drdr.virginia.edu/sea/ivysea.html
Ivy Landfill Contamination

http://jacksonville.com/tu-online/stories/092597/2a1Navy_.html
Landfill to Park Project

http://www.zerowasteamerica.com/WasteDispCap.htm
Waste Disposal Capacity

http://www.schwarze.com/Secure/v6n2/v6n2landfills.html
Future Waste

http://www.zebu.uoregon.edu/1996/ph161/l19.html
Nuclear Waste

http://www.sm.rim.or.jp/~kasuya/eng.html
Radioactive Waste(+Links)

http://www.ultranet.com/~dleger/recycle.htm
Recycling

http://www.webdirectory.com/Pollution/
Waste_Management/
Waste Management Links

http://www.epa.gov/OGWDW/Pubs/14ground.html
Ground Water Contamination

http://www.greenpeace.org/~usa/toxics.html
Greenpeace

CLEAN WATER

Goal: This lesson provide a hands-on, cooperative learning activity related to water filtration. Students gain an awareness about water supply, filtration, and purification in their community.

Overview: Student groups are challenged to create and test a filter system using only a handful of items made available. Each group shares its filter and its results with the class. The teacher shares a successful model that uses all of the items that make sense. Filtration is discussed. As a final step, students research local water filtration systems.

Materials: Bag containing cups, sand, rocks, cotton balls, carbon chunks, filter paper, and some random materials (marbles, pencils, etc.); a faucet water filter; dirty water in a large container (Dirty water = water, soil, and vinegar)

INVITATION
Show students a container full of dirty water. On a table have the sand, rocks, cotton balls, carbon chunks, filter paper, faucet water filter, and random materials (marbles, pencils, etc.). Ask students to name which of the items on the table they would use to clean the dirty water. Allow time for a few students to propose some ideas (record these on the board). Isolate the sand, the cotton, the rocks, and the carbon chunks. Briefly discuss these items, then inform students that their challenge is to create a filtration system using some or all of these items.

EXPLORATION
Have students work in groups. Present each group with a bag containing the lab materials. Student teams should create a filtration device using any or all of those items. They should then test their filters and summarize their results.

EXPLANATION
Each group presents its filter to the class and shares the results of its test. After all presentations are complete, the teacher shares/presents a model utilizing all of the materials except the random ones. Discussion should focus on the reasons for the filter's success and the various items it is composed of. The teacher's role is to lead the discussion and intervene as needed.

TAKE ACTION
Students could watch an informative video about water purification. They could also learn how home water purification systems work. Finally, students could research and visit a local water purification plant and/or conduct research on the cleanliness of the local water supply. Students could even get involved in a community-based project. Be creative—this lesson lends itself to a great many activities.

Internet Resources

http://www.waterforlife.com/solution.html
Clean Water Solutions

http://www.goodwaterco.com/pglg/shortcou.htm
Water Purification

http://www.globalx.net/ocd/directions/9424.html
Career: Water Treatment Plant Operator

http://www.sdcwa.org/
San Diego Water Authority

http://www.gkss.de/G/MM-Description.html
European Monitoring

http://es.epa.gov/oeca/water/index.html
EPA–Water

HYDROELECTRIC POWER

Goal: This activity raises student awareness of the various sources of energy available to humans. Students come to recognize that water is a renewable resource that is an important source of electricity. Creativity, experimentation, and cooperative learning are enhanced in the process.

Overview: Students brainstorm about the various energy sources available to humans. In groups, they design and build their own basic small water turbine, which are tested and presented to the class. Final models and summaries are displayed.

Materials: Bags containing pins, cork, cardboard, tacks (and other potential building materials); scissors; tape; paper; other basic supplies

INVITATION

Students brainstorm about the various energy sources available to humans. In groups, students determine the pros and cons of each of the energy sources. A few of these are shared with the class. This leads into a discussion of the pros and cons of hydroelectric power, and the basic principle behind a hydro-powered turbine.

EXPLORATION

Groups receive their bags containing the building materials. Each group designs and builds its own basic small water turbine. Models should be tested under running water from the faucet. Each group records its design notes, observations, and so on.

EXPLANATION

Each group presents its model and summary to the class. Class discusses models and, by extension, issues involving hydro-powered plants. Final models and summaries are displayed in the classroom or in the school. By now, it should be clear to students that the potential energy of water is harnessed to produce mechanical energy, which can be used directly or indirectly to generate electricity.

TAKE ACTION

Students could investigate their local source of electricity. They could also make posters about alternative sources of energy—ones that are environmentally friendly—and place them in their school to raise awareness.

Figure 9.14
Water turbine

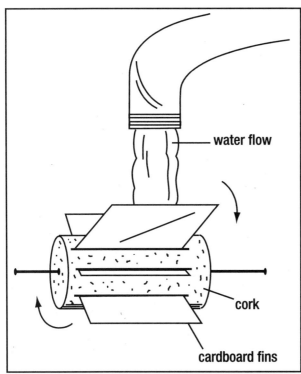

water flow

cork

cardboard fins

Internet Resources

http://www.calpoly.edu/~ashan/
Hydroelectric Power

http://www.energy.ca.gov/html/hydro.html
Hydropower in California

http://www.his.com/~mesas/loren1.htm
Hydropower in India

http://h20.usgs.gov/public/watuse/wuhy.html
Hydroelectric Water Use in the United States

http://www.hooverdam.com/workings/main.htm
Hoover Dam

Life Science Lessons

- Endangered Species

- Dinosaur Biographies

- Dinosaur Defense

- Life in a Seashell

- Fossils

- Fossilization: Making a Plaster Mold

- Classification Systems

ENDANGERED SPECIES

Goal: This activity raises student awareness of endangered species. Students become aware of the needs of such animals by doing a practical, cooperative, and fun activity that encourages creativity and hones research skills, including those involving the Internet.

Overview: Students are asked to discuss endangered species and what is being done to protect them. In groups, students research an endangered species and design a habitat in which that species could live in captivity, for the purpose of reproduction. Projects are shared with the class.

Materials: Bags containing a picture of an endangered species (a different endangered species in each bag); books; computer(s) with Internet access

INVITATION
On the board make two columns, one labeled "Yes" and the other "No." Without telling them why, ask students to name some animals. List any animal that is endangered in the "Yes" column, and any nonendangered animal in the "No" column. Challenge students to guess how the animals are being categorized. This should lead to a general discussion of endangered species and what is being done to save them. In preparation for their research, let students know that many interesting Web sites can be used to obtain excellent information on endangered species. One of these is the SeaWorld/Busch Gardens Animal Information Database site.

EXPLORATION
Divide students into groups. Each group receives a bag with one endangered species inside. Groups research their species in-depth and design an enclosure, or a habitat, in which that species can mate in captivity. Habitats

should reflect student knowledge of and sensitivity to the animal's needs. Students prepare a final written report, that includes drawings, images, models, and so on. Creativity should be encouraged. NOTE: To give students ample time to research and be creative, it may be beneficial to allow two to three days for this lesson.

EXPLANATION
Each group presents to the class its endangered species, including the species' current condition, chances of survival, particularities, etc. The groups should also present their designed habitats. NOTE: It may be a good idea to create a rubric, such as the one shown in Figure 10.1, and allow students to evaluate their classmates' presentations and created habitats.

TAKE ACTION
Students could contact local zoos or animal organizations and find out what, if any, steps they are taking to save endangered species from extinction.

Internet Resources
http://www.fws.gov/~r9endspp/vertdata.html#Mammals
U.S. Fish and Wildlife Service: 300+ Endangered Species Links

http://www.ritslab.ubc.ca/libe477/group2topic5.html
Elephants: Endangered

http://www.applink.net/cpollard/endangered.htm
125+ Links to Endangered Species

http://www.nceet.snre.umich.edu/EndSpp/ES.law.html
Legislation on Endangered Species

http://www.bev.net/education/SeaWorld/endangered_species/esactivity.html
Endangered Species Activity for Students

Figure 10.1 Rubric

Criteria	3 Points	2 Points	1 Point
Presentation	Clear, structured, and varied presentation. All members were involved. It kept my attention.	Presentation was structured yet not too clear. Had some variety. Most of the members were involved.	Group may have learned the material well, but it only incorporated it fairly simply into the project and did not expand on it.
Content Material	Group displayed clear mastery of scientific material and expanded upon it in its project.	Imagination was clearly in evidence, yet project lost its feeling of reality and seemed fantastical.	The group was very organized, but the project was not well structured. Project had an objective, but no clear method.
Use of Imagination	Project showed a great deal of imagination, while maintaining a realistic focus.	Presentation was confusing and uninteresting. There was little variety or order to it. Not all members were involved.	There was only a superficial mastery of scientific scientific material. It was incorporated very generally into the project.
Organization	The group was very organized, and the project was well structured from concept to method.	Project was replicative as opposed to original. It had a few novel ideas, but the general scope was not novel.	The group lacked organization, and the project was not fluid. The project had an objective, but it was not carried into method.

http://www.ru.ac.za/saep/cntry/namibia/namlink.html
Southern Africa Environment Page

http://www.orecity.k12.or.us/ochs/species/
Endangered Species Project

DINOSAUR BIOGRAPHIES

Goal: This lesson has students think back to an earlier time on Earth. In the process, they learn about dinosaurs and utilize cooperative learning and inquiry skills.

Overview: Students watch a portion of *Jurassic Park*. As a class, students create a list of questions they would like to ask a dinosaur, if they could. Then, in groups, students "interview" one specific dinosaur to discover how it lived. Groups then present their interview results and findings to the class orally and in a written report. All group reports are bound into book form and given to the library as a resource.

Materials: Bags containing a plastic dinosaur (put a different dinosaur in each bag), paper, markers, binding materials (staples, string, rings, etc.); the video *Jurassic Park*, books, computer(s) with Internet access

INVITATION

Play the portion of *Jurassic Park* with the friendly dinosaurs. Have students suggest questions they would like to ask the dinosaur if it could speak. On the board, write down five to fifteen questions. Divide the class into groups and distribute the bags containing dinosaurs. Have each group identify its dinosaur (this may require teacher assistance). Write the dinosaur names on the board. In preparation for students' research and to help them with dinosaur identification, you may want to project the following Web site on an overhead.

EXPLORATION

Instruct each group to "interview" its dinosaur. Groups should choose five questions to ask their dinosaur (they can create their own questions or use questions on the board). To answer these questions, they must conduct research (on the Internet). They then make a written report of their findings that will become a chapter in a class-made book. Encourage students to be creative and to treat the report as if they had actually interviewed the dinosaur to obtain the responses. The Internet can be an excellent source of information on dinosaurs. In addition to the site in Figure 10.2, see the many sites listed at the end of this activity.

EXPLANATION

Student groups present their dinosaur to the class, including the questions they asked it and the responses they received. Each group also turns in its interview report/chapter to the teacher. NOTE: To ensure better quality, you may want to allow students an extra 1 to 2 days to complete their chapter.

TAKE ACTION

Once the interview reports/chapters have been turned in, the class works to bind them into a book. Each one of the groups is also responsible for one of the following items: cover, table of contents, index, glossary, pictures, references, "about the authors" page, and so on.

Internet Resources

http://www.clpgh.org/cmnh/doe/dino/intro.htm
Age of Dinosaurs Lives On

http://www.ucmp.berkeley.edu/diapsids/
dinolinks.html
200+ Great Links

http://www.mines.utah.edu/~wmgg/Video/
Dinosaurs.html
20+ Links–Tours

http://www.ntu.edu.sg/home1/s7632986i/
Dino Info

http://www.nationalgeographic.com/features/96/
dinoeggs/museum/resources/resource.html
National Geographic (17 Dinosaur Articles)

http://www.gl.umbc.edu/~tkeese1/dinosaur/
gallery.htm
Dinosaur Gallery

http://www.nmmnh-abq.mus.nm.us/nmmnh/
footprints.html
Dinosaur Footprints

http://www.geocities.com/CapeCanaveral/4459/
Dinosaur Reconstructions

http://home1.gte.net/friendly/linkpg_1.html
Dinosaur Links (100+ Links)

DINOSAUR DEFENSE

Goal: This lesson introduces students to dinosaurs while it teaches them about sound scientific inquiry. It implements active cooperative learning methods and exercises observational and inference-making skills.

Overview: In groups, students make observations about different dinosaur models. Each group shares with the class the feature it feels was most significant to the dinosaur's survival. The class

Figure 10.2
Dinosaurs! home page from
www.hcc.hawaii.edu/dinos/dinos.1.html Web site.
Reprinted by permission of Honolulu Community College.

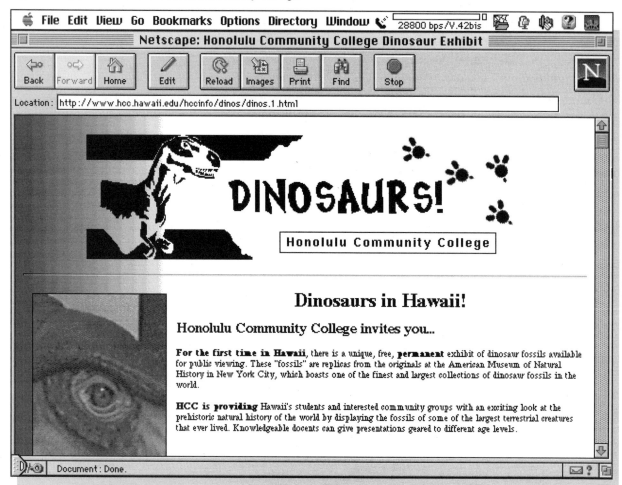

engages in a teacher-assisted discussion about each dinosaur. As an extension, students make inferences about other animal features.

Materials: Bags containing a model/image of a dinosaurs; newsprint, markers, access to the Internet

INVITATION

Begin by holding a brief discussion on the following: "What is indirect investigation?" This should lead nicely to a discussion of this question: "How do scientists study dinosaurs . . . or other subjects that are not available for direct study?"

EXPLORATION

Teacher divides students into groups by having them select pieces of paper with the names of dinosaurs written on them. All those with the same dinosaur are on the same team. The bags containing the corresponding model dinosaurs are passed out. Each group works to list as many features as it can about its dinosaur during a 3-minute period. The bags are rotated and work commences for the next 3-minute period, and so on.

EXPLANATION

Each group selects the feature it feels was most important to each dinosaur's survival. On newsprint or chalkboard at the front of the class (one sheet/grid per dinosaur), a representative from each group writes down the feature selected for each dinosaur. The class then discusses each dinosaur and the teacher expands on/corrects the features as needed. The Internet sites listed at the end of the lesson can be integrated into this stage as explanatory resources. Alternatively, certain sites can be assigned to each team, with the teams doing additional research on their respective dinosaurs. Research on themes such as extinction, the Earth's history, carnivores vs. herbivores, and the like should prove profitable.

TAKE ACTION

Students could be given photos of other animals, archaeological finds, bones, remains, and so on. from which they make additional inferences. Encourage inferences about the animals' habitat, food source, social habits, and so on, depending on the item/photo analyzed. Endangered animals might also be researched.

Internet Resources

http://www.nationalgeographic.com/features/96/ dinoeggs/museum/resources/resource.html
National Geographic (17 Dinosaur Articles)

http://www.gl.umbc.edu/~tkeese1/dinosaur/ gallery.htm
Dinosaur Gallery

http://www.nmmnh-abq.mus.nm.us/nmmnh/ footprints.html
Dinosaur Footprints

http://www.geocities.com/CapeCanaveral/4459/ *Dinosaur Reconstructions*

http://home1.gte.net/friendly/linkpg_1.html *Dinosaur Links (100+ Links)*

LIFE IN A SEASHELL

Goal: This lesson aims to familiarize students with seashells and the types of animals that live in shells. The activity also gives students an opportunity to make observations and inferences, and thus to learn about indirect means of study.

Overview: In groups, students make inferences about the animal that lived in the shell they are examining. Each group selects the observation and inference they feel is the most accurate. One by one, groups present their observations and inferences to the class. Teacher then leads an informative discussion on each shell.

Materials: Bags containing one shell and one small ruler; also, newsprint and markers

INVITATION

Teacher asks students to name ways in which scientists conduct research. The brainstorming should lead to indirect means of study, such as that relying on fossils, remains, bones, habitats, and so on. Teacher records brainstorming ideas on newsprint. Invitation phase ends with the introduction of the idea of using a shell to make inferences about the animal that lived in it. Teacher then explains the activity and distributes the materials.

EXPLORATION

Students are divided into groups. Each group receives a bag containing one shell and a small ruler. Each member of the group makes one observation about the shell, which should be recorded on newsprint by a group member. After each student has had a turn, each student makes a second observation. Based on his or her observation(s), each student then makes one inference about the animal that lived in the shell. The group reviews all of the inferences and selects the observation-inference pair it feels is most significant/accurate. Final observations and inferences should be recorded on newsprint as well.

Figure 10.3
"Dinosaurs in Cyberspace: Dinolinks" page from
www.ucmp.berkeley.edu/diapsids/dinolink.html Web site
Reprinted by permission of the John R. Hutchinson.

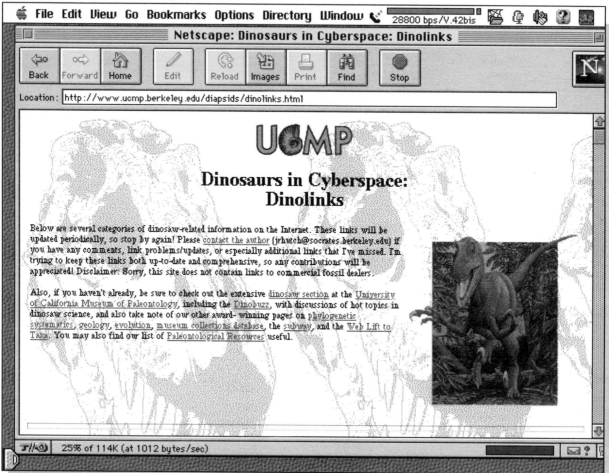

EXPLANATION

Each group makes a brief class presentation, sharing its shell and the final observation-inference it selected (in their presentations, groups may mention some of the other observations and inferences as well). In a teacher-led discussion, information about that shell and its inhabitant is shared, discussed, and related to the groups' observations and inferences.

TAKE ACTION

Teacher hangs up the newsprint from the initial brainstorming session. All the items listed that deal with indirect means of study should be highlighted. Students could then be asked to research one of these methods or another method involving indirect observation.

Internet Resources

http://www.univaq.it/~sc_amb/pesce/shells.html
Seashells: Phylum Mollusca

http://www.coralcay.org/critters/seashell.html
Coral Cay Conservation: Shell Shape and Color

http://www.mpm.edu/collect/shell.html
Seashells: Identification Photos

http://www.acmepet.com/club/bboard/fish/
messages/6515.html
Seashells and Small Fish . . . Don't Mix?!

http://museum.nhm.uga.edu/GSC/
The Georgia Shell Club

Figure 10.4 Table of Inferences

Observation 1	Observation 2	Inference
Shell has a hole.	Shell has ridges.	Animal was consumed.
Shell has several colors on outer covering.	Color pattern resembles camouflage.	Animal had predators.

http://middleton.sowashco.k12.mn.us/N/4/
95-96/bomsta/poem/sarah/poem.html
Shell Poetry

FOSSILS

Goal: This lesson gives students an overview of how fossils are used to make hypotheses about prehistoric life. Students learn about and utilize indirect methods of investigation, utilizing computers and the Internet.

Overview: Students discuss archaeology as a means of solving a mystery from a set of clues. In teams, students make observations and inferences about a fossil, and share them with the class. Students then prepare a factual short report (using the Internet as a resource), which they share with the class. As an extension, students search the Internet or the library for means of dating fossils and for the names of pioneering archaeologists.

Materials: Bags containing a fossil; a mystery-type "Who Done It?" picture; informational sheets about each of the fossils; newsprint and markers; textual resources; computer(s) with Internet access

INVITATION
In teams, students are given a "Who Done It?" picture (picture of a crime scene with clues). Team members discuss the clues in the picture and propose a solution. As a class, students discuss their solutions and then professionals other than detectives who "solve mysteries." Teacher-led discussion leads to archaeology as a means of solving some types of mysteries.

EXPLORATION
Each team receives a bag containing a fossil. Teams make observations and inferences about their fossil, using a two-column format. For every observation in column 1, they should make at least one inference/hypothesis in column 2. After sufficient time, each group shares its observations and inferences with the class.

EXPLANATION
Teams are given a factual information sheet about their fossil, including its site of extraction, life form that made it, age, and so on. Teams prepare a short report to share with the class about their fossil. In it, they should include some ideas about how that factual information was inferred/hypothesized from the fossil. After discussion of fossils, if time permits, groups can conduct research, via the Internet, using the following Internet sites. Students might initiate specialized searches by theme or participate in scavenger hunts within these sites. Findings can be summarized and shared by the students.

http://ctcnet.net/treasure/fossil.htm
Treasures of the Earth: Fossils and Bones

http://www.collectorsguide.com/ab/g360.html
Fossil Gallery

http://www.extinctions.com/catalogs.htm
Web Site for Fossil Collecting

http://www.intersurf.com/~heinrich/laffossil1.html
Louisiana Fossil Page

http://www.flmnh.ufl.edu/natsci/vertpaleo/
resources/res.htm
Paleontological Resources

TAKE ACTION
As an extension, students could search the
Internet or the library for means of dating fossils, for the various types of fossils that we know
of, or for information about pioneering "mystery-
solving" archaeologists. Teams could also
research any local fossil activity that would be of
particular interest.

Internet Resources
http://www.cruzio.com/~cscp/index.htm
Fossil Evidence: Human Evolution

http://www.halcyon.com/rdpayne/jdfbnm.html
Fossil Beds National Monument

http://www.uh.edu/~jbutler/anon/histpal.htm
Paleontology Resources

FOSSILIZATION: MAKING A PLASTER MOLD

Goal: This lesson introduces students to the
process of fossilization. Using the Internet and
laboratory procedures, students discover how fossils are used to learn about history, adaptation,
ancestry, and so on. Observational and indirect
inquiry skills are enhanced.

Overview: Students compare a fossilized snail
with a modern snail. This comparison leads to a
discussion of how fossilization occurs, and how
fossils are used by scientists. Students then make
a fossil out of plaster of Paris. To finish, students
discuss other forms of preservation.

Materials: Bags containing a fossilized snail
shell and a "modern" snail shell, a small amount
of plaster, containers and utensils for making
plaster, plastic containers for making molds;
also, newsprint and markers; computer(s) with
Internet access

INVITATION
In groups, students are given a bag containing a
fossilized shell and a modern shell. Groups compare and contrast the two shells, recording their
observations on newsprint. Groups then make
inferences about each shell, again recording
these on the newsprint. Students should focus on
the similarities and differences between the two
samples.

Figure 10.5
Making Fossils

EXPLORATION

The various observations in inferences are discussed as a class. Discussion should include the process of fossilization and the importance and use of fossils. Internet-based research can be conducted on how fossilization occurs and how fossils are studied. If time permits, you might involve students in a virtual scavenger hunt wherein they discover how and where major dinosaur fossils have been found, who found them, and how they have been utilized by scientists. For example, students might conduct an Internet search of the Yellow River in Wyoming to discover why the conditions of the river have led to such amazing fossilized specimens (see the Web sites listed at the end of the lesson).

EXPLANATION

The groups make a fossil out of plaster. Various materials can be placed on the item to be fossilized to simulate pressure-inducing layers of rock. A crystallized sugar sample might be used to make the fossil; that way, when heated and/or submerged in water, it will disappear, leaving only its "fossil" markings.

TAKE ACTION

Students could discuss other forms of preservation, such as amber or ice, or gather information about the "Ice Man." Students might also inquire into short-term preservation, such as organ/blood preservation.

Internet Resources

http://www.science.ubc.ca/~geol313/lecture/
fossil/fossil.htm
Fossilization

http://emrs.chm.bris.ac.uk/Susan/Preserve.html
Preservation/Fossilization

http://www-odp.tamu.edu/mrc/mrcpage.HTML
Microfossils

http://pw1.netcom.com/~carl5/fossils.html
Fossil Sites in the USA

http://www.ucmp.berkeley.edu/FAQ/faq.html
FAQ's About Paleontology

http://nmnhwww.si.edu/paleo/
Smithsonian: Paleobiology

http://www.ucmp.berkeley.edu/collections/invert.
html
Berkeley Invertebrate Fossils

http://www.amnh.org/Exhibition/Amber/index.html
American Museum of Natural History: Amber

http://www.emporia.edu/S/www/earthsci/amber/
amber.htm
World of Amber: Emporia State University

http://sapphire.surgery.wisc.edu/home.html/
Organ Preservation

http://worldwidenews.net/HEALTH/
MEDICINE/ORGANTRA/SUBJECT.HTM
Guide to Organ Transplant

CLASSIFICATION SYSTEMS

Goal: Students are introduced to classification systems to learn why such systems are necessary and their place in our lives.

Overview: Student teams compete to locate certain buttons from various sets of classified (and unclassified) buttons. Students share their experience and discuss how the classification system, or lack thereof, affected their performance. Students then create their own classification system for the buttons, which they share with another group. Teams brainstorm about scientific and everyday classification systems.

Materials: Bags containing many different kinds of buttons (one bag should contain buttons that are all mixed up; the other bags should have smaller bags within, with buttons classified by random categories, such as color, size, shape, number of holes, material, etc.); newsprint and markers

INVITATION

Students are divided into small teams. One team receives a large bag full of buttons in no order whatsoever. The other teams receive a bag containing smaller bags of classified buttons (see above). All teams are challenged to locate specific buttons (e.g., a red button with four holes). After five to ten searches, teams discuss the ease with which they located the buttons and in what way the button classification system that they inherited affected the process.

EXPLORATION

Student teams create their own classification system for the buttons they receive. They detail their system on newsprint. Teams then trade newsprint sheets. One team applies the other team's system to its buttons and provides an analysis.

Figure 10.6
Button Classification Scheme
Use this classification system to classify any set of buttons.

SHAPE	○				□				△			
COLOR	Blue Green		Yellow Red		Blue Green		Yellow Red		Blue Green		Yellow Red	
SIZE	Big	Small	Big	Small	Big	Small	Big	Small	Big	Small	Big	Small
HOLE (H) OR NO HOLE (NH)	H NH	H NH	H NH	H NH	H NH	H NH	H NH	H NH	H NH	H NH	H NH	H NH

EXPLANATION

Teams pair up with their partner team to share their experience and analyze the other team's system. As a class, students discuss their experience in the initial button search and in creating a classification system. Teacher-led discussion should uncover the advantages and importance of classification systems in science and in our lives, in general. Examples abound, including the periodic table, animal/plant kingdoms, matter (solid, liquid, gas), rock types, musical instruments (wind, percussion, etc.), grocery store shelves (canned, frozen, etc.), and clothing sizes.

TAKE ACTION

Students could be asked to observe their activities for one week and note how many classification systems they encounter. They should analyze and critique those systems for functionality and adequacy. New systems could then be proposed. Student teams might also research a scientific classification system and prepare a brief report for the class.

Internet Resources

http://www.uen.org/utahlink/lp_res/TRB017.html
Plants and Animals (Classification)

http://www.wesleyan.edu/libr/wlibstkg.htm
Library Classification Systems

http://www.public.iastate.edu/~CYBERSTACKS/CTW.htm
Organizing the Web: Classification Systems (30+ Links)

http://turva.me.tut.fi/cis/chemcode/03.htm
Classifying a Chemical as Hazardous

http://www.vegasindex.com/ufo/topic/sighting/class/
UFO Sighting Classification

http://www.wetlands.ca/wetcentre/wetcanada/implementation-guide/guideap1.html
The Canadian Wetland Classification System

PHYSICAL SCIENCE LESSONS

- Electromagnetism

- Power: Watts in the Water

- Pendulum Variables

- Gravity

- Mixtures: Iron in Cereal Flakes

- Evaporation Is Cool

- Magnetic Fields

- Surface Tension: The Stress H_2O Feels

- Water and Air Surface Interactions: Bubbles

- The Visible Spectrum: A Rainbow

ELECTROMAGNETISM

Goal: Students gain insight into the relationship between electricity and magnetism. Working in cooperative groups, they conduct a hands-on inquiry experiment in which they use basic laboratory equipment.

Overview: In groups, students are challenged to create a scenario in which a compass needle wouldn't point north. Each group then investigates how an electric current affects the direction of the needle on a compass. Groups share their results. Students extend their knowledge by investigating electric cars.

Materials: Bags containing a 6-volt battery, wire, a compass

INVITATION
Students are divided into groups. Groups are challenged to write about a situation in which the needle of a compass would not point North.

Figure 10.7
What happens to the compass needle when a wire, connected to a battery, is wrapped around the base of the compass?

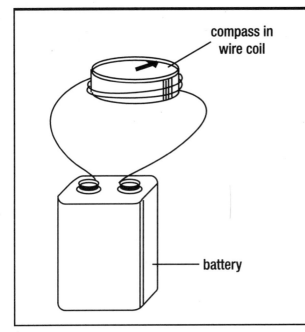

compass in wire coil

battery

Groups should be given just a few minutes for this activity. Each group briefly shares its scenario. The teacher comments on the ideas, then mentions that another method (if not already mentioned) exists.

EXPLORATION
Bags are distributed to the groups. Groups are challenged to find a way to alter the direction of the compass needle using the contents of the bag. Each group records with drawings, each of its attempts and the results.

EXPLANATION
After sufficient time, any group that discovered a means of altering the direction of the needle with the battery and wire presents its findings to the class. Teacher involvement at this stage consists of providing the class with correct information (wrapping the wire around the compass), as needed. After the presentations, the remaining groups should be given a short time to test the correct setup.

TAKE ACTION
As an expansion activity, students could conduct research on electric cars. What are their benefits? their drawbacks? Are there any in the United States? How much do they cost? Are they being used more extensively outside the United States? How do they benefit the environment? How do they work?

Internet Resources
Electric Cars

http://www.car-stuff.com/carlinks/future.htm
Alternate Fuel Cars (40+ Links)

http://www.automatch.com/related/ted/Comm/elecC.htm
Electric Cars: The Future

http://www.hev.doe.gov/
Department of Energy

http://www.mvhs.srvusd.k12.ca.us/~bdahlin/
electric.html
Electric Car Models

http://kearnykomets.sdcs.k12.ca.us/programs/
ec/e_c.html
Electric Car Project and Links

POWER: WATTS IN THE WATER

Goal: In this activity, students gain insight into power and work by actually measuring it in a cooperative activity. Activity requires data collection and mathematical calculation, as well as creativity.

Overview: Students are asked to propose ways in which the human body's power can be measured. In groups, students test their power by raising the temperature of water. Calculations are made to determine the power each group emitted. As an extension, an inquiry into the cost of power is made.

Materials: Bags containing a one-stopper standard-sized test tube and a thermometer

INVITATION
Students are asked to suggest ways to test/measure the power of a human body. Ideas are recorded by the teacher on the board. With each suggestion, the units in which human power would be measured should also be given. By the end of the discussion, the teacher should introduce or highlight using temperature as a means.

Figure 10.8
Pendulum Terminology

Heat/Power Terminology

Calorie: Unit of heat; defined as the amount of heat necessary to raise the temperature of 1 gram of water by 1 degree Celsius

Work: Force applied to an object in a certain direction; measured in Joules
Work + Force (Newtons) x Distance (meters)

Power: The rate at which work is being done; measured in Watts
Power + Work (Joules)/time (seconds)

Joule: Unit of work; defined as 1 Newton-meter; 4.19 Joules/calorie

Watt: Unit of power; defined as 1 Joule/second

Steps to Calculate Power from the Change in Temperature of Water in Tube

1. Convert temperature change, which is in degrees Celsius, to Heat, measured in Calories. (number of degrees Celsius) x (grams of water in tube) = (number of Calories)

2. Convert Heat, which is in Calories, to Joules of Work. (number of calories) x (4.19 Joules/Calorie) = (number of Joules)

3. Convert Joules to watts to obtain measurement of Power. (number of Joules)/(number of seconds it took to raise water temperature) = (number of Watts)

EXPLORATION

Students are divided into groups. Each group receives a bag containing a test tube and a thermometer. Students should pour 10 to 20 mL of water into the test tube. The initial temperature and mass of the water (1 mL = 1 gram) should be measured. When the signal is given, one student in each group begins doing whatever he or she has decided to do in order to warm up the test tube. Students can shake it, rub it, blow on it—whatever they want, so long as they use only their body. After 5 minutes, time is up! Take and record the final temperature of the water. Repeat as many times, with as many different students, as time allows.

EXPLANATION

Each group calculates the power it generated. The temperature change is converted into calories by multiplying each degree gained by the number of grams of water. If 10 g of water gained 8 degrees, then 80 calories of heat was added to the water. The work done in raising the temperature of water can be found by multiplying the calories added to the water by 4.19 joules. Power in watts can then be calculated from the work (joules/second). Each group should calculate its total power and share it with the class. One group should emerge as the winner!

TAKE ACTION

Students could contact their local power company to inquire into the cost of a kilowatt hour of power. They might then review their figures and place a dollar value on the power they generated.

Internet Resources

http://www.jademountain.com/hydro*.html
Hydroelectric systems

http://www.iaw.com/~falls/power.html
Niagra Falls–Hydropower

http://www.efi.sintef.no/NEF/enfo/clean.htm
Norway: Energy Supply

http://www.windpower.dk/tour/econ/tariffs.htm
Wind Power

PENDULUM VARIABLES

Goal: Students learn to identify pendulums at work around them. By designing a basic experiment and presenting their results, they recognize how a change in one of the pendulum's features affects its motion.

Overview: Students brainstorm about different types of pendulums, including their motion and their function. In groups, they design a basic pendulum and test a variable. They present their experiment to the class. In an extension activity, students gather information about a specific pendulum in operation today.

Materials: Bags containing string, many washers of all sizes, a ruler, a stopwatch (if available); chalkboard/newsprint

INVITATION

Have students brainstorm and come up with a list of different types of pendulums that exist in the world around them (clocks, swings, cranes, *The Flying Dutchman* amusement ride, tree tire swing, etc.). Using one of these examples, ask the class questions related to length and weight: What would happen if you shortened the length of the rope?" "What would happen if twice as many people got on the swing?" Allow students to suggest answers to such questions without verifying what is correct. Write two to four of the questions on the board.

Figure 10.9
Pencils & Washers Pendulum

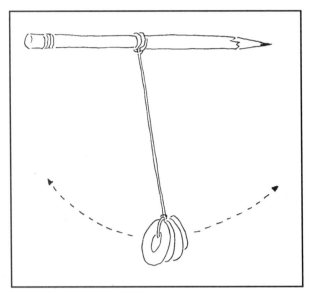

EXPLORATION

Divide students into groups of four or five. Distribute the bags containing the laboratory items. Instruct students to build a basic pendulum and then design a basic experiment testing one of the pendulum's features. Suggest features such as length of string, weight on the end of the string, release point, period of time, and so on. Circulate about the room and assist groups on experimental design, as needed.

EXPLANATION

Each group prepares a written report that includes its pendulum design, variable tested, method used, number of tries, measurements, results, conclusions, and so on. Each group shares its findings with the class in a brief oral report. After the presentation, ask the students as a class to answer the questions you first asked them in the Invitation portion of the lesson. Alternatively, assign this as homework.

Figure 10.10
Pendulum Terminology

Pendulum Terminology

Speed: Rate of change of position, or the distance over time

Velocity (v): Speed + direction (a vector quality)

Acceleration: The rate of change of the velocity

Weight (w): The force of gravity upon a body times the quantity of its mass

Mass (m): Equivalent to the inertia of a body (the amount of work necessary to move it or to stop it, without regard to gravity)

Work: Force times distance

Kinetic energy (k): The energy a body (of mass m) has by virtue of being in motion (at velocity v). The quantity of work k can perform is $k = \frac{1}{2}mv^2$.

Potential energy (p): The "potential to do work" a body (of weight w) has by virtue, for instance, of its position (h) within a gravitational force field: $p = w \times h$

The total energy of a dynamical system (E) is the sum of its kinetic and potential energy:

$$E = k + p \text{ or } E = (\tfrac{1}{2}mv^2) + (w \times h)$$

In a pendulum, raising the h of the weight increases its p. This injects energy into the pendulum. Releasing the bob creates an oscillating relation between p and k. As h decreases to 0, v increases to a maximum; as h increases to a maximum, v decreases to 0. Here, k and p are in direct inverse proportion.

Figure 10.11
Experimental Planning

Experimental Planning

Independent variable: Factor or condition being tested

Dependent variable: Factor that responds to the change in the independent variable; its response is measured as data

Controlled variables: All other factors that are kept constant during the experiment

TAKE ACTION
Students could select one of the real-life pendulums from the list on the board and prepare a brief report explaining a few of the following: function, principle feature, how it works, size, weight, designer, cost, maximum capacity, and so on.

Internet Resources
http://www.sedl.org/scimath/compass/v02n01/
pendulum.html
Pendulum Lab

http://english.ttu.edu/courses/5343/pendulum.htm
Physics of the Pendulum

http://galileo.imss.firenze.it/museo/a/erelazs.html
Galileo's Pendulum Clock

http://physics.nist.gov/GenInt/Time/revol.html
Pendulum Clock Invention

http://www.paris.org/Kiosque/nov96/foucault.html
Foucault's Pendulum

http://www.iit.edu/~smile/ph95p3.html
Periodic Motion Lab

Goal: This lesson introduces students to the concept of gravity, including the concepts of acceleration and mass. Students experience the principles of gravity in a hands-on cooperative activity that requires measurement and data collection.

Overview: Students, working in groups, make predictions about how quickly different objects will reach the ground when dropped from the same height. Tests are run and results are analyzed with respect to gravity, acceleration, and mass. The groups are then challenged to apply their knowledge to other scenarios and conduct further tests.

Materials: Bags containing a tennis ball, a baseball, a sponge ball (such as a Nerf™ ball), a marble (can be any four different objects), a stopwatch, a meterstick

INVITATION
Students are divided into groups of four or five. Each group is asked to predict the order in which the four balls (tennis ball, baseball, Nerf ball, marble) will hit the ground when dropped from the same height. Each group writes a brief statement containing the group's prediction and the reasoning behind that prediction.

EXPLORATION
Each group tests its prediction by dropping the four balls and recording each time of fall—dropping the balls first individually and then simultaneously—and the height. Each group summarizes its results and discusses them.

Figure 10.12 Recording the Falls

TIME OF FALL (SEC)

Item Dropped	First Drop from 5 Feet	Second Drop from 5 Feet
baseball	.37	.30
tennis ball	.32	.29
marble	.22	.38
sponge ball	.42	.49

EXPLANATION

The teacher leads a class discussion focusing on the experiment. Each group briefly presents its prediction and its results. The teacher should keep a master tally of the groups' predictions and results on a chalkboard or chart in front of the class. The class goes on to discuss the results, touching on such concepts as mass, gravity, force, and acceleration. The teacher's role is to reinforce correct predictions with factual information and untangle incorrect predictions by discussing common misconceptions.

TAKE ACTION

Groups could research a real-life scenario involving gravity, mass, and/or acceleration. Examples might include parachuting, escape velocity from the Earth's atmosphere (space shuttle), a penny falling from atop a tall building, hail, and so on.

Internet Resources

http://www.windows.umich.edu/people/
enlightenment/newton.html
Isaac Newton

http://www.blackhole.net/
Blackhole Info Page

http://acs5.bu.edu:8001/~mapotter/
Educational: Escape Velocity

http://www.grayphics.com/~jamess/
Escape Velocity

http://www.glenbrook.k12.il.us/gbssci/phys/
Class/newtlaws/u2l3e.html
Free Fall Explained

http://www.npac.syr.edu/REU/reu94/williams/
ch3/subsection3_3_3.html
Falling Objects

http://www.ksc.nasa.gov/shuttle/missions/
missions.html
NASA Space Shuttle

http://www.amdahl.com/internet/events/shuttle.html
Hot Topic: Space Shuttle

http://www.usafa.af.mil/pa/media/facts/
parachut.htm
Parachuting

MIXTURES: IRON IN CEREAL FLAKES

Goal: This lesson reviews the properties of mixtures and helps students to understand that the components of a mixture retain their own identities. Students use a physical method to separate a mixture, in the process gaining insight into the difference between physical and chemical changes.

Overview: Students brainstorm about the composition of a cereal flake. Substances and physical properties are identified. Students then physically remove iron from wet, crushed cereal with a magnet. As an extension, students discuss and research water pollution.

Materials: Bags containing a bar magnet, $1/2$ cup iron-fortified cereal in a sealable plastic bag, tissues, magnifying glass; water

INVITATION

Students are asked to reflect on the following question: "What is in a cereal flake?" Teacher should record students' ideas on the board and lead the class to include iron as a component. Teacher should ask for physical properties of the substances students list. Ideally, iron will emerge as a component and magnetism will eventually emerge as a physical property. Teacher-led discussion of physical properties of mixtures should generate student interest in the possibility of separating iron from cereal with a magnet, thereby proving one basic feature of mixtures: individual components retain their identities. To expand your Invitation-stage discussion, distribute a copy of the side of a cereal box (Figure 10.14) and discuss the contents and how they are combined in every flake.

EXPLORATION

Small groups receive a bag containing the laboratory materials. Cereal should be crushed in the bag until it is a fine powder. Water should be added to the bag, and the mixture stirred with the bar magnet for 5 minutes. At the end of this

Figure 10.13
Nutritional information
Courtesy Kellogg's Product 19

American Heart Association

Meets American Heart Association food criteria for saturated fat and cholesterol for healthy people over age 2.

Diets low in saturated fat and cholesterol may reduce the risk of heart disease.

Nutrition Facts

Serving Size 1 Cup (30g/1.1 oz.)
Servings per Container About 11

Amount Per Serving	Cereal Alone	Cereal with 1/2 Cup Vitamins A & D Skim Milk
Calories	100	140
Calories from Fat	0	0
	% Daily Value **	
Total Fat 0g*	0 %	0 %
Saturated Fat 0g	0 %	0 %
Cholesterol 0mg	0 %	0 %
Sodium 210mg	9 %	12 %
Potassium 50mg	1 %	7 %
Total Carbohydrate 25g	8 %	10%
Dietary Fiber 1g	4 %	4 %
Sugars 4g		
Other Carbohydrate 20g		
Protein 2g		
Vitamin A	15 %	20 %
Vitamin C	100 %	100 %
Calcium	0 %	15 %
Iron	100 %	100 %
Vitamin D	10 %	25 %
Vitamin E	100 %	100 %
Thiamin	100 %	100 %
Riboflavin	100 %	110 %
Niacin	100 %	100 %
Vitamin B6	100 %	100 %
Folate	100 %	100 %
Vitamin B12	100 %	110 %
Pantothenate	100 %	100 %
Phosphorus	4 %	15 %
Magnesium	4 %	8 %
Zinc	100 %	100 %

*Amount in cereal. One half cup skim milk contributes an additional 40 calories, 65mg sodium, 6g total carbohydrate (6g sugars), and 4g protein.
**Percent Daily Values are based on a 2,000 calorie diet. Your daily values may be higher or lower depending on your calorie needs.

	Calories	2,000	2,500
Total Fat	Less than	65g	80g
Sat. Fat	Less than	20g	25g
Cholesterol	Less than	300mg	300mg
Sodium	Less than	2,400mg	2,400mg
Potassium		3,500mg	3,500mg
Total Carbohydrate		300g	375g
Dietary Fiber		25g	30g

Calories per gram: Fat 9 • Carbohydrate 4 • Protein 4

Ingredients: Milled corn, sugar, whole oat flour, wheat flour, rice, defatted wheat germ, salt, high fructose corn syrup, malt flavoring, sodium ascorbate and ascorbic acid (vitamin C), alpha tocopherol acetate (vitamin E), niacinamide, zinc oxide, annatto color, reduced iron, calcium pantothenate, pyridoxine hydrochloride (vitamin B6), riboflavin (vitamin B2), thiamin hydrochloride (vitamin B1), BHT (preservative), vitamin A palmitate, folic acid, vitamin B12, vitamin D.

Corn used in this product contains traces of soybeans.

time, the bar magnet should be removed, allowed to drip, and then carefully wiped on a white tissue. Examination of the tissue with a magnifying glass should reveal the presence of small dark specks: iron. Groups should record their procedure, observations, and results.

EXPLANATION

Each group briefly presents to the class a summary of its results and any problems encountered during the activity. A teacher-led class discussion should reinforce the idea that each component in a mixture retains its identity. Discussion should inspire students to suggest other ways to separate other mixtures.

TAKE ACTION

As an extension, students might discuss and research water pollution, water purification systems (local and home), and what can be done about any home, local, or global issues of water purification that emerge. The ocean might also be studied in the context of its properties as a mixture/solution.

Internet Resources

http://www.gwpca.org/
Georgia Water & Pollution Control Association

http://www.iawq.org.uk/spgroups/wetland.htm
The International Association on Water

http://www.engineering.usu.edu/Departments/ cee/classes/envir/fw551.html
Water Pollution Effects

http://ntp-server.niehs.nih.gov/htdocs/Results_ status/ResstatC/M88022.html
Chemical Mixture—Drinking Water Contaminants

http://www.primeline-america.com/crystal/
Water Distillation Purification

EVAPORATION IS COOL

Goal: This activity gives students a hands-on opportunity to discover why we sweat. Students work in cooperative groups to learn that the evaporation of liquid from skin cools the skin. In the process, heat stroke awareness may also be raised.

Overview: Students brainstorm about the idea of utilizing heat in order to cool. Groups then experiment with a few materials to show how the human body utilizes heat in order to cool. Groups reach one final observation, which they share with the class. Teacher expands on how the human body cools by heating.

Materials: Bags containing cotton balls, small containers of isopropyl alcohol, small containers of water

INVITATION

Ask students to consider the following puzzle: "I utilize heat in order to cool, what am I?" Working in groups, students brainstorm for ideas and decide on a possible solution. Solutions should be shared with the class, but no final conclusion arrived at.

EXPLORATION

Teacher tells the student groups to experiment with the materials in the bag in order to solve the puzzle. Teacher then instructs the students to use the cotton balls to rub the back of one hand with alcohol and the back of the other with water, to wait a few seconds, and then to record their observations. Group members should share their observations with each other, and each group should arrive at one final observation.

EXPLANATION

Each group shares its final observation with the class. The class then revisits the initial puzzle.

The teacher provides the final solution— "the human body"—as needed. He or she goes on to explain that the hand rubbed with alcohol will feel cooler because alcohol evaporates faster than does water. Heat from the skin provides the energy for the evaporation of liquids such as perspiration. When heat is used this way, it is removed and the body becomes cooler.

TAKE ACTION

Students could research animals, such as pigs, that do not have sweat glands. Alternatively, they could research heat stroke and methods of cooling that humans have devised in extremely hot areas of the world. Students might also make a pamphlet or handbook on avoiding heat stroke and distribute it within the school.

Internet Resources

http://www.urbanlegends.com/science/hot_water_freezes_faster.html
Hot Water Freezes Faster

http://hammock.ifas.ufl.edu/txt/fairs/29587
How the Body Handles Heat

http://www.healthtouch.com/level1/leaflets/diet/diet005.htm
Sports Health

http://www.eb.com/cgi-bin/g?keywords=perspiration
Perspiration—Animals

http://www.umr.edu/~umrshs/heat.html
Heat Stroke

http://www.aes.purdue.edu/AgAnswrs/1995/7-21Sweat_Keep_Pigs_Cool.html
Pigs Don't Have Sweat Glands

MAGNETIC FIELDS

Goal: Students directly observe and come to understand the direction of a magnetic field.

Students work in cooperative learning groups and gain experience in making and recording observations.

Overview: In groups, students make predictions about a magnetic field. Groups then discover the shape of a magnetic field by utilizing iron filings on a plate. Groups record their observations and present their predictions and results to the class. As an extension, the concept of magnetic fields is related to issues such as solar activity and electricity production.

Materials: Bags containing a few magnets, a plate, iron filings, a compass, chart paper, newsprint, markers

INVITATION

Students are divided into groups. Each group receives a bag containing the laboratory materials. Using only the magnets from their bags, groups make predictions about the magnetic field, including direction, shape, and relationship to the magnet's poles. They can manipulate the magnets to assist the prediction-making process. On a sheet of newsprint labeled "Prediction," each group describes its prediction (diagrams strongly encouraged).

EXPLORATION

Groups now use the remaining materials from their bag to make predictions about magnetic fields. The iron filings should be spread out on the plate. By placing magnets underneath, above, on, and around the plate, the directions of the magnetic field of each magnet will be revealed by the filings. Each group should record its findings and make a Results poster that includes descriptions and diagrams.

EXPLANATION

Groups present to the class their Prediction poster followed by their Results poster. After each brief presentation, small discussions can be held, in which questions are asked and answered. The teacher provides any corrections or information

Figure 10.14
Magnetic Fields

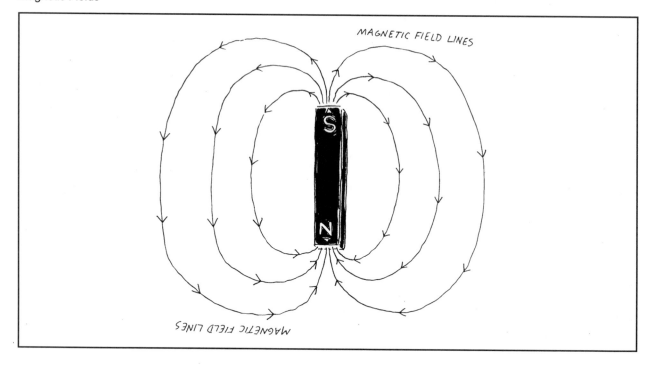

that may be needed to properly explain magnetic fields. Posters are displayed in the classroom.

TAKE ACTION
Students could research the effect of magnetic fields on our lives. Examples include the following: the relationship between electricity and magnetic fields (including the direction of electron flow), the purpose of magnets in televisions and speakers, solar activity due to the sun's magnetic field—and its results (sunspots, flares, solar wind, comet tails, auroras, etc.), the Earth's magnetic field, and so on.

Internet Resources
http://www.ultranet.com/~jkimball/BiologyPages/M/MagneticFields.html
Do Magnetic Fields Cause Cancer?

http://www.ncsa.uiuc.edu/Cyberia/Bima/flares.html
Solar Flares

http://www.ngdc.noaa.gov/seg/potfld/
Earth–Sun Geomagnetic Data

http://hurlbut.jhuapl.edu/NEAR/Education/lessonMag/lpmag.html
Lesson Plan on Magnetic Fields

http://www.stlpark.k12.mn.us/sh/physics/magnets.html
Electricity and Magnetism

http://www.exploratorium.edu/learning_studio/auroras/seethem.html
Auroras

SURFACE TENSION: THE STRESS H₂0 FEELS

Goal: This lesson provides students with a hands-on, cooperative learning experience in which they investigate water surface tension. Students utilize scientific inquiry and experimental design as they create their own experiment.

Overview: Students are introduced to water surface tension with a striking class demonstration.

Figure 10.15
Surface Tension

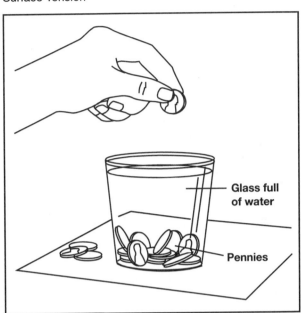

Glass full
of water

Pennies

In groups, they test surface tension by designing and conducting their own experiment. The results are shared with the class.

Materials: Bags containing diverse lightweight objects (paper clips, wires, cardboard, pennies, plastic chips, etc.) and containers of various sizes; water (cold and hot)

INVITATION
Students are asked to guess how many pennies will fit into a full cup of water without causing the water to spill over. Student guesses are recorded on the board. The teacher then begins to drop pennies into the cup of water, one by one. Once the cup overflows, the teacher leads a discussion focusing on why things happened as they did. The concept of surface tension is introduced.

EXPLORATION
Students are divided into teams. Each team receives a bag of laboratory materials. Each team designs an experiment utilizing the lightweight objects and any of the containers available. The experiment should in some way test water tension. (Suggestions: placing objects on top of the water, hot water vs. cold water, shape of container, depth of water, placing objects on water surface and in glass, etc.) Experiments should be recorded as they are carried out.

EXPLANATION
Groups prepare a brief presentation of their procedure and results and share it with the class. Each group should arrive at one final conclusion regarding surface tension, which they should write on the board/newsprint. After the presentations, the teacher leads a discussion about the results, the final conclusions, and water tension in general.

TAKE ACTION
As an extension activity, the class could research the local water supply, or the condition of local lakes or rivers. Pollution, water supply, water distribution, water towers, and so on, might be looked at specifically, depending on the area.

Internet Resources
http://www.worldbank.org/html/research/ipps/home.html
Industrial Water Pollution

http://w3.ag.uiuc.edu/liberty/isil/pollution.html
The Pollution Solution

http://www.brad.ac.uk/acad/civeng/emtpg.html
Research on Groundwater Pollution—U.K.

http://irsa1.irsa.rm.cnr.it/s_qua.html
Water Research Institute

http://pwn.com/~pwn/guide.html
EPA—Drinking Water Filters

WATER AND AIR SURFACE INTERACTIONS: BUBBLES

Goal: This activity demonstrates surface interactions between water and air. Students work in cooperative groups to discover properties of water and air. Observational and recording skills are enhanced.

Overview: In groups, students are asked to speculate on how it might be possible to make a raisin or a grape rise to the top of a glass of water, without touching it. Groups are given materials with which to conduct an experiment showing that the object may rise in carbonated water. Results are shared, and the class discusses the relationship of the air bubbles to the rising raisins and the grapes.

Materials: Bags containing raisins and grapes, a clear carbonated beverage, 2 beakers; tap water

INVITATION
Ask students in groups to speculate on how it might be possible to make a raisin or a grape rise to the top of a glass of water, without touching it. Have each group propose a plan and briefly share it with the class.

Variation: Many teachers have successfully utilized a scenario in which students are initially told they will be studying a species of sewer lice, a variation that seems to truly engage the students in the activity. The sewer lice are being studied, students are told, because they are very efficient at cleaning dirty water, including sewer water. Show the students a beaker containing (dark) cola and yellow raisins. Inform the students that they are looking at dirty water with a few sewer lice in it. Then show students a beaker containing a cola/clear cola mixture and some yellow raisins. Tell the students that the lice have been in that beaker for a week; make

the observation that the water is clearly cleaner. (The raisins should be rising and falling in the liquid periodically.) Finally, show the class a beaker containing clear cola and yellow raisins. Tell the class that the sewer lice have been in that beaker for 3 weeks; observe that it is perfectly clean. You can even drink some of the "water" to prove how clean it is. Give the students a small beaker with dark cola and some raisins in it, and ask them to make observations that they have actually seen eyes and tiny legs on the sewer lice. Now you can go ahead and inform the students that they are really observing yellow raisins in cola. Following a short debriefing, move into the explanation-stage discussion of the phenomena observed.

EXPLORATION
Distribute the bags. Have each group fill its two beakers, one with water and one with carbonated water. Instruct the groups to place raisins, grapes, and/or peeled grapes in one or both of their containers. Each group should record its observations.

EXPLANATION
Once all groups have completed their test, each group should present its observations to the class. A teacher-led class discussion provides a forum in which groups attempt to explain the phenomena they observed. The teacher should inform the students that in a carbonated beverage, the raisins and the unpeeled grapes will periodically rise to the surface, "riding" on the bubbles, and then fall. The peeled grapes do not rise because the bubbles cannot adhere to their surface. From here, discussion can turn to the properties of air and/or water.

TAKE ACTION
Students could research the dangers involved in scuba diving, and how these relate to the properties of air and water.

Internet Resources

http://www.discoveringhawaii.com/Medical Advice/ScubaDivingFlying.html
Scuba Diving Dangers

http://www.medscape.com/Medscape/OrthoSports Med/1997/v01.n09/mos3036a.campbell/mos303 6a.campbell.html
Decompression Illness

http://www.jtan.com/antibubble/
What Is an Antibubble?

http://www.healthlink.com.au/nat_lib/ htm-data/htm-supp/SUPPS28.HTM
Divers—"The Bends"

http://math.ucr.edu/home/baez/physics/fizziks.html
FAQs About Carbonation

THE VISIBLE SPECTRUM: A RAINBOW

Goal: Students become familiar with the diffraction of light through a prism. They come to understand that different colors have different wavelengths and that white light consists of all the colors combined. Students use scientific inquiry and observational skills to complete this activity.

Overview: In groups, students are challenged to describe how a rainbow is formed. Each group records its ideas and shares one with the class. Groups then test light by passing it through a prism and a glass of water. Results are recorded and shared. The class reaches a consensus on the formation of rainbows.

Materials: Bags containing a prism, flashlight, white cardboard, drinking glass; water

Figure 10.16
Prism

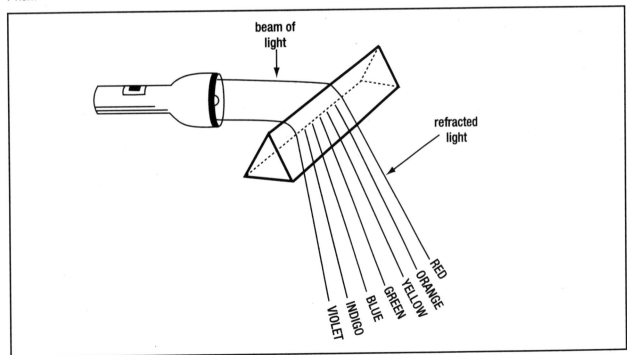

Figure 10.17
Visible spectrum

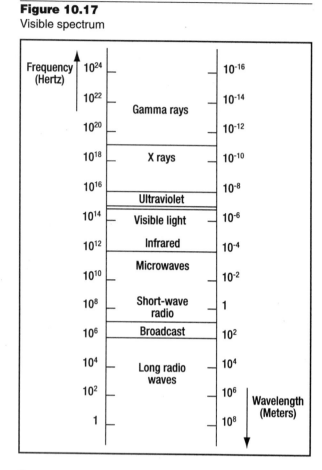

INVITATION

In groups, students are challenged to describe how a rainbow is formed. Each group records its ideas with diagrams. It selects the idea it feels is most accurate and shares it with the class. The various explanations are recorded by the teacher on the board or on newsprint.

EXPLORATION

Groups receive a bag containing the lab materials. Groups test light by passing it from the flashlight through the prism and/or the glass of water, onto the white cardboard. Students record their results with drawings and explanations.

EXPLANATION

Each group shares its findings with the class. Teacher-led discussion clarifies the separation of the different wavelengths of light. The class then reaches a consensus on the formation of rainbows, comparing its latest ideas with those originally proposed.

TAKE ACTION

Students could study the entire electromagnetic spectrum and see where visible light fits in. Research into other forms of electromagnetic waves might focus on X rays, UV light, infrared light, radiowaves, and so on; students could learn about the functionality and importance of these invisible waves.

Internet Resources

http://www.geom.umn.edu/education/
calc-init/rainbow/
Circles of Light

http://www.unidata.ucar.edu/staff/blynds/rnbw.html
What Is a Rainbow?

http://www.sciam.com/askexpert/environment/
environment14.html
Why Are Rainbows Curved?

http://www.deltatech.com/rainbowx.html
FAQs About Rainbows

http://www.ncsa.uiuc.edu/Cyberia/Bima/
spectrum.html
Visible Spectra

http://www.purchon.co.uk/science/electrom.html
Electromagnetic Spectrum

http://www.netwalk.com/~fsv/homepage2.htm
Radio Wave

SCIENCE ACTIVITY BOOKS

Bochinski, Julianne Blair. (1991). *The Complete Handbook of Science Fair Projects.* New York: John Wiley & Sons, Inc.

Cothron, Julia, Ronald Giese, and Richard Rezba. (1993). *Students and Research: Practical Strategies for Science Classrooms and Competitions* (2nd ed.). Dubuque, IA: Kendall/Hunt Publishing Company.

Downing, Charles R., and Candace J. Aguirre. (1994). *Cranial Creations in Physical Science: Interdisciplinary and Cooperative Learning Activities.* Portland, ME: J. Weston Walch, Publisher.

Downing, Charles R., and Owen L. Miller. (1992). *Cranial Creations in Life Science: Interdisciplinary and Cooperative Learning Activities.* Portland, ME: J. Weston Walch, Publisher.

Epstein, Lewis Carroll. (1993). *Thinking Physics.* San Francisco, CA: Insight Press.

Great Explorations in Math and Science (GEMS). Lawrence Hall of Science, University of California, Berkeley, CA 94720. Tel: 415-642-7771. Following are some teaching units that may be of interest:
>   Acid Rain
>   Animals in Action
>   Chemical Reactions
>   Crime Lab Chemistry
>   Discovering Density
>   Global Warming and the Greenhouse Effect
>   Mapping Animal Movements
>   Mapping Fish Habitats
>   Paper Towel Testing

Hassard, Jack. (1989). *Adventures in Geology.* Alexandria, VA: American Geological Institute. To order: AGI, 4220 King Street, Alexandria, VA 22302. Tel: 703-379-2480.

Hassard, Jack. (1990). *Science Experiences: Cooperative Learning and the Teaching of Science.* Menlo Park, CA: Addison-Wesley.

Hassard, Jack, and Weisberg, Julie. (1999). *Environmental Science on the Net: The Global Thinking Project.* Parsippany, NJ: Good Year Books.

Hillman, Lawrence, E. (1989). *Nature Puzzlers.* Englewood, CO: Teacher Ideas Press.

Liem, Tik L. (1991). *Invitations to Science Inquiry.* Chino Hills, CA: Science Inquiry Enterprises. To order: SIE, 14358 Village View Lane, Chino Hills, CA 91709. Tel: 714-590-4618.

Nature Scope, Natural Wildlife Federation, 1400 Sixteenth Street, N.W., Washington, DC. Series of science teaching modules. Here are some titles that may be of interest:
>   Amazing Mammals I & II
>   Astronomy Adventures
>   Birds, Birds, Birds
>   Digging into Dinosaurs
>   Discovering Deserts
>   Diving into Oceans
>   Endangered Species
>   Geology: The Active Earth
>   Incredible Insects
>   Pollution: Problems and Solutions
>   Rain Forests: Tropical Treasures
>   Reptiles and Amphibians
>   Wading into Wetlands
>   Wild About Weather

Samples, Bob, Bill Hammond, and Bernice McCarthy. (1985). *4MAT and Science: Toward Wholeness in Science Education.* Barrington, IL: Exell, Inc.

Stepans, Joseph. (1994). *Targeting Students' Science Misconceptions: Physical Science Activities Using the Conceptual Change Model.* Riverview, FL: Idea Factory.

VanCleave, Janice. (1993). *A+ Projects in Chemistry: Winning Experiments for Science Fairs and Extra Credit.* New York: John Wiley & Sons, Inc.

VanCleave, Janice. (1990). *Biology for Every Kid: 101 Easy Experiments That Really Work.* New York: John Wiley & Sons, Inc.

VanCleave, Janice. (1991). *Physics for Every Kid: 101 Experiments in Motion, Heat, Light, Machines and Sound.* New York: John Wiley & Sons, Inc.

PROFESSIONAL DEVELOPMENT BOOKS

American Association for the Advancement of Science. (1993). *Benchmarks for Science Literacy.* New York: Oxford University Press.

American Association for the Advancement of Science. (1989). *Science for All Americans: A Project 2061 Report on Literacy Goals in Science, Mathematics, and Technology.* Washington, DC: AAAS.

Assessment in Science Education: The Middle Years. (1994). Washington, DC: The National Center for Improving Science Education.

Brooks, Jacqueline G., and Martin Brooks. (1993). *The Case for Constructivist Classrooms.* Alexandria, VA: Association for Supervision and Curriculum Development.

Building Scientific Literacy: A Blueprint for Science in the Middle Years. (1992). Washington, DC: The National Center for Improving Science Education.

Chaille, Christine, and Lory Britan. (1991). *The Young Child as Scientist: A Constructivist Approach to Early Childhood Education.* New York: HarperCollinsPublishers.

Champagne, Audrey, Barbara Lovitts, and Betty Calinger. (1990). *Assessment in the Service of Instruction.* Washington, DC: American Association for the Advancement of Science.

Harmin, Merril. (1994). *Inspiring Active Learning: A Handbook for Teachers.* Alexandria, VA: Association for Supervision and Curriculum Development.

Hassard, Jack. (1992). *Minds-On Science: The Art of Teaching Middle and High School Science.* New York: HarperCollinsPublishers.

Hein, George. (Ed.). (1990). *The Assessment of Hands-On Elementary Science Programs.* University of North Dakota: Center for Teaching and Learning.

The High Stakes of High School Science. (1991). Washington, DC: The National Center for Improving Science Education.

Modell, Harold, and Joel Michael. (Eds.). (1993). *Promoting Active Learning in the Life Science Classroom.* New York: The New York Academy of Sciences.

Osborne, Roger, and Peter Freyberg. (1985). *Learning in Science: The Implications of Children's Science.* Aukland, New Zealand: Heinemann.

Ruopp, Richard. (1993). *LabNet: Toward a Community of Practice.* Hilldale, NJ: Lawrence Erlbaum Associates.

Shapiro, Bonnie. (1994). *What Children Bring to Light: A Constructivist Perspective on Children's Learning in Science.* New York: Teachers College Press

ONLINE AND INTERNET RESOURCES

Armstrong, Sara. (1994). *Telecommunications in the Classroom.* Palo Alto, CA: Computer Learning Foundation.

Brooks, David B. (1997). *Web-Teaching: A Guide to Designing Interactive Teaching for the World Wide Web.* New York: Plenum.

Cohen, Karen C. (1997). *Internet Links for Science Education: Student-Scientist Partnerships.* New York: Plenum.

Eddings, Joshua. (1994). *How the Internet Works.* Emeryville, CA: Ziff-Davis, Press.

Gilster, Paul. (1997). *Digital Literacy.* New York: John Wiley & Sons, Inc.

Gilster, Paul. (1994). *The Internet Navigator: The Essential Guide to Network Exploration for the Individual Dial-Up User* (2nd ed.). New York: John Wiley & Sons, Inc.

Glossbrenner, Alfred. (1995) *The Little Online Book: A Gentle Introduction to Modems, Online Services, Electronic Bulletin Boards, and the Internet.* Berkeley, CA: Peachpit Press.

Hahn, Harley, and Rick Stout. (1994). *The Internet Complete Reference.* Berkeley, CA: Osborne McGraw-Hill.

Harris, Judi. (1994). *Way of the Ferret: Finding Educational Resources on the Internet.* Eugene, OR: International Society for Technology in Education.

Kehoe, Brendan P. (1996). *Zen and the Art of the Internet: A Beginner's Guide.* Englewood Cliffs, NJ: Prentice-Hall.

Krol, Ed. (1994). *The Whole Internet User's Guide and Catalog.* Sebastopol, CA: O'Reilly & Associates, Inc.

Kurshan, Barbara, and Deneen Frazier. (1995). *Internet (and More) for Kids.* Palo Alto, CA: Computer Learning Foundation. To order: CLF, 2431 Park Blvd., Palo Alto, CA 94306.

Lichty, Tom. (1994). *The Official America Online Tour Guide: Everything You Need to Begin Enjoying the Nation's Most Exciting Online Service.* Chapel Hill, NC: Ventana Press.

Negroponte, Nicholas. (1995). *Being Digital.* New York: Vintage Books.

Pfaffenberger, Bryan. (1996). *Web Search Strategies.* New York: MIS Press.

Science Internet Curriculum Guide. (1997). Lancaster, PA: Classroom Connect.

Seiter, Charles. (1994). *The Internet for Macs for Dummies.* San Mateo, CA: IDG Books Worldwide, Inc.

Stout, Rick, and Morgan Davis. (1996). *The Internet Yellowpages: Science, Research, and Technology.* Berkeley: Osborne McGraw-Hill.

Tapscott, Don. (1998). *Growing Up Digital: The Rise of the Net Generation.* New York: McGraw-Hill.

Web Guide: Instant Access to the Best Internet Web Sites— Science. (1997). Lancaster, PA: Classroom Connect.

Williams, Bard. (1996). *The World Wide Web for Teachers.* Foster City, CA: IDG Books Worldwide, Inc.

ONLINE SERVICES

There are hundreds of online Internet service providers. Here are three that you might investigate as a potential service provider.

1. Netcom. Netcom is an online communications service that offers full Internet access for about $19.95 per month, for unlimited access. Netcom software includes Netscape, e-mail, Usenet reader, FTP, Internet Relay Chat, and Gopher. Contact Netcom at P.O. Box 2839, San Francisco, CA 94126, or at 1-800-382-4633, or at http://www.netcom.com/.

2. EcoNet. EcoNet is part of the Institute for Global Communications, a nonprofit organization dedicated to linking people around the world who are interested in environmental and human rights issues. You can obtain an application to join EcoNet by writing: Institute for Global Communications, 18 de Boom Street, San Francisco, CA94107, or via the Internet at http://www.igc.org/. When you open an account with EcoNet, you can obtain special telecommunications software giving you full access to the Internet. The cost is $19.95 per month for unlimited access. EcoNet has hundreds of conferences (EcoNet calls bulletin boards conferences) dealing with environmental issues and research. Contact EcoNet at 1-415-561-6100 or at http://www.econet.org/.

3. MindSpring, Inc. Mindspring is a user-friendly full Internet access service provider. MindSpring uses Netscape and other key Internet applications that you will want to access, including FTP e-mail (Eudora Light), Newsreader, and Chat. Contact MindSpring at 1-888-677-7464 or at http://www.mindspring.com/.

SCIENCE TEACHING ORGANIZATIONS

International Society for Technology in Education (ISTE), 1787 Agate Street, Eugene, OR 97403. A leading organization helping you stay in touch with online learning resources and new developments in technology. Membership includes the journal *Learning and Leading with Technology* or the journal *Research on Computing Education.* To join, call 1-800-336-5850 or contact ISTE at http://www.iste.org/.

National Science Teachers Association (NSTA), 1840 Wilson Boulevard, Arlington, VA 22201. The largest organizations of science teachers in the world, NSTA offers four journals (elementary, middle, high school, and college), area and national conferences, and access to resources in science teaching through its members bookstore. For more information, call 1-703-243-7100 or contact NSTA at http://www.nsta.org/.